STARTING EVEN

*An Equal Opportunity Program
to Combat the Nation's New Poverty*

BY

ROBERT HAVEMAN

A Twentieth Century Fund Report

SIMON AND SCHUSTER

New York   London   Sydney   Tokyo   Toronto

Simon and Schuster
Simon & Schuster Building
Rockefeller Center
1230 Avenue of the Americas
New York, New York 10020

Designed by Irving Perkins Associates
Manufactured in the United States of America

1   3   5   7   9   10   8   6   4   2

Library of Congress Cataloging in Publication Data
Haveman, Robert H.
Starting even : an equal opportunity program
to combat the nation's new poverty / by Robert Haveman.
p.   cm.
"A Twentieth Century Fund report."
Bibliography: p.
Includes index.
1. Income distribution—United States.   2. Transfer payments—
United States.   I. Twentieth Century Fund.   II. Title.
HC110.I5H37   1988
362.5'82—dc19   88-15875
CIP
ISBN 0-671-66762-9

To Beth, Jon, Andrea, Jenny,
and Ari, and to the memory
of Dirk, who so loved life.

Foreword

From the 1970s to the 1980s the percentage of people living in poverty rose; so did the perception that the distribution of wealth and income was more unequal. Social scientists became increasingly aware that the growth in the number of people in need of welfare resulted from the programs begun in the 1960s in order to ameliorate poverty, the policies pursued by the Reagan administration, and the effects of international economic problems.

Since the growing polarization of American society, particularly the growth of a welfare-dependent class, would clearly be one of the major issues facing the next administration, the Trustees and staff of the Twentieth Century Fund sought an author who could examine the history and effectiveness of the federal government's welfare policies and propose a strategy for reform that would break new ground. It was a tall order.

In Robert Haveman of the University of Wisconsin, a scholar who has devoted most of his professional life to an examination of government redistributive policies and the effects of those policies on the performance of the economy, we found the ideal writer for such a study. Haveman believes that the government is responsible for dealing with inequality, that it should intervene to reduce poverty and to improve the opportunities available to those who have benefited least from prosperity. Yet he has always been conscious of the economic and political limits on what governments can do.

Haveman's book is likely to arouse controversy, to bring to the forefront of public debate the question of what has happened to the American dream. He proposes measures that will help those who are now at the bottom of the income barrel—the long-term unemployed, displaced workers, single mothers on welfare, and children growing up without traditional family ties. These measures would help them escape from poverty without creating the kinds of disincentives to work that have characterized many of our past welfare programs.

What Haveman has done is point out a road to equal opportunity. We hope his vision will gain wide acceptance.

M. J. Rossant, *Director*
The Twentieth Century Fund
June 1988

Contents

Preface

The idea for this book was first conceived by Gary Nickerson, who was then at the Twentieth Century Fund. It came in a letter nearly four years ago, proposing that I write a monograph tying together various strands of my work on and thinking about anti-poverty policy, especially labor market policy toward poor people. In the give and take that ensued, the theme of economic inequality and redistribution policy evolved. The basic notion that the nature of the poverty problem had fundamentally changed, and that the nation's existing policy strategy was no longer up to the task of effectively combatting it, came to form the core of the envisioned book. The bold idea that I outline a new way of achieving the nation's goals of reducing poverty and inequality—a strategy that would allow us to reduce inequality with efficiency—followed naturally. The project that ultimately resulted contained all of these themes.

The research and writing of the book involved a close working relationship with Ross E. Finnie, a young economist at the University of Wisconsin–Madison. His fresh view of the issues regularly confronted my ideas which have grown out of two decades of research and writing on the problem of poverty and policies to reduce it. As a result of his stubborn urging, the book delivers a broad "equal opportunity" message. The tabulations that form the heart of Chapters 2 and 3, and much of their interpretation, are his work, and the other chapters reflect our conversations and his comments. He is the author of the Appendix.

Early drafts of the book were read by several people. Sheldon Danziger, Irwin Garfinkel, Robert Lampman, and Barbara Wolfe were especially persistent in questioning my basic premises, challenging my conclusions, and forcing me to rethink and reformulate. I owe each of them a great debt. For different—and sometimes contradictory—reasons, certain parts of the volume still do not sit well with them. Other readers whose helpful comments improved the manuscript are William Gormley, Flip de Kam, Sar Levitan, Gary Nickerson, Joseph Pechman, Richard Sinopoli, and Eugene Smolensky.

The job of turning turgid prose into common, lively language fell to Carol Kahn. Every academic should be forced into the humbling experience of working with a person of her skills with a pen. Betty Evanson also read parts of the book with an editorial eye, and the structure of the Appendix largely reflects her suggestions. At the head of this activity was Beverly Goldberg, assistant director of the Twentieth Century Fund. Her editorial skills, her writing standards, and in equal measure her spirit and commitment are reflected throughout. Robert Asahina at Simon and Schuster was a pleasure to work with; he handled the book professionally and with skill.

In addition to the Twentieth Century Fund, the Institute for Research on Poverty deserves recognition. For nearly two decades, it has provided an intellectual home—and stimulation—for my research on poverty and inequality. The basic themes in the book reflect the multitude of discussions and collaborations with my colleagues there. Early drafts of the manuscript were typed at the Institute—Catherine Cameron, Cathy Esser, and Nancy Rortvedt were prompt, accurate, and tolerant. Administrative machinery was greased by Joyce Collins, Jack Sorenson, and William Wambach.

I am grateful for the patience and encouragement of my wife and colleague, Barbara Wolfe. Much of the time for this project came at her expense. Finally, Charles Murray, George Gilder, and Lawrence Mead deserve acknowledgment. Without the frustration that their influential and conservative writings generated, I would not have been budged from writing for scholars into writing for a broader audience. Surely a more positive, more research-based, and more forward-looking message than theirs deserves to be aired. While government antipoverty efforts could have been more effective than they were, I do not find evidence that they made things worse. This rich nation can, I believe, effectively combat the intolerable and persistent poverty among a portion of its population. To do so, however, requires a new policy strategy—one which emphasizes equal opportunities, promotes individual responsibility, attends to economic incentives, and builds upon the findings of research studies. The recently passed welfare reform legislation is one such change. It is my hope that this book will provoke the debate necessary to secure additional changes consistent with such a strategy.

Robert Haveman
June 1988

Introduction

As individuals, Americans tend to be a generous and helping lot. We respond to loneliness, impoverishment, and hardship through our communities, churches, and secular charities. As a nation, the story is somewhat different. Given the persistence of poverty and serious social problems in the face of affluence, it is difficult to argue that we have a deep and long-standing national commitment to social justice and equality, even though we claim to believe in both. While we insist that we hold tightly to the principle of equality of opportunity, we tend to take collective action to improve things only when advocates of the disadvantaged generate sufficient political pressure to make us uncomfortable.

Historically, such calls to action tend to follow a cyclical pattern.[1] Every thirty years or so, the pendulum seems to drift away from pro-welfare attitudes and policies, and there is a significant decrease in attention to so-called equality issues until the pendulum completes its swing. In the 1930s, for example, mass unemployment, soup lines, and widespread evictions strengthened the voice of advocates, and the nation responded with the New Deal. It happened again in the mid-1960s, when the War on Poverty–Great Society programs were enacted and carried out in response to the plight of those living in urban ghettos and rural poverty, to black privation amid white affluence, and to a large elderly population living in poverty, many without benefit of Social Security.

Today, as we approach the 1990s, Americans have awakened to the dramatic increase in the long-term unemployed population, in displaced workers, in single black mothers on welfare, and in children growing up without traditional family ties. Recent polling data show that a majority of Americans now believe government should do more to help the poor.[2] But this latest swing in the cycle seems to be somewhat different. There is an awareness that the social programs expanded in response to the last swing of the pendulum are unable to deal effectively with the problems created by the radical changes in population and economic patterns and social values of the past two decades. Thus, what is being heard is not so much a cry for still more social policies but a cry for reform. The Great Tax Reform of 1986 reflected this concern by granting substantial tax relief to those at the bottom of the distribution, effectively exempting the poor from income taxation. President Reagan, in his 1986 State of the Union speech, issued a call for welfare reform in response to this rising tide of concern. Robert Reischauer, an economist, says that "reform is back on the nation's agenda. . . . The problems of the poor, once again, [are] the focus of policymakers' attention."[3]

This new perception has opened the door to a wide variety of special interest groups, who have organized panels and commissions to formulate policy proposals. Reports were issued by such groups as the National Governors Association, the American Public Welfare Association, Governor Mario Cuomo's Task Force on Poverty and Welfare, Governor Bruce Babbitt's Project on Welfare and Families, and the Working Seminar on Family and American Welfare Policy.[4] All of these reports recognized that the problems of work, welfare, inequality, poverty, family disintegration, mother-only families, and failed education had increased in severity. By early 1987, without much fanfare, the House passed a reform bill that permitted states wider discretion to experiment with work-for-welfare initiatives and expanded efforts to secure child support from absent fathers.

Then, in the summer of 1987, Senator Daniel Patrick Moynihan put forth his program for reform, including demands for work in return for welfare, that would not have received serious consideration fifteen years ago. The discussions that ensued indicate that Americans are aware that something needs to be done about the current tax and benefits system. As a result, the question of how to improve the redistribution system we already have, how to make it better serve those it was intended to help, is again high on the nation's agenda.

While these discussions and proposals are a start, they are not enough. Indeed, they only patch up an approach to social policy that is fundamentally flawed—a strategy that cannot cope with the problem of growing inequality and its siblings, poverty and dependency. But before we can replace the existing system, we need to examine our past efforts to discover both what went wrong and what went right.

Where We Stand

Today, as a result of a variety of social programs established in the past decades, most Americans face less economic insecurity than ever before. The impact of income losses from whatever source—disablement, death of an income-earning spouse, retirement, unemployment, a lack of employable skills—has been cushioned by the benefits of income-support programs. Publicly supported education and training programs have helped millions of Americans become productive participants in the labor force, moving them toward the mainstream of economic life. Retraining programs have helped American workers adjust to technological change, and to the job losses caused by the changes, which have often meant abandoning long-held occupations and community ties.

While these various benefit programs have had their successes, they have also had their failures, and those who evaluate them do not always find that the social gains clearly outstrip the costs. Overall, an assessment of "good with flashes of excellent" is the highest praise offered.[5] Some observers find much to criticize. For example, Robert Nozick, one of the leading spokesmen for those who view the transfer of resources through taxes as unjustifiable "taking," questions whether the redistribution policies that comprise the current strategy violate our fundamental constitutional principles.[6] George Gilder finds that the social policies of the 1960s and 1970s have undermined the functioning of the basic institutions of our civilization.[7] In his view, family, church, community, and the workplace no longer offer stability and support, in part because changes in our society have encouraged permissiveness and social programs have increased dependence. Marital breakup, out-of-wedlock births, the demand for public child care, youth unemployment, and the erosion of individual initiative and respect for others can, he believes, all be laid at the doorstep of the War on Poverty–Great Society programs.

These policy analysts and others have examined the efforts to reduce poverty and found that, instead, they created more poverty. Some argue that the programs begun in the 1960s were structured in such a way that they created incentives for reduced work, increased childbearing by the poor and unwed, and a propensity among those covered by the programs to become and remain "welfare dependent." Charles Murray, in *Losing Ground,* has made the case that, in addition to these results, those assisted have become alienated, and those whose work brings them barely above the poverty level have come to view themselves as "chumps."[8]

The "Big Tradeoff-Retrenchment" Message

Such negative critiques began to strike a resonant chord in the mid-1970s, and by 1980 the political atmosphere reflected a general disillusionment with government efforts to reduce poverty and inequality. It appeared that the greater the efforts, the greater the loss of economic efficiency and progress. High and persistent unemployment, sluggish economic growth, and the erosion of our international competitive position, we were told, were in large part a legacy of rising social spending, supported by the transfer of public funds raised from high taxes. We could not have both equality and efficiency, and our emphasis on the former sapped the latter.[9] The result of this perception was the harsh and hurtful prescription to retrench, cut, eliminate.

These claims fell on the ears of a polity that had experienced a decade of stagnation, a decade during which earnings failed to increase as fast as taxes and prices.[10] Polls showed that families dependent on a paycheck found an increasing number of things they aspired to but could not afford—vacations, new cars, and remodeled homes were becoming unaffordable luxuries; why, then, should they be made to pay for a growing tax and benefits system?

And so twenty years of growing government intervention focused on the poor and disadvantaged slowed down in 1978–1979 and came to an end in 1981. The Carter administration curtailed spending for social programs; the Reagan administration made such curtailments official policy. In the first two years of the Reagan administration, cuts in "human resources" programs (in the early 1980s, they cost $500 billion a year) reduced federal expenditures over the 1982–1986 period by over $100 billion, or about 5 percent a year.[11] Because welfare, disability, food stamps, and training programs absorbed the bulk of these reductions, the effects of the cuts fell primarily on those who had least. (CETA, a manpower training program, was cut 100 percent, Social Security hardly at all.) The case for retrenchment—and in part the justification for "supply-side economics"—was built on the view that the government was too big and too intrusive; social intervention had not been effective and may even have made the problem worse; social programs eroded private initiative and traditional institutions. This period of retrenchment was the inevitable down phase of the political cycle; it followed twenty years of continually expanding social welfare expenditures.[12]

A Time to Rethink—An Alternative Assessment

This period of negative appraisal of social programs has left basic questions regarding both the validity of the objectives of these strategies for reducing poverty and inequality, and their effectiveness. While I argue that the Big Tradeoff–Retrenchment message preached in 1980 is not only wrong but pernicious and destructive, there were other problems that the federal government's social policy was not dealing with. For example, the social problems that were believed to have been fostered by lives lived in poverty—drug use, out-of-wedlock births, crime, youth unemployment, alcoholism—remain serious. In addition, there is incontrovertible evidence that disincentives to work are built into the redistribution system and undermine individual—and ultimately national—productivity and, to some extent at least, savings.[13] But perhaps most damaging, long-term dependency has become more concentrated and pathological.[14]

The War on Poverty and the Great Society began with a worthy rationale: in President Johnson's words, to provide "a hand up and not a handout."[15] The problem of poverty and inequality was seen as the result of some combination of slow economic growth, a population that was in many cases not sufficiently skilled or trained to be employable, and obstacles to full participation of blacks and Hispanics in the economy. Macroeconomic policies designed to attain full employment were the central part of the plan, which also included programs to provide better education, training programs, and affirmative action. To stress the need to provide equal opportunities to achieve success, a new Office of Economic Opportunity (OEO) was set up.

Programs with optimistic titles such as Head Start, Job Corps, Community Action, and Upward Bound were put in place; affirmative action regulations were established and enforced. The results of these efforts were noticeable: from 1965 to 1973, the adjusted poverty rate fell by one-half[16]; education, medical care, unemployment, and income gaps between blacks and whites and rich and poor were narrowed; housing, health, and nutrition indicators rose.

But the rationale of equalizing opportunities that motivated the early War on Poverty–Great Society planners was not sustained by the policies that evolved. Much of the increased spending went for a quite different purpose—to relieve income poverty. As Robert Lampman has put it, the War on Poverty established a "What does it do for the poor?" test for national policy.[17] Increasingly, efforts to help the poor took the form of income transfers. Welfare (e.g., AFDC: Aid to Families with Dependent Children; SSI: Supplemental Security Income), food stamps, Social Security, and health care subsidies (through Medicare and Medicaid) were increased, using monies raised from taxpayers and transferring it to eligible recipients—the aged, the disabled, the needy. The big surge in the years 1965–1975 was in income transfers and not in programs that increase human capital or improve skills (education and training), and assure equal opportunities (affirmative action). The initial commitment to "even starting lines" and "level playing fields" turned into operational strategies to reduce income poverty, thereby equalizing outcomes.

These strategies of taxing and transferring income require continual government intervention for the gains to be sustained. There is nothing inherent in them to enable recipients to become more self-sufficient, to assure their independence through their own efforts. Long-term and permanent progress against poverty and inequality is possible only through programs that make it possible for individuals to acquire sufficient skills and training to become economically independent, and give them the incentives and hope to make the effort.

This, then, is where we stand—retrenchment as the result of disillusionment at the end of the 1970s, and acceptance of the Big Trade-off. We, or at least our political leaders, have become convinced that social programs (and the higher taxes they imply) have ended up reducing work and savings—and these reductions hurt the economy. As a result, we have not pursued or even seriously considered more effective—or efficient—ways of reducing poverty and inequality.

As I will demonstrate later, the nature of the inequality-poverty problem has changed significantly over the past twenty years. There have been successes and failures, the latter resulting in a group of "new unequals"—minority youth, single mothers, and children living in one-parent families. These people confront basic constraints on their efforts to achieve economic success that cannot be relieved simply through income transfers. Theirs is truly a problem of unequal starting lines. Hence, if less poverty is the objective, efforts to redress the balance need to be directed away from income transfers toward programs that will foster more equal opportunities, self-sufficiency, and independence. The initial opportunity-based objectives, so clearly stated by President Johnson in 1964, must again be adopted as a basis for doing the nation's income redistribution business.

Breaking Out of the Old Mold

What is required is a new way of doing business: a reorientation—and replacement—of the current strategy toward poverty. I propose a plan—parts of which are little more than minor changes in programs already in place but much of which is new—that will provide more effective ways of dealing with poverty and inequality. The five major provisions, all of which will be explained later, are:

- An income safety net for individuals and families, accomplished through a refundable tax credit;
- A minimum income in retirement provided through a social security program, in tandem with assistance for working people to make individual provision for a standard of living in retirement in excess of this minimum;
- A national child-support program that requires absent parents to assume financial responsibility for their children, and enforces this requirement through the tax system;
- An employment subsidy to increase jobs for workers with little or no academic or vocational background; and
- A capital account for youths, enabling them to make choices to achieve more and better education, training, and health care.

This program will foster independence and self-reliance, individual choices, and accountability for these choices. It will do so by expanding the opportunities available to many of those who have few. And it will enable those likely to end up in poverty or on welfare to increase their incomes through their own initiative instead of through government transfer programs.

The Book and Its Goals

This book, then, is about economic inequalities among people, about government, and about what government does to reduce these inequalities. It does not question the government's right to intervene to reduce poverty and race- or gender-based inequalities. Rather, it supports options that will enable the government to do its job better.

This book is motivated primarily by the need to examine what has been happening to the level of poverty and inequality in the United States since the 1960s—and to gain an understanding of why these changes have taken place. At the same time that the nation, and especially the federal government, has spent huge amounts of money to reduce disparities, the size of the poor population has not shrunk, and economic inequality—the gap between the haves and the have-nots—has increased.[18] Why? What is working to offset the equalizing effects of social policy?

The second purpose of the book is related to federal government policy, a policy well described as "muddling through." Our legislators have never faced the issue of "what degree of inequality is acceptable." Dozens of programs have been established in recent years, each with its own equalizing-disequalizing, pro-rich or pro-poor, effects, each with its own approach to resolving social problems. At some level, policymakers perceive this uncoordinated mélange of efforts to be valid, and sanction the implied changes that result. But because the questions of the level of inequality we are willing to accept and the most effective way of achieving less inequality are never explicitly dealt with, decisions on poverty and social programs are made on the basis of quite extraneous, often political, considerations. Little systematic thought is devoted specifically to identifying the most effective and efficient means of reducing inequalities through expanding opportunities.

What is the consequence of this disjointed approach to social policy? I believe that we are spending hundreds of billions of dollars to buy less poverty and inequality reduction than we could. Using my proposed strategy as a starting point, we could reform the current tax-benefits system, developing programs that encourage independence and self-reliance, programs that would achieve the desired outcome of reducing inequality and poverty—with fewer of the adverse side effects that accompany our existing strategy.

PART I

Inequality and Efficiency

Equality is a complex and controversial concept, and it is an ideal that is beyond our grasp. Moreover, even if it could be achieved, we probably would not want it. From the moment of birth, physical, physiological, and intellectual differences set us apart. These natural differences are destiny, and they can neither be altered nor eliminated. But equality in a social context does not deal with unalterable differences; rather it involves economic opportunities and economic outcomes. To what extent do families have different incomes or wealth and why? To what extent do people have the same chance to earn income and move up the ladder of financial success, and if they do not, why not? As a society, we seem to accept inequality of outcome when it is the result of individual choice and achievement, but we find inequalities due to external forces (inequalities of opportunity) basically wrong.

This section looks at economic inequality and its causes. For many, racial and gender discrimination still preclude equal access to education, training, and jobs—the traditional routes to economic betterment. Discrimination causes both unequal opportunities and unequal outcomes. In addition, a decreasing proportion of children and youth have family structures and support systems that encourage achievement. Growing up in homes headed by a single parent receiving welfare is commonplace today for many children in our society. And unfortunately, the result is an environment in which innate potential may well be thwarted by the lack of both incentives and examples. These situations reflect the unacceptable inequalities of opportunity that underlie inequalities of outcome.

This part of the book will consider many basic inequality issues, emphasizing those that are amenable to policy changes. Welfare and distribution policies will be distinguished from those that could help "level the field," that is, give all a chance for an equal position at the economic starting gate. It will focus on how we can spend our fiscal resources to simultaneously secure both a reduction in inequality and an increase in economic efficiency, keeping in mind that the object of social policy is not to guarantee a certain life-style, but rather to guarantee that we all have access, on equivalent terms, to that life-style. Until that principle is reflected in policy, inequality reduction will come at the cost of efficiency.

Conventional wisdom holds that there is necessarily a tradeoff between equality and efficiency; this seems to me demonstrably wrong. The adverse inefficiency consequences of current policy can be reduced, and greater equality of opportunity gained, without a major increase in the expenditures already allocated to social welfare policy. In 1987, that amount was in excess of $600 billion. Given that total, and different policies, inequality and poverty can be reduced at the same time that efficiency and growth can be achieved.

The Appendix to Chapter 7 ("How Much Would All This Cost?") supplies some of the cost numbers on which this claim is based. It is fairly technical; it is also speculative. Nonetheless, I include it to show that reasonable cost estimates of the policy agenda sketched out are possible, even though the assumptions on which they are based rest on both political and economic choices.

Chapter 1

Economic Differences Among Us: Some Perspectives on Inequality

Economic differences among people are far larger in the United States than in most Western industrialized countries.[1] The image of the poor and the homeless living in the midst of affluence has long plagued both our national conscience and our international esteem. And it is precisely on such images that the case for the superiority of the market system model for economic development falters.

Clearly, the problem of poverty—of the economic "underclass"—in the United States is a serious one; just as clearly, economic differences among us have not decreased, even though the nation has devoted substantial resources to fighting poverty and redistributing income. As a matter of fact, since 1980 these gaps have grown, and we do not fully understand the reasons for that growth.[2] While we have come to live with such differences, they nevertheless make us uncomfortable. The discrepancy between the life-styles of the haves and the have-nots makes this society a less pleasant, less satisfying place to live than it could be.

Some Inequality Distinctions

The common notion of inequality concerns the overall gap between rich and poor, usually based on income but sometimes also on wealth and social status. Recent figures show that the poorest 20 percent of the people in the United States receive less than 5 percent of the nation's income; the richest 20 percent receive nearly one-half.

While the overall level of inequality is relevant, I will concentrate on the gaps between specific socioeconomic groups: between blacks and whites, males and females, youths and older workers, children and the aged, and between mother-only and two-parent families. These categories seem to be the most significant in terms of both social and political considerations.

Inequality of Outcome/Inequality of Opportunity

Many of the arguments in this book depend on the distinction between inequality of results (or outcomes) and inequality of opportunity.[3] Inequality of results refers to gaps in levels of living, as indicated by income or wealth. The black-white income gap, for example, and the male-female earnings ratio indicate the degree of inequality in living standards between these groups.

Inequality of opportunity is much more difficult to define and measure because there is no commonly accepted notion of the extent of opportunity. The basic concept, though, is clear: it has to do with having the same chance to run the race for economic success as others with similar talents and drives. Equality of opportunity exists if a black youth and a white youth have the same access to education, training, jobs, earnings, and incomes, according to their abilities. Racial discrimination, therefore, implies inequality of opportunity. So does discrimination based on gender, age, family background, or family structure.

It is difficult to deal with the idea of inequality of opportunity in a consistent manner. Is the failure of the military to include women in the draft an inequality of opportunity? Does the disparity between the percentage of blacks and whites in attendance at private colleges reflect inequality of opportunity? Is there inequality of opportunity when some children have trust funds established for them and others do not? The answer is yes. Each of these represents an inequality of opportunity, but since the elimination of all such disparities is quite out of reach, at least over any reasonable period of time, my approach will be more pragmatic. I will leave many differences in opportunity unchallenged, focusing instead on several particularly pernicious and socially disruptive disparities. These include black-white gaps in access to jobs and wage rates; male-female gaps in occupation, employment, and earnings; the unemployment (or inactivity) differentials among black and white youths; and the poor life chances of children in mother-only families.

The consistent theme of this book is my judgment that inequalities of opportunity are basically wrong. It is a judgment with which I believe most citizens agree, although there are differences among us in the lengths we are willing to go to in order to guarantee everyone an even start.

There is also the judgment that inequalities of opportunity are more fundamental and long-term—ultimately more serious—than are inequalities of result. In terms of result, the income of a thirty-five-year-old millionaire by inheritance may be very different from that of a thirty-five-year-old factory laborer, but few among us would call for confiscation of the income of the rich man in order to transfer it to the worker. We would immediately recognize the major costs of such a transfer—costs involving the disruption of an accepted system of property rights, the incentives created by such transfers, and the intrusive role of government that is implied.

This inequality can be compared with that of a thirty-five-year-old millionaire and a thirty-five-year-old unemployed mother on welfare. Here a new aspect of inequality is introduced. While the children of the millionaire have all the education and connections required for success, the children of the single mother have a far smaller chance of becoming educated, productive youths and adults.

The plight of the mother-only family disturbs our sense of fairness and justice more than the situations of the millionaire and the factory worker. Her children lack a fair start in life because of poverty; the mother lacks a fair chance because of constraints on her ability to work. They are being deprived of opportunities that our society believes should be generally available.

The most recent spurt of social policy—that begun in the 1960s with the War on Poverty—was focused on opportunities. Education, training, jobs, and equal opportunity were hallmarks of that effort. What started as an attempt to equalize opportunities has become side-tracked. The current tax-transfer basis of social policy has ceased to focus on opportunities. Cash disbursements may help meet immediate needs, but their effects are short-term and ameliorative. Moreover, this approach carries with it a set of adverse economic and social side effects that increase faster than poverty is relieved and inequality moderated. For these reasons, the system has exhausted its potential to achieve further reductions in poverty and inequality efficiently.

Our focus must shift from attempting to equalize outcomes to improving access to opportunities. Only then can we secure an authentic and lasting reduction of those differences that we as a society find so troubling.[4]

The Sources of Inequality

Where do inequalities come from? What characteristics of individuals or of the economy or society lead to the creation of these gaps? What role is played by nature as opposed to social environment, by choices as opposed to fate?

Although researchers have studied these questions for decades, the only clear conclusion is that inequality can neither be simply explained by nor easily partitioned among its various sources. I will try to convey some of its primary causes, distinguishing those that seem amenable to change through public policies from those that do not. At the same time, I will identify some as contributing to inequalities of opportunity, others as resulting in inequality of outcome.

Basic talents, intelligence, and capabilities are unequally distributed among people, and these differences are reflected in market payments—wages and earnings; they are essentially beyond the reach of public policy measures. The same is true for basic levels of motivation and physical appearance, although these characteristics also pay off in the market. The notion of effecting a major change in the distribution of these characteristics by policy is too macabre to be worth considering.[5]

Given a set of unequally distributed basic abilities, children are raised in families that differ enormously in their capacity to provide love and care. Some grow up in families with substantial income and wealth; others are raised in poverty. Many children live with two parents, some with one or none. Clearly, the nature of nurture has an important effect on how children develop. It is possible to alter some of the conditions of family life—income and the incidence of single-parent arrangements, for example— but much more difficult to influence attitudes, aspirations, perceptions of self-esteem, and the family's capacity for love and affection. These differences in the quality of family life represent inequalities of opportunity.

Children are also affected by the schools they attend and the length of time they remain in school. Decades of research have established the close tie between schooling and economic success, and access to education can be readily influenced by public policy measures. The maldistribution of the quantity and the quality of schooling is a basic inequality of opportunity. The "rate of return" on education (viewed as earnings increases from investments in human capital) has been competitive with investments made by private businesses in physical plant and equipment. And apart from increased earnings potential, there is a wide variety of other personal and social benefits, such as improvements in health, in the "quality" of one's children, in the greater efficiency of consumer choices, in reductions in criminal activity. When all is added up, the rate of return on schooling may be far above that of other investments.[6] The inequality of the distribution of our educational resources contributes strongly to the gaps among us.

Community environment and peer group influences also have deep and long-standing effects on ultimate economic success. To some extent, these conditions are subject to the influence of public policy (community action and neighborhood rehabilitation programs, for example) but only over the long term, and in any case they do not exist in a vacuum. The great discrepancy in community environments, then, also represents inequality of opportunity.

The results of these early years appear most clearly when youths try to enter the job market. Some take a job immediately, some hold out for better offers, some get no offers. Some choose a job with low starting pay but with substantial training and opportunity for moving up; others opt for higher starting pay but little chance for advancement. Some choose dangerous or unpleasant jobs that pay well; others choose safe and attractive lines of work that pay less.

To some degree, all of these choices reflect preferences, and all of them imply wage differences. When the differences are dominated by rational and deliberate choices, policy has a limited role. Few would encourage people who are averse to taking risks to take steeplejack jobs just because those jobs pay more. But more than preferences are at work. To the extent that these wage differences are based on the "external" inequalities of opportunity encountered, they deserve the attention of public policy.

Differences in pay are the result of more than just entry-level choices. In nearly all occupations there is an age-earnings profile. Higher wages go with experience, making age a factor in earnings inequality. Health is another one: workers with serious health problems will earn less over the long run, as will women who drop out of the labor force because of childbearing and child care. Pay differences based on these differences may be amenable to change by policy.

Discrimination in the labor market is a much discussed source of inequality in earnings. Women and racial minorities often earn less than male and majority workers with the same qualifications.

While such discrimination would appear to be subject to the influence of government policy, it has in fact been powerfully resistant to change—and it represents inequalities at the starting gate.

Many of these inequalities are reinforced by the wage policies followed by businesses. Firms in the United States often pay those in the top earnings decile more than ten times as much as they pay workers in the bottom decile. While economists tend to attribute these differentials to supply, demand, and marginal productivity considerations, there is nothing that says such gaps are necessary for productivity or efficiency. In Western Europe and Japan there are far smaller wage differences within firms, yet labor appears efficiently allocated and production seems cost-effective.[7] Thus, there is something about the wage structure in the United States, whether due to labor unions, management strategies, or competition for a mobile work force, that leads to wide disparities in earnings. In principle, public sector efforts to moderate wage structures would seem possible; in fact, this has never been seriously considered as part of the nation's political agenda.

On top of earnings inequalities, disparities in family or household income may be a function of whom one marries—what social science researchers call "assortative mating." The fact that college-educated females and males tend to marry each other tends to boost them up in the income and wealth distributions. Similarly, the decision to stay married or get divorced influences the level of family earnings and income.

Government transfer payments also affect the distribution of family incomes. Some families qualify for public income transfers—a family whose principal breadwinner is disabled, for example, or a family with an unemployed or retired worker. Such payments are, by and large, equalizing in nature and are thus a powerful instrument for reducing income inequality.[8] In fact, the public redistribution system involving transfer payments and taxes is the government's main tool for reducing poverty and inequality. But this kind of redistribution is aimed only at redressing the inequality of results; it does little to equalize opportunities.[9]

There is a final source of disparities which should be mentioned: the wealth holdings of families. These are distributed very unevenly; most derive from the efforts and accumulation of parents and grandparents, through bequests and inheritances. As with incomes, the government can influence the extent of this wealth through tax policy, but in fact, it does little to alter holdings by this means.

What we have, then, is a rather long catalog of reasons for much of the inequality that we see about us. After all other reasons have been accounted for, some inequality can only be attributable to random forces, to just plain good or bad "luck."

How Much Inequality Is Best?

Government social policies, affirmative action regulations, social insurance programs, and education and health care programs are the primary means of countering the basic inequalities that the interaction of tastes, talents, and markets generates. These policies are the result of a democratic process, reflecting a consensus that the measures are "socially correct," and the resulting distribution of income "optimally unequal," or at least closer to the optimum than it would be if the market system were allowed to operate without fetters. It then follows that unaltered "market inequality" is greater than most people desire.

Although this position is not radical, it has not been accepted by many who have thought deeply about it. The debate over the ideal level of inequality is similar to the debate over how many angels can dance on the head of a pin—neither has a resolution. The inequality debate boils down to a conflict over values. A brief discussion of the nature of this debate—and of the wide variety of positions—is in order before taking a deeper plunge into this emotionally charged issue. I will adopt the perspective of "standard economics" in order to lend some structure to the discussion.

Let's begin with the hypothetical assumption that all people agree on the nature of the "good life." Let us also assume that everyone's goal is to achieve the greatest level of well-being for themselves. If all people are similar in their tastes and in the satisfaction they get from consuming, it follows that everyone should have the same amount to consume.[10] In this hypothetical world, the distributional prescription is perfect equality.

A uniform allocation of resources rests on the fundamental economic principle of "diminishing marginal utility of income." If the amount of enjoyment from one additional dollar of income goes down as a person's income goes up, taking a dollar from a rich person and giving it to a poor one will result in an overall improvem nt in the well-being of the society. The well-being lost by the rich person will be less than that gained by the poor person.

This extreme "egalitarian" position is open to attack on a variety of fronts, but, mainly, because people are not alike. Because they are different and have different tastes and abilities, they are able to take actions that allow them to satisfy their distinctive wants. Those with expensive tastes will tend to work harder, be more active, and be more successful than others. Society benefits from the fruits of their energies and activities.[11] In an egalitarian society, there would be no incentive for these achievers to be so productive.

Another anti-egalitarian argument goes back to the observation that basic natural and biological talents are distributed unequally. Given that humans are biologically unequal, why is it important to make them economically equal? To attempt to do so, it is argued, requires a constant and ultimately fruitless battle against nature.[12]

One of the most prominent of the arguments against the egalitarian position rests upon the fundamental sanctity of property rights, and of certain civil and political rights.[13] According to its advocates, people have a right to what they own and to the produce of these possessions, and this right is inviolable. "To each according to what he and the instruments he owns produces," as the economist Milton Friedman puts it. What we guarantee to each other is an equal right to be involved in the social process, as represented by the market system, the political system, the judicial system, and so on. If these processes are judged to be fair, then the results which are generated by them are also fair, no matter how unequal these results are. This strong principle, it is argued, is the bedrock on which a society rests. Accepting it leads to the view that efforts by government to alter inequality—by taxes, by welfare, by social security, by public education, by affirmative action—are a violation of fundamental rights.[14]

This libertarian position coincides with the logic of standard economic thought, namely that there be a "correct" set of incentives if society is to get the most out of its limited resources. Only if the "right" signals are conveyed—the right prices assigned to different goods and services, and the right wages for different jobs—will the right amounts of work, saving, investment, and risk taking get done. To secure these "efficient" prices, businesses must be allowed to compete for talent and to pay each individual what he or she is worth in the job he or she is best qualified for. That is the only way to prevent surgeons from doing the tasks that sweepers should do, and engineers the jobs of clerks. Hence, wages must differ in line with productivity, as must interest rates and profits, and these differences generate efficiency—but also inequality—in a free market economy. Efficiency demands that property rights be enforced, and efficiency usually means substantial inequality.

The egalitarian position and the libertarian-efficiency position establish the two poles in the debate over the appropriate level of inequality. Both positions are part of the political debate, but neither has been fully accepted in Western societies. Public decisions have, in fact, been based on a more pragmatic stance, one which views policy interventions to reduce inequality as carrying a cost in terms of sacrifices of liberty and efficiency. This perspective recognizes both the costs of interventions to reduce inequality, and their benefits.

Philosophers and political theorists have searched for principles that would help define this "optimal" level of inequality. One prominent British economic historian, R.H. Tawney, focused on the inherent "powers" possessed in varying degrees by all people ("initiative, decision, common sense, imagination, humility, and sympathy") and based an egalitarian position on this perception. There is a social benefit to having these capacities developed to their fullest, he argued, but that can occur only when there is equality of "circumstances, institutions, and manner of life." The existence of differences among people in character and capacity,

Tawney wrote, "is no reason for not seeking to establish the largest possible measure of equality of environment, and circumstance, and opportunity. On the contrary, it is a reason for redoubling our efforts to establish it, in order to ensure that these diversities of gifts may come to fruition."[15]

Harvard philosopher John Rawls also presented a distributional rule—like Tawney's, a highly egalitarian one—that would embody a "principle of justice."[16] Rawls proposed a mental experiment that he believed would yield a guiding distributional principle that could avoid the influence of wealth and status on views of social justice. Each person would decide on the ideal degree of social inequality behind a "veil of ignorance," as if the economic process had not yet started, and he or she could end up being the least well-off person in society. Operating behind such a veil, all would agree that the least well-off person should be the one whose interests are considered, and any social and economic inequalities that are allowed to exist must be to the benefit of the least well-off members of society.

This "maximin rule," as it has come to be known, is a strong egalitarian position. Because no increase in the well-being of the more affluent people in society can compensate for even a small decrease in the well-being of the least fortunate, it raises the plight of the poor to a high level of concern. It has had an important impact on the equality debate.

The point here is that there are no generally accepted principles for determining the "best" level of inequality. What the debate has done, though, is to alert us to the most important things that have to be considered in taking a position. It forces us to identify the nature of the social gains of redistributing income or opportunities and to stipulate the costs (in freedom or economic efficiency) associated with redistribution. It forces us to identify the available options for altering inequality and to measure, to value, to compare the gains and losses associated with each.

The Gains and Losses of Redistribution: The "Leaky Bucket" View

The issue then is redistributive policy—interventions by government to change the level of inequality and poverty. The task is an economic one—evaluating the gains and losses from alternative strategies in order to reach informed decisions.

A great deal has been written on the costs of redistribution policies, most of which involve losses of economic efficiency due to taxes and transfers.[17] These measures are said to distort private decisions and to thereby impose costs on the economy. This view derives from the "model" on which economics rests—that individual decisions based on prices generated by an unfettered private market economy will yield the most efficient allocation of resources. From this it follows that decisions based on prices that are altered by government redistribution policy deviate from this private competitive norm and hence generate excess costs and inefficiencies.

Efficiency and growth, according to basic economic theory, are secured only if specialized skills and talents are allocated to the tasks and functions to which they are best suited; price and income differences help secure that allocation. This simple idea has given the discipline of economics a basically conservative cast, implying that interference with the process of choices motivated by economic incentives creates inefficiency and slow growth. Government redistribution and regulation is interference.

The conflict between efforts to reduce economic inequality and sustain economic progress has become known as the tradeoff between equality and efficiency, or simply as the "Big Tradeoff." Its most vivid description was presented by Arthur Okun of the Brookings Institution over a decade ago in *Equality and Efficiency: The Big Tradeoff*.[18] The volume caricatured the process by which government diverts income from those who have earned it to those who have not, emphasizing the losses of output and growth that occur along the way—the image became known as "Okun's Leaky Bucket."

This image and framework established the language used by politicians, economists, and citizens in discussing redistribution or antipoverty policy. As government seeks to "buy" additional equality, some efficiency—some economic growth, some goods and services—is sacrificed. To the extent that the losses from reduced inequality exceed the benefits, additional redistribution carries with it a net efficiency loss. Okun stated it this way:

> Some economic policies designed to reduce the scope and magnitude of inequality weaken incentives to produce and otherwise impair economic efficiency. At many points along the way, society confronts choices that offer somewhat more equality at the expense of efficiency or somewhat more efficiency at the expense of equality. In the idiom of the economist, a tradeoff emerges between equality and efficiency. [p. vii]
>
> A nagging and pervasive tradeoff [is] that between equality and efficiency. It is, in my view, our biggest socioeconomic tradeoff, and it plagues us in dozens of dimensions of social policy. We can't have our cake of market efficiency and share it equally. [p. 2]
>
> If both equality and efficiency are valued, and neither takes absolute priority over the other, then in places where they conflict, compromises ought to be struck. In such cases, some equality will be sacrificed for the sake of efficiency, and some efficiency for the sake of equality. But any sacrifice of either has to be justified as a necessary means of obtaining more of the other.... In particular, social decisions that permit economic inequality must be justified as promoting economic efficiency. [p. 88]

This tradeoff idea is central in contemporary economics: without tradeoffs, we could eat our cake and have it too. But the "Big Tradeoff" conclusion is a troubling one. It suggests some immutable, negative-sum economic conflict; it makes discussion over the future of the redistribution system highly divisive. It implies that if we attempt to provide more support to those at the bottom of the heap by, say, increasing Medicaid benefits, the rest of society will be heavily burdened. Each dollar of gain secured by the poor will come at a cost to the nonpoor that is some multiple of a dollar. Those who are relatively well-off not only have to pay the extra dollar in taxes, but will also bear the burden of the distortions—the losses associated with the work and savings reductions—which the taxes and transfers create. The magnitude at the margin of these costs relative to the gains is the critical comparison which the "Big Tradeoff" highlights. It is this comparison which, in a perfect and rational world, would guide decisions on whether to expand or contract the redistribution system. If the benefits of expanding the system are large relative to the costs, a larger redistribution effort is called for. Conversely, if the costs of expanding the existing system are known to be large relative to the gains, one would conclude that the system has been exhausted as an instrument for further combating poverty and inequality.[19] In a political context, such exhaustion would not bode well for those at the bottom of the heap, whom the rest of us at least claim we wish to help.

The Basis of the "Big Tradeoff": Exploring a Red Herring

But is this "Big Tradeoff" perspective an appropriate way of looking at the problem? As I see it, the basic premises on which this notion rests are at the least misleading, and often wrong in the case of social welfare or redistributive policy. It forces errors by restricting choices and generating erroneous information on the options available. A different and more realistic set of premises will lead to a different framework, a framework that poses an opportunity rather than a straitjacket.

Making this break with the "Big Tradeoff" is a form of economic heresy. It amounts to denying the validity of the basic conventional wisdom on which economists rely in thinking about public policy.

The basic premise of the "Big Tradeoff–Leaky Bucket" view is that decision makers are well-informed, consistent, and rational —that they have clearly defined objectives, well-defined options for achieving them, accurate knowledge about how each option contributes to the objectives, and that they choose among the options so as best to attain the objectives. In such a situation, tradeoffs are inevitable because not all objectives can be obtained simultaneously.[20] Some balance among them must be chosen, and as a result, some options will be pursued extensively and others hardly at all. Applied to the world of public policy, this view leads to Okun's "Big Tradeoff." It suggests a leaky redistribution bucket: more efforts to reduce inequality will cause efficiency leaks; it generates the question of how far redistribution policy should be expanded so as to balance equality gains and efficiency losses optimally.

But, the basic premise of the "Big Tradeoff" view is false; the "world of Okun" simply does not correspond with the functioning of the U.S. political system. Hence, the "Leaky Bucket" perspective does not give us much guidance for policy in our world. In our political system, there is no consistent government decision maker, whose job is to set the most rational policy. There is a Congress with a changing cacophony of voices and interests, which is checked and balanced by an administration that changes over time, sometimes rather radically, and by a judiciary that also changes, though not so fast.

These public decision makers help themselves by helping their clients and the vested interests who contribute to their support.[21] They have little or no well-defined notion of a social welfare objective writ large, nor of the components of that objective, nor of how individual policies affect these components. And even if they have a set of public interest goals which they profess, they are constrained in their efforts to achieve them by a political system dominated by powerful private interests. They often lack information—especially about interactions and consequences. Their knowledge about the effects of the policies they undertake is so crude as virtually to eliminate the possibility of rational choices. Perhaps most seriously, social movements and leaders change over time; tastes and perceptions change, and new and better knowledge comes to replace the old. Both the nature of the tradeoff and judgments about priorities are far from static.

In short, under optimal (ideal world) conditions, there would be some frontier-like curve to define society's equality-efficiency tradeoffs, much as Okun envisioned. Thinking in terms of this framework would clarify decisions and improve policy. But unless the basic requirements for this tradeoff relationship—consistent and rational decision makers, full information, the absence of political motives, and so on—are met, there is no such effective tradeoff curve. In an imperfect world, the "Big Tradeoff" is a red herring. It focuses debate on a simple, narrow, and miscast question: Shall we expand the nation's redistribution system, or shall we—in the interests of efficiency and growth—cut it back? Another framework and another set of questions will prove more fruitful and more enlightening.

Toward Equality with Efficiency: A New Framework

I believe that an alternative view—call it an "equality-with-efficiency" view—is a more appropriate way of viewing our public policy options. In this view, both equality and efficiency can be pursued simultaneously; there is no fixed tradeoff relationship to which we are tied. This perspective follows directly from the imperfect world in which policy is made. In such a world, the policies in place will not trace out some ideal tradeoff. Some of these policies will simultaneously contribute to both equality and efficiency; others may sacrifice both equality and efficiency. Still others will emphasize efficiency while sacrificing equality and vice versa.

In this alternative view, then, the trick is to identify and implement those policies that simultaneously promote both efficiency and equality. Those that sacrifice both should be abandoned. This view emphasizes the *reorientation* of the policy, rather than considering only the retrenchment-expansion options. It advocates substitution of public policy measures that will secure inequality reduction simultaneously with efficiency for those that score poorly on both accounts.[22]

The basic problem with Okun's "Big Tradeoff–Leaky Bucket" notion is that its domain is too limited. It presumes that the existing redistribution policy mix is fixed and that all we can do is to expand or contract that system at the margin. On the other hand, the alternative view holds open the possibility that policy can be radically redesigned. While the "Big Tradeoff" perspective causes myopia and limits efforts to identify new and different policies with quite different effects in the effort to achieve social well-being, the equality-with-efficiency view forces a search for innovative approaches. It holds open the possibility that policies with more favorable efficiency *and* equality implications can be substituted for those that do not score well at either—a case of eating one's cake and having it too.[23]

It is this perspective that motivates much of the remaining discussion in this book. The successes and failures of the present redistribution system lead to my proposal, which is designed to reduce inequality while simultaneously creating positive incentives for productivity-increasing, growth-inducing behavior. By moving toward a new system, divisive debate over whether to expand or contract the existing system can be reduced.

This equality-with-efficiency view, then, implies that existing programs and policies may have to be abandoned and that alternative strategies should be experimented with. It demands a search for a new approach for reducing inequality—a program consistent with and supportive of an economically competitive environment.

My proposed strategy is based on the judgment that such a reorientation is possible. It will achieve equality with efficiency by (1) targeting gains on the "new inequalities"; (2) substituting measures to increase opportunities for a strategy aimed at reducing differences in outcome; (3) increasing the wages of low-skill workers while expanding the demand for their services; (4) substituting individual choices and accountability for bureaucratic determination of services and benefits; (5) substituting parental for state responsibility for the support of children; (6) reducing the flow of public benefits for nontarget group recipients; and (7) fostering independence and self-support rather than reliance on public support. These are the objectives which it seeks, and by which it must ultimately be judged.

This package of new approaches is consistent with Professor William Baumol's recent admonition:

I do *not* conclude...that the search for...increased equality is quixotic. What is called for is an exercise in imagination and ingenuity, to find some alternative ways to go about this quest. We are not...wasting our time in looking for new and more heterodox means to reduce inequality without imposing an unacceptably high income loss upon society.[24]

The Gains and Losses of Redistribution: Toward Eating Cake and Having It[25]

The equality-with-efficiency view offers a radically different perspective on public policy and the choices that are available to us, but it does not reduce the need to focus on the costs and the benefits that are associated with the measures pursued. In truth, making a wise choice among the various options requires that the gains and losses of each—both in terms of equality and efficiency—be carefully assessed. Consider some of the most important of these gains and losses:

- Reduced or misallocated labor supply is the most often cited efficiency leak caused by public redistribution policies. Both taxes and social programs may reduce the returns from additional work effort by imposing marginal tax (or benefit reduction) rates. As a result, the gain in income from more work is less than the wage that is paid, and the incentive to work is weakened. Reduced labor supply and initiative lead to reduced output and growth.

- The adverse effect of redistributive taxes and social programs on savings and investment is regularly the target of the business press and economists; it is another potential leak. The argument is that corporate or property taxes reduce the returns from savings and investment; decrease the capital available for new machinery, plants, and equipment (the driving forces in the growth process); and slow down economic progress. Productivity gains are lower than they would otherwise be, and income is diverted from productivity-enhancing investment toward excessive consumption— yachts, cars, and vacations. The capital market is distorted; interest rates are unable to perform their allocative function.

- A negative argument is also leveled against programs such as the Social Security system. Because of Social Security, it is claimed, individuals no longer find it essential to save for retirement. Private savings fall, and because benefits are paid out of current payroll tax receipts, there is no increase in government savings to offset the loss. As a result, total savings and investment are reduced, output and economic growth are lower, and these losses destroy potential well-being.

- Similarly, social programs—especially welfare—have been accused of encouraging "dependence." Recipients, it is asserted, come to rely on government largess, rather than making a go of it on their own. Income support policies are also viewed as causing the migration of low-income families from low-benefit southern states to higher benefit northern cities. It is now not unusual for observers to accuse the welfare system of concentrating the poor in northern urban ghettos, hence heightening racial tensions. These effects, too, are efficiency leaks attributed to the existing system.

- The assertion that the incentives in redistribution policy have contributed to the increase in both divorces and births out of wedlock is based on the same logic: because of welfare payments which are available only to single parents (primarily, through the Aid to Families with Dependent Children program), women separate more readily from their spouses and receive government benefits. For a similar reason, husbands may feel freer to leave a relationship, realizing that their wives will receive welfare benefits if they no longer provide them with support. Some of the most strident attacks on the income redistribution system have suggested that unmarried mothers on welfare actually have more children because another child assures the retention of benefits.

The focus so far has been negative, emphasizing efficiency losses that might be attributed to redistribution policy—the leaks in Okun's bucket. But a wide variety of positive effects of social policy have also been established. The losses emphasize deviations from some idealized economic model; the gains, however, point to longer-term possibilities that are more likely to be achieved in the economy if more equal opportunities generate more equal outcomes. The losses focus on today's performance shortfalls; the gains point to the horizons and prospects for tomorrow.

- The primary benefit of redistribution policy, of course, is that it reduces the poverty and tempers the significant inequality that is generated by an unfettered market system. The overwhelming majority of citizens find these levels of market poverty and inequality unsavory. It is of value to citizens to have them reduced.

- A second and long-term benefit of redistribution policy is that it contributes substantially to the economic well-being of individuals by reducing the risks they confront in a world filled with uncertainties. Because redistribution policy tends to set a net under those who experience large losses from unemployment, illness, or the loss of an income-earning spouse, the uncertainty present in a market economy is diminished.

- A third important gain from redistribution policy—especially those programs concerned with education, health care, nutrition, housing, environmental quality, and occupational health and safety—is their contribution to human investment. They enable some people who would otherwise be ill-housed, ill-clothed, ill-fed, and ill-educated to become productive and contributing citizens. The relationship between these provisions and the wage rates that people command in the market is well-established.[26]

- To the extent that the redistribution system sustains demand in bad times and tempers it when there is inflation, it promotes economic stability. While certain aspects of the system may tend to stimulate inflation or push some prices and wages above their competitive levels, they are also likely to contribute to buoying that largest bloc of aggregate demand—consumption—when other sectors fail.

- Redistribution policies may also facilitate technological change. The phenomena associated with economic change, and thus with social resistance to it, are well-known—displacements from jobs; changes in the structure of families and roles within families; alterations in caring for children, the elderly, and the sick. The protection offered by the redistribution system may well ease the resistance and forestall conflict; it can grease the wheels of change. It softens the harshness of competition and tames the winner-loser character of the market. The Unemployment Compensation program is an important example: by cushioning the adjustments required in a market economy, it increases efficiency while reducing inequality. In the United States, this contribution of the income redistribution system is seldom emphasized; in Western Europe, it is taken for granted and serves as a primary rationale for the system.

These, then, constitute the positive and negative effects of any constellation of redistribution policies or of any policy strategy.

For both the existing redistribution strategy and any radically different alternative to it, an assessment of these sorts of gains and losses is necessary. With respect to the existing strategy, there is considerable evidence to suggest that poverty is reduced and economic gaps are moderated, and that by redistributing incomes, we have succeeded in helping millions of Americans. There is, however, equally compelling evidence that these redistribution policies have a variety of adverse resource allocation or efficiency consequences. Labor supply reductions, savings decreases or diversions, increases in dependency, and undesirable migration and family structure can, in varying degrees, all be laid at the doorstep of our existing redistribution efforts. In proposing an alternative strategy for this approach, my goal is to extend the gains that have been achieved while reducing the losses. This is what pursuing equality with efficiency is all about.

Statement of Position

My position is that the market system and the institutions surrounding it generate too much income inequality. This judgment is apparently shared by an overwhelming majority of American citizens, since the federal government now allocates over $600 billion a year to social welfare spending, much of which is designed to reduce these gaps. I have no difficulty accepting this level of public spending, or even more, to reduce the inequality and poverty which is the legacy of our market economy.

Saying this, however, in no way ratifies the nature of the strategies now being pursued. In fact, much of this book is a critique of the measures now in place. I argue that current strategy has come to focus too much on the reduction of inequalities of outcome (results), when the main problem is one of basic and serious inequalities of opportunity. Many of these latter inequalities need not exist; they are without justification in either economic or social terms. Consequently, I describe an alternative strategy that shifts the emphasis away from outcomes and toward the reduction of inequalities of opportunity. This strategy, I believe, will avoid many of the adverse side effects of the existing strategy and accomplish many of the objectives which, back in the 1960s, served as its basic rationale. It is designed to return social policy to its original vision.

In the game that determines how our national income is distributed, there are winners, there are losers, and there are those who aren't even part of the action. The winners are those who are successful in the marketplace or who receive enough help from the government to secure economic self-sufficiency. The losers are those who fail in the market or those for whom government policies, either directly or indirectly, are inadequate; the market supplemented by public transfers fails to raise them above the poverty line. They "fall between the cracks" of both the private and public systems, vulnerable and overlooked.

Unfortunately, the private economy has become an increasingly disequalizing force over recent decades. Overall inequality and poverty have crept up rather than leapt up only because of government efforts to help the losers. Nevertheless, the gap between the rich and the poor is widening: today nearly 70 percent of the wealth in the United States is held by the richest 10 percent of the population.

Government social policies since the mid-1960s have clearly helped many elderly, blacks, and women, the relative winners among the nation's most vulnerable groups. But on the other end of the success/failure spectrum are those groups whose relative status has actually worsened over the past two decades: minority youth, children living with single mothers, and those among the elderly who have inadequate retirement support. Except for the elderly, simple income support is not enough to change their plight. What is needed are policies that deal with the inequalities of opportunity that determine the economic prospects of these "new unequals."

The challenge for the nation's redistribution system is to return the losers to the economic mainstream. While some of the problems may correct themselves as demographics change and economic growth improves, the new inequalities that have emerged in recent decades will not evaporate. Trends currently under way suggest that many older people will fare better in the future than in the past, but that minority youth will not fare well at all without the technological skills that will make them attractive employees. The prospects for mothers and children in mother-only families are the bleakest of all. The so-called feminization of poverty will not go away without major reductions in out-of-wedlock fertility and divorce, or major increases in remarriage rates. And there is no evidence that these shifts are taking place.

For those whose economic position depends on government support, the outlook for ultimately achieving economic independence is not good—unless there is a shift in policy that favors measures that will provide them with far greater opportunities than they have had in the past.

Chapter 2

The Changing Patterns of Inequality: The Successes*

While the overall level of inequality in the United States changes with glacial slowness, the composition of the poverty population can shift rapidly. Some groups gain and move out of poverty; others lose. Government, through its redistribution system, works to help some of the losers, but its efforts to adapt to the changing economic and distributional patterns in our society do not keep pace with the changes. The reasons for the changes in the poverty population are complicated, involving fundamental issues of demographics, social movements, mores, and governmental policy.

Before looking at the "new unequals," those now at the bottom of the economic ladder, this chapter analyzes income distribution nationwide, including changes affecting particular social and ethnic groups, and examines the gains made by the "old unequals." For such an examination, it is necessary to discount inequalities that simply reflect normal life situations. For example, young workers earning less than more experienced ones present a distinct, well-known inequality, but not a serious or long-term

---

*Chapter 2 has been coauthored with Ross E. Finnie, who is responsible for many of the tabulations included in it.

problem. Unless the gap between two groups indicates an important inequality of opportunity, it does not reflect a sustained level of hardship for the group in question. If newcomers to the labor force lack the education and training to ever advance, the resulting gap will be sustained and serious. Similarly, children born into poor single-mother families are of concern: through no fault of their own they face a low level of economic well-being and a sharply limited set of long-run opportunities. For those of us concerned with even starting lines, those falling at the low end of these gaps are clearly confronted with an inequality problem.

How Unequally Is Income Distributed?

A few numbers paint a simple picture of how unequal the overall distribution of earnings and income is in the United States.

	1967	1983[1]
Share of income received by the bottom 20 percent of families	4.7	4.2
Share of income received by the top 20 percent of families	43.0	44.3
For working age (below 65) families, share of income received by the bottom 20 percent of families	5.3	3.9
For working age (below 65) families, share of income received by the top 20 percent of families	41.4	43.5

The share of the nation's total income pie which is captured by the richest people in society is large and growing, while the already slim slice going to the poorest of the nation's citizens is shrinking. Thus, the gap between the rich and the poor is widening. The figures indicate that the gap is growing faster for the younger (below 65) population than for the total population. Between 1967 and 1983, the Gini concentration index (a standard measure of inequality) increased by 4.2 percent for the total population; it increased well over 10 percent for nonaged families.[2]

While this discrepancy in income distribution is large, it pales in comparison to statistics on the inequality of assets and wealth.

	1962	1983[3]
Share of total wealth of the "super rich" (top 1 percent)	32.3	31.5
Share of total wealth of the "very rich" (next 9 percent)	32.3	35.1
Share of total wealth of everyone else	34.9	33.4

Nearly 70 percent of the wealth in the United States is concentrated in the hands of the richest 10 percent, and as with income, the concentration is increasing. The percentage share held by the very rich increased by nearly 19 percent over the 1962–1983 period; the share held by the bottom 90 percent fell by about 5 percent.

Although overall inequality is high, its growth, while troubling, is relatively small. For example, the growth in the Gini index for income is less than 0.25 percent per year for the entire population and less than 0.5 percent per year for families headed by a person under sixty-five. While we are trending toward more inequality, we are doing so slowly. Even the relatively rapid increase in inequality after 1980 does not invalidate this conclusion. This slow trend, however, camouflages some radical changes in the position of important groups in the economy over this period. Underneath the smooth surface is a boiling cauldron.

How Have Some of the Old Inequalities Fared?

In the early 1960s the inequality between blacks and whites was seen as the shame of a nation. The War on Poverty was begun in 1965, in part to aid the black population; it was spurred on by the same basic instincts as the civil rights movement of that period.[4]

A second visible and shameful inequality was that between the elderly and the working age populations. Like blacks, the elderly had poverty rates that were orders of magnitude greater than those of other groups.[5] While discrimination served to highlight the plight of blacks, the fact of poverty after retiring from a lifetime of work highlighted the unfairness of the plight of this group amidst a growing and affluent society. The elderly, like blacks, were targeted for help in the mid-1960s.

Gender-based inequality has also been on the front burner of national concerns over the past two decades. Women of the same age and educational background as men earned substantially less than men, and were denied access to occupations and jobs for which there were no gender-based requirements.

The policies of the federal government toward these three groups—blacks, elderly, and women—are well documented and need only be mentioned here. Much of the War on Poverty–Great Society initiative was, in fact, targeted on the special problems of blacks and the ghettos and rural areas in which they lived. Head Start, Job Corps, Upward Bound, and the Community Action program were all expenditure programs designed to increase the access of blacks to education and training. Affirmative-action and equal-opportunity guidelines were set and enforced in order to eliminate bias and discrimination in employment and housing. More generous benefits and easier access to welfare programs, especially the Aid to Families with Dependent Children program, were legislated. Finally, Medicaid was passed to provide health care coverage to the poor on welfare and to the disabled.

For the elderly, benefits in the Social Security retirement program were increased substantially, and ultimately indexed to the rate of inflation. The Supplemental Security Income program was passed to effectively ensure that no elderly person—even those without Social Security coverage—need live below the poverty line. And Medicare was enacted, over the opposition of the medical profession, to cover the largest and most feared of the unexpected expenses that older people often confront.

The gender-based inequalities were addressed as part of general affirmative-action and equal-opportunity legislation. Regulations and their enforcement (rather than expenditures) were the main line of attack on this front.[6]

These, then, are the primary "old inequalities" that prompted governmental action beginning in the early 1960s. What has happened over the course of two decades? Have we made progress in pulling these groups back into the mainstream of American life, or have we failed?

The Elderly—Depauperization on Average

The economic plight of the elderly was an important catalyst for the War on Poverty—Great Society efforts initiated in the 1960s. And their experience is an important success story.

The elderly of 1960 had low incomes and high poverty rates largely because their earnings during working years were low, and their accumulated savings negligible. Moreover, private pension plans were virtually nonexistent, and the ones that did exist provided only minimal income. In addition, many newly retired people in the 1960s were not covered by Social Security retirement benefits. For others, failing health and other unexpected expenses consumed much of their remaining income and wealth. The irony was that many who had worked hard for many years, raised children, fought wars, and suffered through hard times were not receiving a share of the nation's income pie that was proportionate to their input. Indeed, it was not even sufficient to raise many of them out of poverty in retirement.

This is no longer the case. Taking income as the best indicator of well-being, the following shows the gains from 1960 to 1985 for elderly couples of both races (in 1979 dollars):

	1960	*1985*[7]
Per capita income of white elderly couples	$5,000	$10,000
Per capita income of black elderly couples	2,300	4,600

For both groups real income approximately doubled—a rate of increase greater than that for prime-age intact families over this period.

This real income growth is also reflected in the poverty rates of the elderly. From the mid-1960s on, the poverty rates of the elderly eroded steadily, while those of other groups held constant or increased. As the following figures show, by 1985 the poverty rate for all elderly people had fallen below that of the rest of the nation's population. As a group, today's elderly enjoy a level of well-being which is at least equal to that of nonelderly citizens.

	1967	1985[8]
Ratio of poverty incidence of elderly to all persons	2.08	0.92
Ratio of poverty incidence of white elderly to all persons	1.95	0.76
Ratio of poverty incidence of nonwhite elderly to all persons	3.75	2.10

The situation of the black elderly is similar to that of blacks in general: while they have made substantial progress, the gap between black and white elderly remains large.

These gains in the economic status of the elderly can be attributed to the deliberate and rapid increases in benefits targeted toward older people, especially to benefits related to past earnings. Consider, for example, the enormous increase in spending on Social Security retirement benefits and Medicare, the two principal assistance programs for the elderly. Social Security benefits nearly tripled in real spending power from 1967 to 1985, while Medicare expenditures rose sevenfold. By way of comparison, spending in the Aid to Families with Dependent Children program was at about the same real level in 1985 as in 1967, despite the fact that the number of poor children needing assistance had risen.[9] This distinct favoring of the elderly population during the last two decades is seen clearly in the data on the real cash transfer benefits (1985 dollars) received by elderly (pretransfer) poor families relative to families in other poor groups over this period.

	1967	1985[10]
Average cash transfers to poor elderly	$4,925	$7,680
Average cash transfers to poor intact families with children	1,897	2,577

Average cash transfers to poor mother-only families	4,047	3,277

While the growth of real transfers to the elderly has been substantial, transfers to poor mother-only families have actually fallen. Elderly poor receive well over twice the assistance received by working age poor families with children. In addition, families with children typically have more members over which to stretch these lesser payments.

Black-White Inequality—A Relative Success Story

While blacks still frequently earn less than whites in comparable positions, the gap between them has narrowed considerably. Like the elderly, though not to the same extent, theirs is a success story. Consider first earnings, for they give the best picture of how the labor market is working. The following numbers tell the critical story in a nutshell:

	1960	*1986*[11]
Black as a percentage of white male earnings	31	73
Black as a percentage of white female earnings	57	89

The earnings of blacks grew dramatically over the past two decades. While parity is coming closer for females, a substantial gap still exists for males. Nevertheless, this represents real progress in reducing what was perhaps the most prominent of the "old inequalities."[12]

These gains in earnings have carried over to the income levels of families. The following numbers compare the total incomes of black two-parent and mother-only families with children to that of traditional white two-parent families:

	1960	*1985*[13]
Black income as a percentage of white income for two-parent families	64	78

Black income of mother-only families as a percentage of white income for two-parent families	33	32

The income comparison shown here reflects both the shrinking gap in labor-market earnings and the effects of the transfer system. From having less than 65 percent of the income of comparable white families in 1960, the income of traditional two-parent black families is now nearly 80 percent of white income. Essentially no gain has been experienced by black families headed by a woman (relative to the income of white two-parent families). The average black mother-only family still has only about one-third of the income of white two-parent families.

A final comparison shows this progress after allowing for the different average sizes of black and white families with children and changes in these sizes over time. Figures regarding the incidence of poverty account for this adjustment, since the poverty line to which a family's income is compared varies by family size and composition.

	1967	1984[14]
Ratio of black-to-white poverty incidence for two-parent families	4.06	1.64
Ratio of black-to-white poverty incidence for mother-only families	1.98	1.49

For intact families, the poverty rate differential has been cut by two-thirds since the start of the Great Society initiatives. The average black family is still far more likely to live in poverty than the average white family, however. While gains have been made for mother-only families as well, they are much smaller.[15]

These gains are impressive; progress has been made. But are they due to government policies, or are other factors also working in the direction of increased black-white equality?

James P. Smith and Finis R. Welch, two prominent labor economists from the Rand Corporation, recently explored the causes of this earnings catch-up for blacks, especially for blacks with strong labor force attachment. The main reason, they found, was the rapid increase in education: higher educational attainment, better quality education, and as a result, improved returns in the labor market. For example, in 1960, black men aged twenty-six to thirty-five had an average of nine years of schooling, about 78 percent of the 11.5 years attained by young white men. By 1980, the two levels were 12.2 and 13.6, respectively, a ratio of 90 percent.[16]

The quality of schooling for blacks has also improved. This improvement increased the monetary return from additional years of schooling; it also raised the level of wages of blacks. While education-based returns for blacks were about one-half the level for whites in 1960, they are now approximately equal, sometimes even higher.

Smith and Welch estimate that higher levels and improved quality of education together account for at least one-half (and up to 80 percent) of the decrease in the male black-white earnings gap over time.

Second in importance to better education, and in many ways inseparable from it, is the role of economic growth. Historically, blacks have been on the fringe of the labor market; their fortunes have risen and fallen dramatically with shifts in general economic activity. It has always been "last hired, first fired." Not only the number but also the quality of jobs open to blacks moves with the business cycle; better jobs and career opportunities open up in good times, and they disappear when the economy falters.

The period from the economic boom of World War II through the mid-1970s was a relatively good one for blacks. Economic growth was strong and many blacks found jobs, even fairly good jobs where their growing levels and quality of education were utilized and rewarded. The faltering economy from 1973 to the present has cut into this progress.[17] Nevertheless, the post-1960 record stands as a period of solid gains for blacks—at least for those with jobs.

The role of economic growth in narrowing black-white differences is also seen in the patterns of regional growth and black migration. Historically, the northern states had stronger economies, more economic growth, and smaller black-white earnings differences. These patterns attracted substantial black migration in the 1950s and 1960s, and migrational shifts played a significant role in the overall narrowing of the black-white differential in the period before 1970. They affirm the importance of economic growth to the growth of black earnings.

Civil rights legislation—affirmative action, in particular—surely played some role in improving the earnings of blacks in the period after 1965. Many observers, however, question the importance of affirmative action as a force in the long-run improvement in black earning power. Secular improvements, they argue, cannot be legislated; they must be grounded in more fundamental economic forces such as education and economic growth. Smith and Welch argue that affirmative action has had little direct effect on black economic status, but acknowledge that a decline in discrimination has been a significant factor in reducing income differentials.[18]

Other researchers, however, have found a more significant effect of antidiscrimination measures.[19] Indeed, affirmative action may have its main effect through changing people's attitudes toward hiring or working with people of other races.

Women—More Work, Stagnant Wages

Women form the third group of the triad of old inequalities. Policy initiatives to bring them into the mainstream of economic life in the United States have persisted over the past two decades, but have not been as visible as those directed specifically to disadvantaged blacks and the elderly. While undeniable progress has been made in the case of blacks and the elderly, no similar claims can be made for women.

To be sure, many more women are now in the labor force—the change is remarkable. In 1960, only 34.8 percent of all women, and 30.7 percent of all married women, were labor market participants. By 1986, these figures had increased to over 55.0 percent. However, while a great deal more female labor is employed, the rate at which women are paid has shown little relative gain, which is reflected in the following figures for the earnings of employed women relative to men:

	1960	1980[20]
Female as a percentage of male earnings for white high school graduates	59	58
Female as a percentage of male earnings for black high school graduates	67	75

Although there has been some improvement since 1980 (see Tables A.2 and A.3 in the Appendix), over this earlier two-decade period there was virtually no gain in the relative earnings of white women. For blacks, both male and female earnings rose substantially, although this trend has abated in the 1980s (see Appendix tables, as noted above).

The economic life of women has also been adversely affected by the breakup of the traditional family unit. At the same time that women increased their participation in the labor force, the incidence of living apart from males also increased. Single-mother households are a new and prominent living arrangement. Because some public income transfer benefits are available only to female-headed families and not to those headed by a male, one wonders if the differential in family incomes reflects the stagnation in female earnings. In fact, the welfare system, by supplementing the incomes of female-headed families, has kept the relative deterioration from proceeding as far as the earnings ratios indicate—especially for blacks. In spite of this, progress for women, in terms of either earnings or family income, is difficult to discern. The following figures show these patterns, again for racial groups:

	1960	1980[21]
White female as a percentage of white male family income, heads aged 35–44	44	45
Black female as a percentage of black male family income, heads aged 35–44	51	45

These comparisons cover the decades from 1960 to 1980; since then, some important (relative) gains have been recorded for women, especially for those who are full-time workers. For white women who work full time, the wage ratio between them and white men has risen by about 10 percent. However, much of this gain for women came at the expense of men. Male wages tended to drift downward during the early 1980s, while those of women held steady. There was, however, little real improvement in the absolute level of women's wages.[22]

It is difficult to understand why women's wages have not responded to the numerous efforts to reduce the gender wage gap. Explanations quickly focus on the difficulties that women have faced in breaking out of their traditional role.[23] Historically, women have specialized (or have been taught to specialize) in what economists call "home production"; in the labor market they have been secondary workers. They were more or less conditioned to choose courses of study, working arrangements, and often occupations that insured that the male-female wage gap would not close. Schools, colleges, and training programs reinforced these choices by offering programs that fostered the traditional female homemaking role.

When these women came to the labor market, they were confronted with low earnings, job insecurity, little advancement, and confinement to "female occupations." Choices made early in life —choices that were themselves largely determined by prevailing values—determined the outcome.

In the 1960s, this traditional pattern began to give way. More women began working outside the home, and a growing number of men and women chose not to marry. Most importantly, marriages began to fail at a rapidly increasing rate. These trends interacted, and in turn had important economic consequences: a failed marriage meant a woman would have to work more; the greater probability of having to work altered earlier education and training choices; being better prepared for work made remaining single more attractive and divorce more feasible. But even well-educated and highly qualified women who are committed to a career still find it difficult to achieve economic parity with males because of the sluggish adjustment of the labor market. Gender-role stereotypes, which determine both supply and demand, have not yet eroded sufficiently for working women to stop being an economic "underclass" of sorts.

Chapter 3

The Changing Patterns of Inequality: The Failures*

The "new inequalities" form a distinct set of serious social problems that have not been addressed well by existing government policy. Our current policy was designed for a different set of inequalities and a different set of economic and social forces. The progress made in reducing the old inequalities was unfortunately accompanied by the emergence of new inequalities caused by new forces.

One important change was that the distribution of earnings in the economy became more unequal. In addition, as those with inadequate educational background or training entered the labor force, it became increasingly clear that their position at the bottom of the economic ladder would be of long duration. And as traditional family structures changed, children, especially those living in mother-only families and the mothers who head these families, found themselves outside the economic mainstream and increasingly dependent on government support.

---

*Chapter 3 has been coauthored with Ross E. Finnie, who is responsible for many of the tabulations included in it.

Youths—Doing Worse While Doing Better

Some inequality in earnings is desirable. For example, one of the most important regularities in economics is the "age-earnings profile." Relatively low earnings early in one's career tend to give way to increases associated with age and experience, and usually peak at or near the end of one's working life.

Figure 3.1
1980 Age-Earnings Profiles for Full-Time, Full-Year
Working White Men, in 1980 Dollars

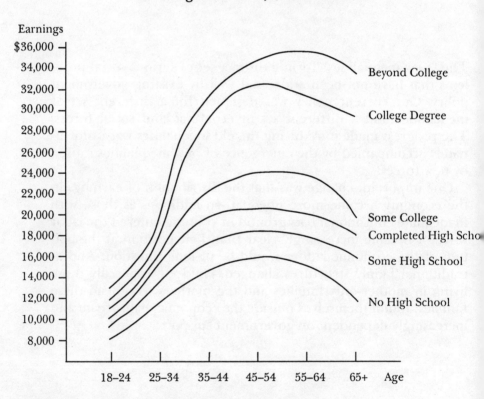

Note: Earnings include wage, salary, and self-employment income.

Source: Special tabulations from the 1980 Census of Population.

Figure 3.1 shows this pattern for white male full-time workers in 1980. It also shows that education makes a big difference in two ways. First, the age-earnings profile for those with more education lies above the profile of those with less. At any age, more education means more earnings.

Second, while we see that something of the classic age-earnings "hump" is visible for all white men, the profiles for those with low education levels are relatively flat. Only a small number of men with low education levels enjoy successful careers involving advancements, promotions, and large salary increases; most are stuck in jobs carrying little or no upward mobility.

The implication of this is very important—over their lifetimes, the earnings of low-education males will be only a fraction of those of men with more education. In addition to limited earnings and career advancement patterns, they will also be denied better jobs in other respects: stable employment, pleasant working conditions, generous fringe benefits, interesting work, and large pensions. Finally, undereducated workers lack the psychological benefit of being able to look forward to persistently increasing earnings throughout their careers and life cycles.

Over the past two decades, youths have fared increasingly poorly relative to older workers, even considering the educational gains of younger relative to older workers and the age differential. There has been a serious deterioration in their relative economic standing; the age-earnings profiles have become substantially steeper over time. The following numbers show the ratio of the earnings of full-time white male workers aged eighteen to twenty-four to the earnings of similar workers aged forty-five to fifty-four; the decline in these ratios is universal, and some of the drops are substantial.

	1960	*1980*[1]
Earnings of white male youths as a percentage of older workers—some high school	61	54
Earnings of white male youths as a percentage of older workers—high school degree	57	52
Earnings of white male youths as a percentage of older workers—college degree	48	41

These statistics partly reflect the entry of the baby boom generation into the labor market. Because there were more youths competing for available jobs in the late 1970s than in the 1960s, the wage rates they could command deteriorated relative to those of other workers. The kinds of entry level jobs that were available to youths also deteriorated. Millions of such jobs were created during the 1960s and 1970s, a disproportionate number of them in the low-paid, service sector. Low-wage jobs became the norm for poorly educated youths entering the labor market.

But these statistics apply only to those who made it—those who actually got jobs. Over the same twenty-year period (1960–1980), a large and growing group of youths were unsuccessful in the labor market. Their plight is reflected in the statistics on unemployment or, even worse, in the category of those "not looking for work." The following numbers suggest how far this deterioration has gone (see the Appendix for more figures); they are stark:

	1960	1986[2]	Percent Change
Unemployment rate of 16–24-year-old black men	13.4	28.6	+113
Unemployment rate of 16–24-year-old white men	8.5	11.6	+36
Unemployment rate of all men	5.4	6.9	+28

For example, through the early 1980s more than one-fourth of all black youths in the labor market were unemployed.

Why has the economic tide turned against youth in general? Why are minority youth especially hard hit? Given that the impact seems to be more on employment prospects than wages, even within racial groups, why are the youth employment burdens shared so unequally?

Identifying the causes of the deteriorating labor market performance of youths relative to adults is a treacherous enterprise. Numerous phenomena interact to result in this new inequality—changes in the strength of the economy, changes in demographic trends, changes in the attitudes and characteristics of youth, and changes in the incentives which they confront. Disentangling the forces entirely is impossible; the most we can hope for is some relatively accurate description of the role played by each of them.[3]

Far and away the most important cause of the discrepancy between youth and adults has been the performance of the economy. It is widely recognized that youth are far more sensitive than adults to swings in the economy. Just entering the labor force, they are the marginal working group, absorbing changes in labor market conditions. When overall economic performance deteriorates, they suffer to a greater extent than adults, and since 1973, U.S. economic performance has been weak.[4]

The demographic and labor force bulge created by the baby boom is often cited to explain the worsening earnings and unemployment experience of youth. It is a simple supply and demand story: the supply of entry-level workers increased rapidly; the natural market response was a downward adjustment in wages, with constraints on free-falling wages, and an increase in unemployment. While studies have found that this demographic development has led to deteriorating youth earnings and wages, it has not been found to have seriously affected their employment prospects.[5]

Two other demographic factors have also been at play: the increasing labor force participation rates of white women and new waves of immigration. There is some evidence that each of these influences has had an adverse effect on both the wages and the employment prospects of youths, especially on lower education and minority youths who always suffer the most immediate consequences of negative trends. And both of these forces are likely to remain in effect, indeed, increasingly so, as an increase in women's participation in the labor force is projected for the foreseeable future.

A third factor relevant to the decline in youth wages and employment prospects comes from a surprising source—the military. All youth, but especially black youth, have been highly overrepresented in the military forces. Since the Vietnam War, the size of the military has been reduced significantly, with a decidedly negative effect on minority youth, who have long found the armed forces a satisfactory alternative to the civilian labor market.[6]

Shifts in the structure of the American economy have also taken their toll on the job prospects of youths. The relative size of the manufacturing sector has declined, while the "service" and "high-tech" sectors have expanded. Structural unemployment is associated with any such change; workers do not move effortlessly and costlessly from one job and sector to another. Those with long ties to declining sectors slide into unemployment; growing sectors attract new labor market entrants. In both cases, young workers have been hit hard by these changes.

Historically, manufacturing jobs (usually covered by union contracts) have paid solid "middle-class" wages. This pattern contrasts with that of the expanding sectors, which have a greater proportion of low-paying jobs and very low entry-level wages. At the margin, youths tend to be overrepresented in these jobs and sectors. In this context, a minimum wage law has both a negative and a beneficial effect. The good news is that some of those who are lucky enough to find jobs will earn more than they otherwise would; the bad news is that fewer of them are likely to find work. Recent research on these effects, however, has found both of them to be small, relative to other effects that have buffeted the prospects of youth.[7]

No one denies that one's family and social environment have important effects on every aspect of life, in particular, regarding success in both school and the labor market. Similarly, few would deny that minorities are generally at a disadvantage in this respect. With minority youths much more likely to come from families characterized by both lower incomes and a higher incidence of single parents, the relatively poor labor market performance of black youths is partially explained.

Supplementing this linkage is the argument that young black men are particularly disadvantaged as a group because the broader social culture of the urban ghettos in which they grow up offers few positive role models and many negative ones. Instead of learning valuable work habits, self-discipline, and goal achievement from fathers in a stable, supportive home environment, some "black boys learn their lessons of manhood from that worst of teachers: the street." Further, when surrounded by the poverty and unemployment and general disaffection that accompanies the erosion of economic activity and the exodus of successful role models in deteriorating ghetto areas, it is not surprising that minority urban youths fail to embrace the middle-class ideal of schooling, a job, and hard work, and instead drop out.[8]

An important study by the National Bureau of Economic Research has found a variety of important links between attitudes, aspirations, environments, and ultimate economic success.[9] "Right" attitudes and aspirations, including churchgoing, were found to be significantly related to black youth employment success. Similarly, having strong career goals, working harder and doing better in school also contributed to getting and keeping jobs. Conversely, where the payoff for criminal activity was high, so was joblessness. Finally, black youths from families dependent on welfare, or living in public housing, or from families in which no one is working (and hence with fewer labor market connections) do far worse than those from other types of homes. The social dislocation often found in black ghettos is consistent with the worsening job experiences of black youths.

Mother-Only Families—The New Social Problem

The ways in which mother-only families are disadvantaged are legion. The facts of these disadvantages need only be summarized: by 1986, there were nearly 4 million mother-only families, up well over 1 million since 1980. More than 12 million people live in such families, and 40 percent of them have incomes below the official poverty line; 50 percent of the children in these families are in poverty, comprising one-half of all children in poverty. The problem is especially great for blacks. Over two-thirds of blacks in poverty live in mother-only families, and three-fourths of all black children in poverty live only with their mothers.[10]

The problem of out-of-wedlock births is intimately related to the problem of the mother-only family. Over three-fourths of all children born out of wedlock are born into mother-only families in poverty. The rapid rise in the rate of out-of-wedlock births, combined with the high rates of marital separation and divorce, have startling implications for the future of this population group. It is now estimated that over one-half of all children born today will live in a mother-only family at some time before they reach the age of eighteen. Indeed, some demographers now project that female-headed families will grow at a rate five times greater than that for traditional intact families.

The facts leave little doubt that the majority of this population of mother-only families represents a serious social problem. The numbers given below track the economic status of mother-only families relative to two-parent families over the twenty-five years from 1960 to 1985. It is impossible to find any improvement in their relative position over this period. Mother-only families are at the bottom of the distribution of well-being, and especially black mother-only families are falling further and further from the mainstream each year. This pattern is just the opposite of black two-parent families, who have closed the income gap between themselves and white two-parent families over the same period.

	1960	*1985*[11]
White mother-only family per capita income as a percentage of white two-parent families	63	57
Black mother-only family per capita income as a percentage of black two-parent families	61	48

It should be noted that the figures for 1985 reflect the major increase in income support and welfare benefits which became available through the expansion of the nation's redistribution system which accompanied the War on Poverty.

This increasing separation of the single-parent family from the remainder of the population can be seen in the trend in poverty statistics. The poverty rates of black and white intact families and the ratio of the mother-only rates to them follow:

The Changing Patterns of Inequality: The Failures

	1967	1985[12]
Poverty rate for white intact families	7.7	9.0
Poverty rate for black intact families	31.3	14.8
Ratio of white mother-only poverty rate to white intact family poverty rate	4.44	4.44
Ratio of black mother-only poverty rate to black intact family poverty rate	2.16	4.04

While the poverty rate for black mother-only families has declined somewhat since 1967 (from 68 percent to 60 percent), it remains at an alarmingly high level. The ratio of the poverty rate of black mother-only families to that of black intact families has nearly doubled; the comparable ratio for whites has remained unchanged at more than four to one.

Why has this increase in inequality occurred? Why have mother-only families—especially black mother-only families—come to constitute a new poverty group, perhaps the most dramatic of the "new inequalities"?

The primary reason is obvious—mother-only families have but a single potential wage earner; two-parent families have two, and in the past twenty years, the number of dual-income families has increased radically. For whites, the percentage of two-worker families increased from 44 percent to 65 percent from 1967 to 1984; for blacks the increase has been from 62 to 72 percent.[13] Mother-only families cannot supplement the family income by putting another adult to work.

A second reason for the development of this new underclass is that even when the mother is working, female earnings stand at about one-half of male earnings for any age and education level. The earning capacity of a typical mother-only family is considerably less than one-half that of the typical intact family.

The third reason is that while single mothers face the same set of labor market problems as all women, they are additionally burdened by child care responsibilities. About two-thirds of all female family heads fail to earn enough to raise their families out of poverty. The comparable figure for the heads of intact families is about one-fifth, and this pertains to the earnings of heads only; most such families have two adults in the labor market.[14]

While conventional wisdom has it that the earnings shortfall of mother-only families is largely made up by child support and alimony payments, in fact, absent fathers are poor providers. Consider the following statistics:

- Only 52 percent of white fathers and 26 percent of black fathers pay any child support.
- Of those who do pay, average annual amounts (1982) were $2,294 for whites, $1,754 for blacks.
- Child-support payments amount to 15 percent of family income for white mother-only families and 13 percent for blacks.
- Only 61 percent of children who live with their mothers are covered by any court-determined child award.
- Of this 61 percent, less than one-half get the full amount; 26 percent receive nothing at all.[15]

Thus, the court-administered child support system in the United States has largely failed in its responsibility to secure the well-being of children confined to mother-only family life by non-marriage or broken marriages. The resulting inequality seems particularly cruel, as the well-being of absent fathers often rises after they leave home.

The final weak link in the chain of mother-only inequality is the role of government transfers—in particular, welfare programs. Since the 1930s, the Aid to Families with Dependent Children (AFDC) program has been in place. Starting in the mid-1960s, there was a general effort to supplement AFDC benefits, resulting in Medicaid, for example, and the food stamp program. By the early 1970s, it was commonly assumed that the most severe hardships associated with single-parent family living were eased by this safety net of public support.

In fact, since 1960 the support provided by the public safety net has fluctuated widely. Table 3.1 documents these changes. During the 1960s, AFDC benefits rose in both per family and per recipient terms; after the mid-1970s, they deteriorated. During the late 1970s, the decrease was steady, and reflected budgetary stringency among state governments. Inflation eroded benefits faster than legislatures raised them. After 1980, the rate of reductions increased. Federal policy emphasized retrenchment in transfer benefits, and the recession of 1981–82 further tightened state government budgets. By 1983, real per family benefits from AFDC were only two-thirds of their level in the mid-1970s.

Table 3.1
AFDC and Poor Families and Children, 1960–1983

Payments per Recipient Families	1960	1967	1973	1979	1983	1983/Peak Year
Monthly Payments per Recipient Family (in 1983 $)	356	463	428	360	312	.65
Monthly Payments per Recipient (in 1983 $)	93	112	123	123	107	.81

Source: U.S. House of Representatives, Committee on Ways and Means, *Children in Poverty,* May 1985, pp. 191–92, 212, and 214.

Table 3.2 summarizes the effect of the changing value of cash transfers on mother-only families. In 1967, at the beginning of the War on Poverty, cash transfers were lifting 25 percent of white, and 11 percent of black, poor mother-only families above the poverty line. By the early 1970s, these percentages increased

Table 3.2
The Antipoverty Impact of Cash Assistance on
Mother-Only Families, 1967–1984

Percentage of Mother-Only Families Lifted Out of Poverty Due to Cash Transfers	1967	1973	1979	1983	1984/Peak Year
White	25.1	29.1	23.6	14.0	.48
Black	11.2	18.0	16.5	9.9	.55

Source: Sheldon Danziger and Peter Gottschalk, "How Have Families with Children Been Faring?", Institute for Research on Poverty Discussion Paper 801–86, University of Wisconsin–Madison, 1986, pp. 31, 41.

to 29 and 18 percent, respectively, before trailing off. By 1983, cash assistance lifted only 14 percent of white, and 10 percent of black, poor families above the poverty line.[16]

Considering these factors, then, the disadvantaged position of mother-only families relative to intact families comes as no surprise. With but one potential earner—and that earner at a substantial disadvantage in the labor market—the relatively low earnings of single mothers constitute a meager economic base. And supplemental income sources—child support from absent fathers and government assistance—have been far less provident than is commonly believed. Since the mid-1970s, government assistance to mother-only families has fallen off drastically—inflation, fiscal austerity in state governments, and since 1980, deliberate retrenchment in federal social spending have all taken a toll.

The deterioration in the status of mother-only families is only one side of the story. The rest of the story concerns the radical increase in the number of these families. In 1967, only about 10 percent of all families were mother-only families; by 1984, over 21 percent; by 1984, over one-half of all black families were headed by a mother.[17]

Clearly, economic and social factors have played a role, and perhaps the structure and generosity of welfare programs have also contributed to the increase in mother-only families. Charles Murray has suggested that welfare benefits encourage women to have children out of wedlock, or if married, to opt out of marriage with modest economic consequences.[18] The research that has been done on this issue shows that welfare benefits may have caused mother-only families to live independently, and may reduce the probability that they will remarry—or remarry as fast as otherwise. Only in this sense, however, has welfare generosity contributed to the growth of the population of mother-only families.[19]

In sum, then, this demographic shift toward mother-only families is largely explained by changed earnings opportunities: positive ones for white women, negative ones for black men. In both cases, the costs of being a single mother (relative to having a spouse) have decreased, and more marital splits for whites and an increased incidence of never-married mothers for blacks has occurred. While general economic conditions and changes in social norms have also played a role, they have not been found to be significant. Finally, while welfare benefits play a trivial role in either causing intact families to split or never-married women to have children, they do have some effect in enabling single mothers to maintain an independent household, and to be more cautious and selective in considering marriage or remarriage opportunities.[20]

Children—Squandering a Nation's Most Valuable Resource?

A nation's children are its most important resource, the bedrock on which future economic growth and prosperity depend. The time and resources that we devote to their development will determine not only their future style and level of living, but ours as well.

We don't often think about how we, as a nation, are treating our children. A few years ago, however, a prominent demographer, Professor Samuel Preston, raised this issue directly and forcefully.[21] Focusing on the government and its spending priorities, he concluded that children are being shortchanged relative to other groups, and increasingly shortchanged over time. Public spending on a wide array of programs aimed at children is being cut back; the quality of the services provided children—education, family income support, health and nutrition—has been deteriorating over time. The nation, he concluded, is neglecting this most valuable of its resources.

While Preston was looking at the commitment of the public sector toward children, other studies were analyzing the overall levels of economic well-being of children and the families in which they live. The findings of these studies were consistent with Preston's conclusion. Consider the following:

	Poverty rate for children under 18	Ratio of children's poverty rate to total poverty rate[22]
1967	16.3	1.15
1973	14.2	1.28
1979	16.0	1.38
1985	20.1	1.44

At the beginning of the War on Poverty, the poverty rate of children was not much above that of the rest of the population. Since then, there has been a steady and inexorable increase in the child poverty rate. At present, children are about 50 percent more likely to be living in poverty than the rest of the population. Over 13 million children are now counted as poor, compared to about 10 million at the end of the 1960s. Over 40 percent of the nation's poor are children.

This poverty is not evenly distributed across the population; it is concentrated in particular racial and family-type categories. For example, in 1984, when the poverty rate for all children was 21 percent, the rate for black children living in mother-only families was over 60 percent. For white children living in single-parent families, the rate was over 40 percent.

These numbers lead naturally to the next question: What has happened to the income of families with children? Figure 3.2 gives an overview of the pattern of inequality among families of different types in 1980. The per capita income of the family is taken as the indicator of economic position. The two high bars for each education level are for white and black two-parent families; the low bars are for mother-only families. Note how the relative differences by race and family type diminish with education; it is a powerful equalizer. The final set of bars, where education is ignored, summarizes the salient point: On a per capita basis, white mother-only families are about 60–65 percent as well-off as white two-parent families, while black two-parent families have about the same level of per capita income as white mother-only families. Black mother-only families have but one-half of this low

Figure 3.2
Per Capita Total Family Income by Education Level of Head,
Race, and Family Type for Heads Aged 35–44, 1980, in 1980 Dollars

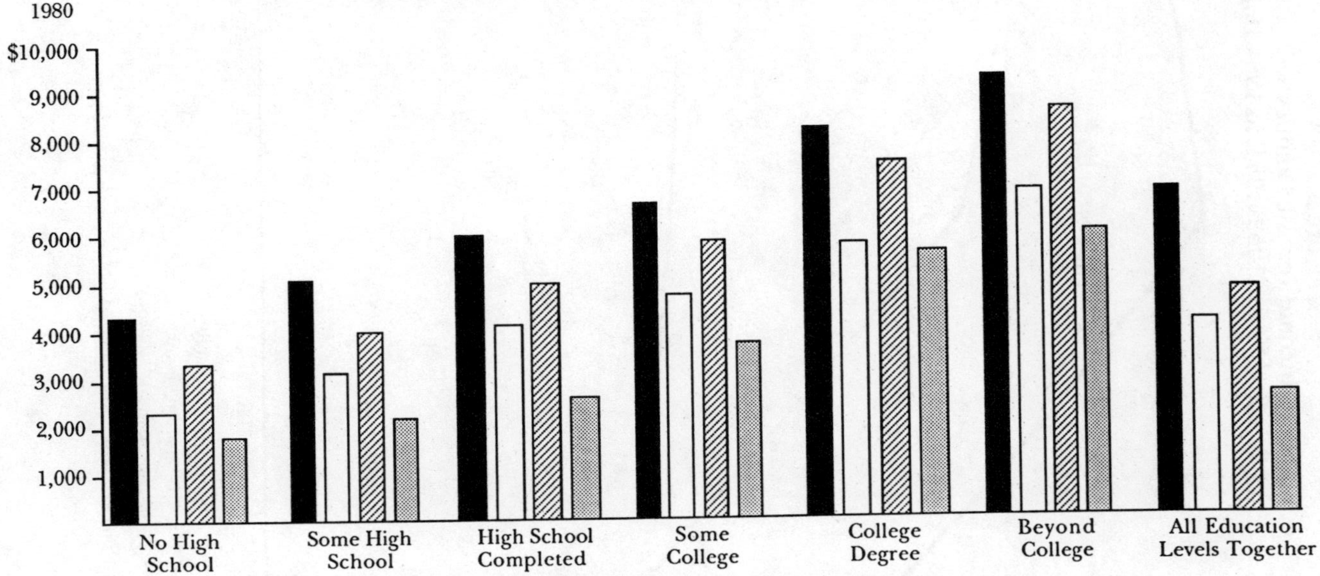

Note: Calculations by the authors from 1980 census; based on total family income for all families with children.

Key: White: 2 Parents Black: 2 Parents
Mother–only Mother–only

Figure 3.3
Total Family Income for All Families with Children, for Selected Years, 1959–1984, in 1984 Dollars

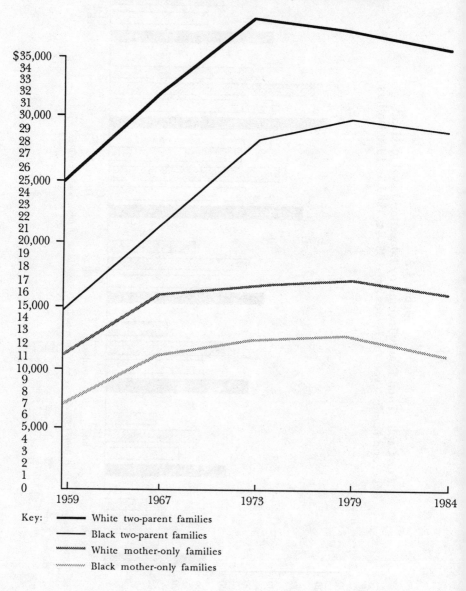

Key:
— White two-parent families
— Black two-parent families
~ White mother-only families
~ Black mother-only families

amount. The problem of child poverty, then, is intimately tied up with the problem of the mother-only family, and in particular the black mother-only family.

Over the past quarter-century, this group of mother-only families has found themselves pulling away from their counterpart two-parent family group. Figure 3.3 documents the general erosion in the position of this group. The trends shown there also indicate erosion of well-being of children as a group. Consider the following patterns:

- The period from 1959 to 1973 was a good one for all of the family types. The last part of this period, however (1967–1973) saw the gains made for mother-only families falling off, while two-parent families continued their steady upward progress.

- The period from 1973 to 1979 was one of relative stagnation for all family types. Interestingly, black two-parent families did the best, and white two-parent families the worst, over this period.

- The most recent period (1979–1984) saw real income decreases for all family types. Again, black two-parent families showed the best performance; they lost less real income than the other family types.

- Over the entire period, two-parent families improved their economic well-being substantially, especially black two-parent families. After keeping pace from 1959 to 1967, mother-only families showed virtually no gains in the 1970s and 1980s. Over these years, they pulled apart substantially from two-parent families.

The income gaps shown for 1984 are substantially larger than they were in 1959. There are greater economic disparities among children from different family backgrounds than there were twenty years earlier—in this important dimension we have become a more unequal people.

There is also more inequality among children within racial and family type categories. The following numbers show the distribution of income within the various family groups:

	Percent of total income of bottom 20 percent of families		Percent of total income of top 20 percent of families[23]	
	1967	1985	1967	1985
All families with children	6.6	4.2	38.5	42.2
White families with children	7.3	4.7	37.8	41.3
Black families with children	5.3	3.5	42.4	46.7
Hispanic families with children	6.0	4.4	40.5	44.2

The story is the same for all of the groups: Those at the bottom of the heap have lost in terms of their share of the income pie throughout the entire two-decade period. In each case, the 1985 share of the pie going to the families with the poorest children is only about two-thirds of what it was in 1967. Conversely, those at the top of the distribution have shown steady gains. Poor families have become relatively poorer; rich ones relatively richer. And this shift has occurred within each racial group. Another, more salient, interpretation exists. Consider a 1 percentage point decrease in the income share of the bottom 20 percent which is transferred to the top 20 percent. Such a shift represents a staggering income loss of about 25 percent for those at the bottom, but a trivial income gain of only about 3 percent for those at the top. The shifts indicated in the table, therefore, represent an enormous increase in inequality among children in the United States.

The Vulnerable Elderly—Falling Between the Cracks

One of the biggest success stories chalked up to the nation's redistribution system is its role in pulling up the average standard of living of the nation's older population. As a group, the elderly are no longer poor—no longer a source of equity or fairness concerns. Indeed, their level of living has come to look very much like that of the rest of us.[24]

But "Beware of the Mean."[25] The Social Security program, which takes the lion's share of the credit for income gains of the elderly, distributes its benefits in a very particular way. Those who have worked all or most of their lives, and especially those who had high earnings when they worked, receive the highest benefits when they retire. When they die, their spouses continue to receive relatively high benefits. But not all elderly people have high-paid working histories. Some were single nonworkers; some were low earners or intermittent workers; some are widows of low-earning men; some are divorced from beneficiaries and have no earnings record of their own. Indeed, as of 1984, over one-quarter of all widows aged sixty-five and over had incomes below the official poverty line. Those living alone had especially high poverty rates.[26]

These elderly groups have fallen through the cracks of the Social Security program. As their peers and friends experienced increased benefits and cost-of-living adjustments that moved them out of poverty, they have been left behind. To be sure, the Supplemental Security Income (SSI) program (a welfare program) may provide them with some income support. But only about 60 percent of the eligible elderly participate, and in many cases these benefits do not boost them above the poverty line. The following real income numbers illustrate the relative poverty and inequality which this has created:

	1960	*1985*[27]
Per capita income of white elderly couples	$5,000	$10,000
Per capita income of black elderly couples	$2,300	$4,600
Per capita income of black widows	$1,900	$4,200

The first row shows how the best-off of the elderly have fared from 1960 to 1985. By 1985, their per capita money incomes were about as high as the average citizen's, but not all have fared well. In 1985, the per capita income of black elderly couples remained at 46 percent of that of their white counterparts; the per capita income of black widows was 42 percent of that of white couples.[28]

The reasons for this pattern are clear. Elderly blacks who are now retired faced a hostile labor market during their working years—discrimination was rampant, their education levels were low, work was intermittent and low-paid. This fate is reflected in paltry retirement benefits today. And the widows of these men fare even worse.[29]

These "left-behind" elderly, then, are surely an inequality of import. Any effective change in the nation's redistribution system must attend to their needs. That they should continue to rest at the very bottom of the income distribution would seem to violate nearly everyone's sense of justice and fairness.

"Two Steps Forward and One Step Back"

The developments recounted in Chapters 2 and 3 show that, as a nation, we are concerned with poverty and inequality and have taken steps to reduce them. Important groups who were out of the economic mainstream in the early 1960s have been brought back in. The elderly and blacks, especially those in intact families, represent the major successes of the past two decades. Progress, however, has been far less than complete.

Even as we continue to improve the lot of the "old unequals," the focus for the future is on a set of new inequalities: groups that have become separated from the mainstream through a variety of causes—demography, economics, values, policies. These "new unequals" form as serious a problem as the traditional inequalities which drove the War on Poverty in the mid-1960s. They represent some of the most vulnerable groups in society— minority youths, children, single mothers, and the elderly who must live with inadequate retirement support. In several cases (notably minority youth and single mothers and their children), the economic inequalities are the result of inequalities of opportunity. The constraints and disadvantages faced by these groups severely hinder their economic prospects. Simple income support will not solve the problem. In subsequent chapters I will argue that the current redistribution system is not up to the task of dealing with these new inequalities and that a new way of doing the nation's inequality reduction business is in order.

Chapter 4

The New Inequalities: Transitory or Persistent?

For reasons of policy, demography, economics, and perhaps culture, the face of inequality has changed in new and sometimes unexpected ways. Children, single mothers, minority youths, and single and minority elderly people are all examples of groups whose relative economic position has recently worsened in spite of massive and—until the late 1970s—growing government income transfers and social programs. Bringing these victims of the "new inequality" back into the mainstream is the primary challenge for the nation's social policies.

The basic questions concern the nature of this new inequality problem: Is it temporary or are those affected likely to be at the bottom of the distribution over the long haul? Are some aspects of it self-correcting? Will economic and demographic changes over the next decades automatically work in favor of these newly disadvantaged groups? These questions must be addressed if redirections in policy are to be as effective as possible, and if they are not to create still other new inequalities.

The task of forecasting future economic and social developments is, of course, a treacherous one. No models exist to reliably guide long-range economic forecasts. Projections must be tempered with judgment. Future demographic changes are somewhat more predictable, as certain aspects of the population are known. For example, forecasts of the ratio of the aged dependent population to the working age population in 1995 or 2000 are likely to be in the ball park—the relevant age groups are alive and counted. For the same reason, forecasts of the relative size of the youth population in, say, 1995 or 2000 are believable.

This discussion of long-term trends in both the population and the economy will yield a number of clues about how the new unequals will fare in the future. The conclusion is not optimistic. Those who have fallen to the bottom of the distribution during the last two decades are not likely to return automatically to the mainstream. Policies must be specifically directed to their particular circumstances.

The United States at the Century's Turn

The structure of the population in the year 2000 will be quite different from what it is now.[1] Consider first the age structure, for it is here that some of the most radical changes in population composition will occur.[2] Whereas the overall size of the population is expected to grow 12 percent from 1985 to 2000 (from 247.6 to 277.5 million), the group aged sixty-five or more will grow by 24 percent—double the growth rate of the general population. Those aged eighty or over are projected to grow by an astounding 62 percent. Interestingly, while growth in this population cohort is expected to be enormous, the ratio of the aged to the working age population will edge up at a much slower pace. This is because the size of the working age population will also expand as those born during the baby boom (about 1945 to 1965) are absorbed by the labor force.[3] By 2000, the number of aged people relative to the working age population (those aged sixteen to sixty-four) will grow from 20.2 percent to 22.1 percent.

The "old-old" (those over 80) are projected to increase from 4.3 percent of the working age population to 6.3 percent. These population patterns are pretty much set. The people who will form the elderly and working age populations in 1995 or 2000 are already born, and except for unexpected contingencies (e.g., wars, natural disasters, epidemics, and other unforeseen changes in mortality rates), these patterns will hold.

The U.S. economy will also increase by the year 2000. While long-term economic growth can be predicted only roughly, the prospects between 1985 and 2000 are good, at least according to the positive changes expected in the labor force—its basic determinant. By the year 2000, the baby-boomers born between 1945 and 1965 will be thirty-five to fifty-five years old, and at the peak of their productivity.

However, the size of the working age population does not accurately predict how plentiful workers will be. The following table shows labor force participation rate projections for the 1984–1995 period:

	1984	1995[4]
Male		
16–24	72.8	73.9
25–54	93.9	93.0
Female		
16–24	62.8	65.3
25–54	68.2	78.1

For men, participation rates will remain high—increasing slightly for younger workers, trailing off slightly for middle-aged workers. For women, the story is quite different. Moderate participation increases are projected for younger women, large increases for mature working age women.

The official projections indicate that the propensity for those over fifty-five years of age to work will continue to decrease over the next decade. For men over fifty-five, the rate is projected to fall from 42 to 33 percent; for women, from 22 to 19 percent. However, this projection is extremely tenuous due to changes both in policies toward retirement and in expectations regarding the length of working lives.

Indeed, the trend toward early retirement that appeared in the 1960s and 1970s may well reverse itself in future years. With life expectancies rising rapidly, the number of potentially productive years after age sixty-five has expanded significantly. There is increasing sentiment, both among policymakers and among members of the older population themselves, that working lives should be extended. Indeed, there is evidence that increasing numbers of older people wish to work longer. The elimination of mandatory retirement, the scheduled increase in the normal retirement age from sixty-five to sixty-seven, and changes in a variety of incentive arrangements in pension programs designed to discourage early retirement all point in this direction. It would, therefore, not be surprising to find that work participation rates for older workers will stop falling over the next decade, and perhaps begin rising.[5]

All of this suggests that the labor force will grow even faster than projected for the working age population.

A second basic determinant of economic growth is labor productivity—output per work hour. During the early postwar period, the underlying conditions for productivity growth were very favorable—the capital stock that workers used in production grew rapidly, the quality of the work force in terms of education and experience improved, and a difficult-to-measure phenomenon, "technological change," was rapid. Productivity in the United States economy grew rapidly—nearly 3 percent per year. Beginning in about 1970, however, these conditions became less favorable. The oil crises in 1973 and 1978, the rapid growth in regulations imposed on businesses, the changes in the age structure, the reduced experience of the labor force (more youths and more women) all helped reduce the amount of output each labor hour yielded. Productivity growth fell off drastically, to effectively zero by the late 1970s.[6]

Looking ahead, the underlying factors supporting productivity growth again appear quite favorable. Savings are likely to expand as the middle-aged cohort (forty to fifty-five), which typically has the highest savings rates, grows rapidly. Without the need to accommodate the entry of a large baby boom cohort into the labor force in the next decades, whatever new investment is generated by these savings can be concentrated on a smaller increment to the work force than in past years; the capital-per-worker trend is favorable.

The work force will embody the recent gains in education,

training, and other forms of human capital that have occurred, and will reflect the benefits of experience that are associated with a maturing population.[7] Finally, if technological developments continue as they have in recent years, this also augurs well for the future.

The projected increase in the productivity and size of the work force suggests good prospects for economic growth until the turn of the century. Together with the relatively slow projected growth of the overall population, *per capita income* (a rough measure of aggregate prosperity) will grow at a rate of about 2 to 2.25 percent from now until 2000.[8] If this happens, the U.S. population in 2000 will be substantially richer than it is today; the "average" citizen will be as much as 40 percent better off than today.

This means that our society will have both income and output that will enable us to do many things we cannot now afford. Government spending could grow substantially with no increase in tax rates; private consumption and savings could also expand. Choices must still be made, of course, but a wide variety of new social and economic policies can be placed on the table for consideration.

However, this relatively rosy picture of the economic future should not be allowed to cover up a wide variety of other problems and issues that the next decades have in store. Most importantly, all groups will not fare equally well. A rising tide does not lift all boats. As Chapters 2 and 3 emphasized, the fortunes of particular groups may differ substantially from that of the population as a whole. From 1960 to 1980, as impressive gains were made by some, we also witnessed a deterioration in the relative economic position of minority youths, those in single-parent families, and other vulnerable groups. While it is difficult and risky to anticipate how the future will deal with these particular groups, in the following pages, I will speculate on how they will fare under the most likely future demographic and economic trends, assuming that our present basic economic structure stays in place.

Future Prospects for Vulnerable Groups: Some Speculations

THE AGED

As Chapter 2 showed, the aged as a group have done very well since the 1960s. On average, their economic well-being was at least equal to that of the nonaged by the mid-1980s, and it surpassed the economic status of children. However, some of the aged—especially widows and minorities—have not fared well, and many of them face a variety of insecurities such as the fear of high medical costs in the face of limited medical insurance (Medicare), or the loss of housing subsidy benefits, or the vulnerability of relying on Social Security benefits as the main source of income.[9]

The future economic prospects of the aged will be buffeted by a number of powerful and sometimes contradictory forces. The most important factor involves changed expectations about the age at which working people are expected to retire. Throughout the postwar period, but especially in the 1960s and 1970s, the trend has been toward increasingly earlier retirement. The Social Security system made provision for retirement at age sixty-two in 1961; during the 1960s and 1970s disability benefits became available on relatively easy terms for people younger than sixty-five with some health problems; mandatory retirement rules became increasingly widespread; and private pension plans encouraged retirement prior to age sixty-five. In general, this trend was supported by both employers and employees. The former saw it as an opportunity to introduce "new blood" into the enterprise; the latter found retirement with income support an attractive alternative to work.

Since the mid-1980s there appear to be powerful forces working in opposite directions. Motivated by both an unexpectedly rapid rise in longevity, health, and fitness among the older population (and by the rapidly rising costs of Social Security), the possibility of longer working lives and a higher retirement age has entered public discussion. This was reflected in the 1983 Amendments to the Social Security Act, which gradually shifts the normal retirement age from sixty-five to sixty-seven by 2022. That act also reduces the generosity of benefits offered under early retirement, increases benefits if retirement is delayed, and reduces the penalty (in the form of decreased benefits) on earnings above the exempt amount. Similarly, in the late 1970s the age of mandatory retirement for most workers was raised from sixty-five to seventy, and the age at which the Social Security "earnings test" ceases was reduced from seventy-two to seventy years of age. In 1986, mandatory retirement was abolished completely, except for a few small groups. Despite some policy changes discouraging continued work, the pendulum has been swinging toward prolonged working lives.[10]

This shift has substantial implications. First, as a group the elderly in the year 2000 will be working more and earning more than today's older population, and projections indicate that they will be more unequal as well. As a result, they will be less dependent on income transfers from Social Security and benefits from private pension plans. Second, as older workers remain on the job—or at least on some job—longer, they will compete with newly entering workers, primarily, youths and women. While the increase in work by older workers will not harm the employment opportunities of these groups in any significant way, to the extent that there is an effect, it will be negative. And particularly for poorly educated youths, who already face very high unemployment rates, any adverse contribution to their employment prospects must be given heavy weight.

In addition, the number of very high income–high wealth elderly will substantially increase, and the income distribution among the aged is likely to become substantially more unequal. The reason for this trend lies in the massive buildup of both private pension wealth and individual retirement savings which have grown in response to a variety of tax-deferred annuity plans. Those with high incomes during their working lives will be able to parlay this into high retirement income.[11]

Workers covered by these pension plans tend to be among the more highly paid and the most steadily employed. For example,

86 percent of regular private sector employees who earned $25,000 or more in 1979 were covered by a private pension, but only 45 percent of those who earned less than $10,000 per year were covered. So the most affluent employees will be eligible for private pension benefits in addition to Social Security benefits, which are also higher for those with high working age wages. As a consequence, those with the highest earnings while working will be receiving the highest Social Security and private pension benefits when retired.[12] There seems little doubt that in the future, the elderly will have a more unequal distribution of income and wealth than the current older population.[13]

This inequality is reinforced by the nature of Keogh plans for the self-employed and individual retirement accounts (IRAs) for employed workers. Until the Great Tax Reform of 1986, these accounts exempted the amount contributed from taxation, allowing the entire contribution to earn interest and to increase in value. Taxes were imposed only on the amounts distributed as benefits. Given these pre-1986 tax provisions, it is not surprising that high paid workers are more likely to have IRAs than low paid workers. In 1982, for example, nearly 60 percent of people earning more than $50,000 per year contributed to an IRA; only about 8 percent of workers earning less than $10,000 were contributors. This disparity is even greater than that for private pension holdings. These private, tax-deferred savings will, like the private pension funds, support new cohorts of retired people in future years, but in a very unequal pattern.

In sum, then, the over–sixty-five group at the turn of the century will, in all likelihood:

- choose retirement at an older age than is now the norm (official projections to the contrary);
- increase their work effort and productivity, and hence their income, during "retirement years";
- enter retirement with substantially increased wealth in the form of private pensions, IRAs, and other private savings;
- receive markedly larger retirement income flows from these private pensions and annuities; and

- will, in addition, receive Social Security retirement benefits which are projected to increase at the same pace as the price level.

This projection, however, is potentially misleading. While the elderly as a group will be doing well, some will continue to fall behind both the other elderly and the rest of the population. Older women, mainly widows, some older men, and minority couples form the largest and most destitute of these groups.[14] Without changes in legislation, it is difficult to imagine how these disadvantaged elderly persons will share in the prosperity expected for the nation in general, and for most of the aged in particular.[15]

YOUTHS

Youths, more than most groups, are buffeted by changes in both the economy and demography. For example, most young people with education and training did well during the low-growth and stagflation period of the 1970s and 1980s, successfully making the transition from school to work and career advancement. Others (largely school dropouts and minorities living in large cities) did poorly and experienced growing unemployment rates and deteriorating levels of well-being. Many were not engaged in any productive activity—they were not working, not looking for work, and not in school. Those with less than a high school education who were working were on flat earnings trajectories reflecting dead-end jobs, long periods without a job, or regular job switches.

The youth population also experienced a decline in its earning and employment performance relative to older workers. The large baby-boom population that entered the labor market contributed to this lagging overall progress. In short, educated youths became differentiated from less-educated ones, and youths in general drifted apart from the older working age population.

The future, however, is a bright one for youths, even with no major changes in policy. Demography is clearly working in their favor: the cohort which will be eighteen to twenty-five years old over the next fifteen years is not a large one. The fertility declines recorded in the late 1960s and 1970s (the baby-bust period) means there will be far fewer youths making the school-to-work transition in the next fifteen years. Job opportunities for youths will tend to increase and youth unemployment rates should fall.[16]

The following numbers indicate the reduced numbers—and increasingly favorable position—of those aged sixteen to twenty-four in 1995, relative to 1975 and 1984, in millions:

| | **1975** | | **1984** | | **1995 (projected)**[17] | |
	Number	Percent of Total	Number	Percent of Total	Number	Percent of Total
Male	12.4	13.2	12.7	11.2	10.5	8.2
Female	10.3	11.0	11.3	8.2	9.6	5.8
Total	22.7	24.2	24.0	19.4	20.1	14.0

While the size of the youth population grew until the mid-1980s, it is projected to fall until the end of the century. The number of youths working or seeking work is projected to be about 16 percent less in 1995 than in 1985; they are projected to fall from nearly one-quarter of the labor force in 1975 to 14 percent by 1995.

While this is the most powerful trend dominating the prospects of youth over the next decade or two, other factors will be at work as well. First, because of current policies—in particular, a restrictive policy on low-income student aid and training subsidies—the distribution of educational attainments will tend to become more unequal in the future. Children from wealthy families will be able to increase their schooling while others are likely to fall further behind. This gap in educational opportunity will of course result in a similar gap in outcomes: Some youth will be better prepared than ever for a promising labor market entry; others will find themselves unable to successfully compete in the labor market.

Second, the reduced support for affirmative action in employment, education, and housing in the 1980s will, if continued, deny additional gains in opportunity to more disadvantaged youths. Even with the supportive policies of the 1960s and 1970s, unemployment rates for low-education and minority youths were disastrously high (see Chapter 3). Continued erosion of this commitment also suggests growing economic gaps in the future.

Increased competition for entry-level jobs may not come from other youths, but competition will still affect their future prospects. Official forecasts suggest that women's labor force participation will continue to increase, although not at the rates experienced in the 1970s. Illegal immigration, despite legislation mandating stricter enforcement, is unlikely to decrease significantly. So long as these trends exist, youths will continue to face stern competition for entry-level jobs, at the same time that older workers stay on the job longer, thus reducing the growth in the jobs available.

A final factor is a big unknown: What will technological developments hold in terms of job prospects for youths? Here, only one forecast is clear—namely, that without training in computer and technology-oriented activities, youths will be at a growing disadvantage, separating still further those without marketable skills from those with them.

Predictions of this sort are not new; a similar forecast was offered in the 1960s and 1970s with respect to the youth labor market of the 1980s. The boom in service jobs at relatively low-skill entry levels which developed in the 1970s and 1980s largely confounded that forecast. The question is: Has that boom now passed, or will it persist until the end of the century? Most observers are not sanguine that the structure of future labor demands will continue to camouflage the low employment qualifications of much of the youth population.

These are only the most important of the factors that must be considered in judging how well youths—black and white, highly educated or not—are likely to fare over the next decades. A variety of other factors will also influence their fate, and most of these are even more difficult to predict. Some can be identified by inquiring as to why, during the 1970s, minority youth employment opportunities eroded so badly relative to those for whites. An exhaustive assessment of this question was undertaken by two economists from Harvard University, Richard Freeman and David Wise.[18] In addition to those mentioned here, their study identified several other important factors:

- The changing structure and size of the military (this was found to account for 20 to 30 percent of the 1970s growth in the black-white male youth employment gap);
- Changing macroeconomic conditions (another 20 to 30 percent of the growing 1970s gap was attributed to the series of recessions during this decade and the general deterioration in economic performance);
- Changing patterns of school enrollment and work while in school (during the 1970s black school enrollment rose relative to that of whites, while white students worked substantially more while in school than did blacks; these factors also partially explain the growing gap of the 1970s);
- Changing family background (because youths from intact families both work more and attend school more, some portion of the decline in relative black performance during the 1970s can be laid to the rapid increase in single-parent families among blacks during this period).

In sum, then, the slow growth in the number of youths seeking employment in future years will improve their overall employment prospects. But this sanguine outlook fails to reflect a multitude of potentially negative forces: the continuation of current policies in education, training, affirmative action, and the military; the expected increase in competition for entry-level jobs by women, illegal immigrants, and older workers; and the likely growth in demand for youths with technical training. The gap between well-educated/poorly-educated and white/nonwhite youths is likely to grow in future decades.[19]

SINGLE PARENTS AND THEIR CHILDREN

In terms of disparate opportunities, single mothers and their children are the most prominent of the "new unequals." That children as a group have fared relatively poorly over recent decades is due primarily to the rapid growth in the number of mother-only families in which they live. Poverty rates for this group are shockingly high (Chapter 3).

Projecting the economic outlook for these families is even

more risky than forecasting the economic future of the aged or youth. The list of factors determining their prospects is long and interrelated in complex ways: the sizes of cohorts; fertility decisions; marriage, divorce and remarriage decisions; work and education decisions; and a long list of public policies including the level of welfare benefits, work and training associated with welfare benefits, and potential changes in the nature and function of schools are all relevant considerations.

But some clues as to what the future holds for mother-only families can be gleaned from recent trends that affect them. The outlook is bleak. The growth of divorce and separation rates, along with the increase in births out of wedlock, is the big story. In 1960, 92 percent of white and 68 percent of black children were living with both parents; by 1980, these percentages had fallen to 83 and 43, respectively. A staggering 57 percent of all black children were *not* living with both parents. Especially among low-income blacks, childbearing has become increasingly separated from marriage.[20] By projecting these trends, some observers have concluded that nearly one-half of all children born today will spend some part of their first eighteen years in a family headed by a single mother.[21]

Accompanying this trend has been the "feminization of poverty." Even though single mothers have a relatively high propensity to work, their wages are low, and, without a husband's income added to their own, the likelihood of poverty is high.[22] Furthermore, it would seem overly optimistic to expect that the nation's court-based child support system would so improve as to increase significantly the incomes of mother-only families. Indeed, as of 1985, about one-half of all those in mother-only families were poor, a far greater incidence than for any other major population group. When this pattern is combined with the rapid projected growth of the single-mother population, nearly one in four American children born today are projected to experience some degree of poverty before reaching the age of eighteen.

As with youths and the aged, the overall economic prospects for single mothers depend in part on the future size of this group. Professor Richard Easterlin of the University of Southern California has examined this phenomenon in terms of his "relative cohort size" view of economic development.[23] In this view, the number of single mothers depends upon divorce rates, which in turn depend upon stresses related to women's work and child-bearing. These phenomena, in turn, depend upon the relative size of cohorts, with larger cohorts facing declining labor market and earnings prospects. As he sees it, the rapid changes in women's work, childbearing, and marital disruption which occurred in the 1970s are all part of a package, and all reflect the fact that the cohort of young adults during that decade was very large.

This "relative numbers" framework leads to some optimism that these adverse trends will be retarded if not reversed in the years until 2000. The growth of marital dissolution—and the resulting increase in the female labor force—should slow down, while childbearing should increase. If Easterlin is right, the growth in mother-only families will be smaller in 2000 than in previous decades.

While some economists and demographers would agree with the general direction of these predictions, there is disagreement regarding their magnitude. Few would forecast a reduction in the number of single mothers, or even a reduction in the number of them falling into poverty. And all would agree that even under the most favorable circumstances, single mothers will be rearing a growing fraction of all American children.[24] Moreover, this more favorable outlook for the mother-only group relates to this population as a whole; little is implied concerning future developments for particular groups of mother-only families, such as blacks or Hispanics, as Professor Easterlin himself is quick to point out.

By the year 2000, then, it seems unlikely that the average mother-only family will experience significant relative improvement in its economic well-being. The number of such families will continue to increase, though perhaps more slowly, as will the trend toward the "feminization of poverty." Only very large reductions in fertility (especially out-of-wedlock fertility) and marital dissolution, combined with a large increase in remarriage rates, are likely to reverse this projection, and such changes have not appeared on the horizon. The high poverty incidence of a growing number of mother-only families seems a fact which policymakers fifteen years from now will have to confront.

Conclusion

This discussion suggests a relatively favorable set of general economic prospects for the United States over the next ten to fifteen years, with an improved labor market outlook for those with the skills and training to take advantage of it. It also suggests that, as a group, the elderly will do quite well with the current set of Social Security policies and institutions in effect. However, at the same time there will be a large number of elderly—women living alone and some nonwhites in particular—who will continue to occupy the bottom of the distribution. As compared to the last decade's experience, a favorable outlook is also forecast for youths entering the labor market. But these gains will be concentrated among those with the education and skills necessary to meet the job demands of the future; poorly educated youths, especially minorities, face a less hopeful outlook than those with skills and training. For single-parent families the prospect is generally unfavorable; while the increase in single mothers might moderate, they will continue to encounter obstacles to their sharing in the projected growth in employment and real wages.

While overall prospects for the elderly and youth seem optimistic, "Beware of the Mean." Only those with high earning capacities will do well; others will continue to be counted among the poor. The elderly with low benefits or without pension coverage, without home ownership or other assets, and youth with little or no education and training will continue to need financial support. They will continue to depend on specifically targeted policies that allow them to move into the mainstream of American economic life.

PART III
Government and Inequality

The federal government is the chief spender, taxer, and redistributor of our national income. Many of its policies are designed to combat poverty and inequality, to transfer resources from the "haves" to the "have-nots." An enormous redistribution system is now in place, including welfare, Social Security, health, and education programs. But even though this system is aimed at the disadvantaged, its results often fall short of its goals.

From 1960 to 1980, the government budget was transformed from a traditional defense-transportation-natural resource enterprise to a major engine for poverty reduction and income redistribution. Although the government redistribution system put in place has narrowed some of the gaps that separate Americans, it has not been able to reverse the trend toward an increase in overall inequality. Nor has the system been effective in dealing with many of the new inequalities that demographic and economic developments have created. Moreover, these policies have had a major effect on the structure of the U.S. economy, its productivity and growth; the size, structure, and location of families; and on labor supplies, migration patterns, and savings and consumption.

These economic effects of the public redistribution system are part of the economist's "efficiency domain." They occur because of the incentives that are created when the government taxes some in order to assist others, and in the process, distorts prices and wages. For example, a tax increase on high-income earners (designed to support higher welfare benefits for the poor) may reduce take-home pay for these workers, and erode the incentive to work longer or harder. Similarly, incentives created by the redistribution system may depress national savings and investment, alter family structure, and induce migration. To the extent that these incentives generate "uneconomic" behavior, they erode efficiency. In fact, there is a variety of potential efficiency losses that can be caused by the redistribution system as people are given incentives (or disincentives) to make choices that may detract from economic growth.

On the other hand, the redistribution system tends to reduce economic insecurity and uncertainty, and to increase economic stability. It is also conducive to facilitating economic change, to creating human capital, and to promoting individual well-being. These efficiency gains from the system need to be set against the economic losses generated by the adverse incentives and distortions that it creates.

To assess the overall efficiency impact of the system, the questions that need to be answered are: At the margin, do the losses associated with expanding the system exceed the gains? Should the system be expanded or cut back?

At this point, additional gains in economic security, welfare, and equality generated by the current redistribution system seem too costly in terms of their harmful efficiency effects to warrant continued expansion. A new way of doing the nations' inequality reduction business must be found if reductions in poverty and inequality are to be achieved along with gains in national efficiency. This section of the book analyzes the reasons for this conclusion.

Chapter 5

Has Government Reduced Inequality?

The federal government is the nation's leading income redistribution machine.[1] Nearly all actions that it takes affect our well-being; some people are affected positively (in the form of benefits), others adversely (through higher taxes). The goals of reducing poverty (or inequality) and of setting a minimum income floor are central to several government programs—for example, welfare, food stamps, and Medicaid. Other programs —for example, Social Security and unemployment benefits— seek to offset income losses. Still other government activities —for example, trade and tariff restrictions—give little deliberate thought to combating poverty and inequality, but also have some bearing on the distribution of income—for example, restrictions that limit competition result in higher prices for consumers.

The transfers—in the form of assets or rights or power, in addition to income—often go from the rich to the poor, but not always. In some cases, the poor are hurt while the rich benefit. But many of the transfers—Social Security retirement benefits are an example—go from those in the middle back to those in the middle; what the government takes with one hand it returns with the other. People's positions in the income line-up change as the pattern of these transfers changes.

This chapter will focus on the government as spender, taxer, and redistributor. Because of these government activities, we are a more equal society than we would otherwise be. But it would be misleading to say that government is consistent and rational in the application of its redistribution policies. For example, government redistribution activity increased radically from 1960 until the late 1970s, but it has since reversed direction.

In 1946, a national War on Poverty was declared; and in the next fifteen years the government initiated a wide range of policies to benefit the low-income population, including equal rights legislation, clearly intended to reduce inequality in access to the polls, jobs, education, and housing.

These actions suggest that government favors "bottom dogs" over "top dogs," but it is also easy to find a host of government policies that move income and wealth toward the "haves" of society—for example, depletion allowances that provide substantial tax savings to holders of oil and mineral rights, water subsidies to large landholders, and trade and tariff restrictions that protect a variety of businesses and industries from competition. The stated purpose of these policies is not redistribution, but they tend to move income, wealth, and power toward the top.

Government policies are pragmatic in making these redistribution choices. A spending program targeted to help poor blacks may be coupled with a tax provision to help owners of corporations, regardless of race. Income shifts to one group may be offset by a flow of some other "currency"—that is, wealth, rights, or power—to another group. Policies that may have hurt one group yesterday may result in a program that will assist that group tomorrow. The "currency" of the hurt and the help may be quite different, and the mechanisms of redistribution may be unrelated—a tax policy yesterday, a subsidy tomorrow—but there are redistributive effects in both cases.

Nobody keeps track of these arrangements; there is no grand scorecard of who gets what from government. But there is some evidence—most of it from economic researchers—on the federal government's overall effect on inequality. The findings are straightforward: while taxes have been mildly equalizing since the 1940s, spending programs increasingly have carried the weight of the government's redistribution efforts. Spending programs aimed at aiding those at the bottom of the income spectrum have grown rapidly.

The basic questions are: Has the government been successful in achieving greater equality? Has it been effective in reducing the gaps that separate us? In general, the answer is yes. But the "new inequalities" that have emerged in the past several years have undermined the government's attempts to achieve a more equitable distribution of income, as well as more widespread access to opportunity. Until recently, the result had been a standoff; since 1980, inequality has won.

Reducing Inequality Through Public Benefits, 1950–1980

Radical changes have occurred during the past three decades in the priority given to reducing poverty and inequality. In 1950, the federal government was largely filling the traditional "macro" functions which most of us associate with public activities—keeping a strong military and national security posture, investing in natural resources, conducting international relations, creating and maintaining a transportation and communication system, and so on. Beginning about 1960, however, government again accepted explicit responsibility for intervening in the social affairs of the nation, reasserting the commitment that was made in the New Deal programs of the 1930s. It responded to issues of poverty, discrimination, and ultimately to riots in the streets. The transformation of government priorities is reflected in the enactment of the War on Poverty, the Great Society, Medicare, Medicaid, Community Action, and expansions in Social Security benefits.[2] By the mid-1970s, however, the enthusiasm for these efforts had waned, and by 1980 the pendulum had swung back. Until then, the government was increasingly concerned with domestic problems of discrimination, insecurity, and gaps among important groups. But the Reagan administration shifted government away from social intervention toward more traditional military-infrastructure activities.[3]

Table 5.1 shows the pattern of government spending from 1950 through 1985. The way the programs are grouped highlights the changes in priorities that have occurred. The bottom part of the table emphasizes the traditional functions of government; the top part of the table shows government's efforts to help individuals through direct income support and subsidies or grants for people to buy essential items like medical care, food, and housing. The programs in this part reflect efforts to alter people's relative well-being; they directly change outcomes.

In 1960, the ratio of traditional programs to social policies was

Table 5.1
Federal Government Expenditures, 1950–1985, by Category
($ current, in billions; percent of column totals in parentheses)

	1950	1960	1965	1970	1980	1985
SOCIAL POLICIES						
Cash Income Support	11.4(27)	24.9	31.2(26)	51.4	216.8	331.5(35)
Income security[a]	4.1	7.4	9.5	15.6	86.5	128.2
Social Security[b]	.8	11.6	17.5	30.3	118.6	188.6
Veterans' benefits[c]	6.5	5.9	4.2	5.5	11.7	14.7
Helping People Buy Essentials	2.8(7)	3.4	4.3(4)	21.8	96.3	133.7(14)
Health services[d]	2.0	2.3	2.1	12.0	56.6	102.3
Education, training, and social services[e]	.4	.4	2.2	9.6	34.1	30.4
Housing	.4	.7	—	.2	5.6	1.0
TRADITIONAL PROGRAMS						
Direct Subsidies to Producers	2.5(6)	4.6	6.8(6)	8.5	19.2	39.3(4)
Agricultural subsidies[f]	1.9	2.3	3.6	4.6	7.4	24.8
Water, air, and ground transportation[g]	.6	2.3	3.2	3.9	11.8	14.5
Defense, Space, Foreign Affairs	18.5(43)	52.0	62.1(53)	91.1	153.9	279.3(29)
National defense	13.7	48.1	50.6	81.7	134.0	252.7
International affairs	4.6	3.0	5.3	4.3	12.7	16.2
Science, space, and technology[h]	.2	.9	6.2	5.1	7.2	10.4

Investments in Physical Environment	1.8(4)	2.1	3.2(3)	4.4	24.1	19.1(2)
Energy	.3	.5	.7	1.0	10.2	5.7
Natural resources and environment	1.5	1.6	2.5	3.4	13.9	13.4
Revenue Sharing	—	.2	.2(−)	.2	8.6	6.4(−)
Other Programs	2.6(6)	4.9	7.8(7)	12.4	39.6	40.2(4)
Net Interest	4.8(10)	6.9	8.6(7)	14.4	52.5	129.4(14)
Financial Allowances	−1.8	−4.8	−5.9	−8.6	−19.9	−32.8
Total	42.6	94.2	118.3	195.6	591.1	946.1

Notes:

  [a] Including Medicaid
  [b] Except Medicaid
  [c] Income payments
  [d] Including Medicare and Veterans' benefits
  [e] Including Veterans' benefits
  [f] Farm income stabilization
  [g] Water transportation plus one-half of air and ground
  [h] Including agriculture

Source: Tabulations by author from U.S. Office of Management and Budget, *Budget of the United States Government,* relevant years: *Statistical Abstract of the United States,* relevant years; U.S. Office of Management and Budget, *Historical Tables: Budget of the United States Government, 1987.*

---

about 70/30. Beginning in 1965, however, the composition of spending changed radically. In the twenty years from 1965 to 1985, federal spending on income transfers increased more than tenfold; programs designed to help people buy essentials increased about thirtyfold. These programs were America's main growth industry during this period.

Why the post-1965 allocation of government spending changed radically is a complex story that can only be touched upon here. The change in national priorities can be seen by looking separately at the upper and lower parts of Table 5.1. Domestic political forces that increased demands for social and antipoverty programs that redistribute income—and domestic political forces that registered disillusionment with military and infrastructure spending—operated in tandem during this period.

Consider first the forces calling for greater social legislation. The Great Depression stimulated the development of income-support policy in the 1930s. The Social Security Act, unemployment compensation, and welfare programs were passed in response to massive unemployment, bread lines, and families being evicted from their homes. They established the principle that the resources of the government are required to deal with those aspects of poverty and insecurity that are not due to personal inadequacies or indolence.

A sweeping combination of poignant events led to a similar acceleration of calls for social legislation during the 1960s and early 1970s. The civil rights movement heightened awareness of the rampant injustice associated with race. Writings of prominent social critics—John Kenneth Galbraith and Michael Harrington, for example—made vivid the abysmal hardship of sectors of the population that could be identified by geography, culture, and race. The assassination of President Kennedy served as catalyst for the social welfare legislation to which he was committed. The War on Poverty and Great Society initiatives of the mid-1960s, signed by President Johnson and passed by Congress, were the legacy of these developments.[4]

These initiatives had a profound if indirect effect on policies that shifted income and services among people, policies that changed people's positions in the economic lineup. By declaring a war on poverty, President Johnson had elevated the question "What does it do for the poor?" to a test for judging government interventions and for orienting national policy.[5] New income transfer programs were enacted; eligibility was extended in existing programs such as Aid to Families with Dependent Children, Social Security, and unemployment compensation; benefit levels were increased; and the number of beneficiaries was expanded. Expenditures increased more rapidly than they had at any time since the mid-1930s. Programs now considered a standard part of the social policy landscape—Medicare, Medicaid, food stamps, Aid to Education, educational grants, Head Start, and various training programs—were all born during this period. Regulations designed to equalize opportunities in the workplace, in education, and in housing were put into place, and enforced. The Vietnam War and the election of Richard Nixon subsequently slowed the growth of these poverty- and inequality-reducing measures in the 1970s, but policy pressures to reduce poverty, inequality, and insecurity persisted until 1980.

These pressures led to the growth of spending shown in the upper part of Table 5.1. At the same time, there were active forces that led to relative stagnation in defense and physical investment spending programs. By the late 1950s, the nation was winding down a major spurt of spending on infrastructure that had been neglected during the Korean War. (The Interstate Highway System is perhaps the most vivid example.) The ratcheting down of military spending after Korea continued until the early 1960s. And while spending for the Vietnam War increased the military budget in the short term, it set the stage for a general skepticism about (and revulsion toward) military spending over the longer term. This skepticism was fueled at the very end of the 1960s by revelations of enormous military cost overruns, and goldplating and waste in weapons system procurement. While the environmental movement grew and peaked during the late 1960s and 1970s, policy in that sphere emphasized regulations (that required private spending) and policing rather than public spending.

The reordering of national priorities, reflected in the table, was tantamount to a revolution. While traditional governmental functions (excluding interest payments on the national debt) absorbed about 60 percent of federal government activities in 1960, by 1980 their share had dropped to about 40 percent. Conversely, social policy measures that are redistributional in character—those in the top part of the table—grew from about a quarter to nearly half of federal activities.[6] The 1960–1980 era saw government transformed from a traditional defense-transportation-natural resources enterprise to a major engine for poverty reduction and redistribution.

This remarkable shift can be seen even more clearly in Figure 5.1. In 1960, military spending accounted for over one-half of total federal expenditures; human resources programs stood at less than 30 percent. By 1980, this "redistribution area" had grown to more than 50 percent of federal spending, while military spending had shrunk to less than 25 percent.[7] By the 1970s, then, the government had established itself as the major redistribution mechanism in the nation—supporting people's income, helping them buy necessities, and insuring security in old age or if disabled or unemployed. This was achieved largely by expand-

Figure 5.1
Percentage Composition of Federal Spending, 1960–1986

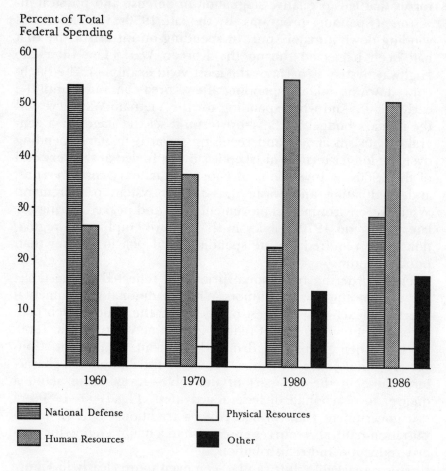

ing that part of the budget devoted to income payments to individuals, most of which are targeted on those at the lower end of the distribution.

The sheer explosion of the governmental redistribution effort, of course, says little about actual results. Several studies have attempted to measure the effect of the main component of this effort—payments for individuals—on the degree of overall inequality. Any estimate of the equalizing or poverty-reducing effect of these expenditures for even a single year depends on a host of assumptions and data which are less than scientific. The problems are compounded when the equalizing effect of these programs is examined over time. However, by drawing on a variety of estimates, it is possible to arrive at a tentative, though fairly solid, appraisal.

Table 5.2 presents this comparison for 1950, 1965, and 1985. To see the equalizing effect of government, compare the share of income the bottom 20 percent of the population receives *without* government benefits to their income share *with* these programs.[8]

Table 5.2
The Share of Total Income of the Bottom Quintile, Without Transfers and With Transfers 1950, 1965, 1985 (in percent)

	Without Cash and In-Kind Transfers	*With Cash and In-Kind Transfers*	*Increase In Share Due to Transfers*
1950	1.5	2.5	67
1965	1.4	3.8	171
1985	1.3	6.0	346

Source: See note 8.

The first column of numbers shows that the bottom quintile has been able to capture only about 1.5 percent of the nation's market income pie, and that this share has dwindled in recent decades. The second column measures the effect of the transfer system on this group. In 1950, when the system was very small, the bottom group ended up with about 2.5 percent of the total income pie—transfers increased their share by about 67 percent. By 1965, the Social Security system had begun to mature, and other redistributive programs were established. Although the share of market income captured was only about 1.4 percent of the total, the bottom quintile ended up with nearly 4 percent of the nation's income pie—the government's transfer and redistribution system had increased their share by about 170 percent.

After 1965, federal payments to individuals grew rapidly, in part because of the War on Poverty and Great Society initiatives. Welfare payments grew in generosity, and eligibility requirements were eased. New programs expanded coverage and benefit levels. The effect of this growth is seen in the last line of the table. Although the bottom 20 percent received only 1.3 percent of the market income generated in 1985, they ended up with nearly 6.0 percent of the nation's total income pie. Government redistribution programs had become a powerful instrument for reducing inequality; by 1985 they led to an increase in the income share of the bottom quintile of nearly 350 percent.

This redistributive impact of government transfers is also reflected in U.S. poverty measures.[9] Table 5.3 shows, first, the percentage of U.S. citizens who would be poor if only market income were available to families. In 1949, about 44 percent of all citizens would have been classified as poor if earnings were their only source of income. "Pre-transfer" poverty fell to 27 percent in 1959 and to 18 percent in 1969, after the first forays of the War on Poverty, but had edged back up to 24 percent in 1983. Column 2 shows what happens to poverty incidence when the benefits of the government redistribution system are added

Table 5.3
Poverty Rates With and Without Government Benefits, 1949–1983

	Percent of Population in Poverty When Income Excludes Government Benefits	Percent of Population in Poverty When Income Includes Government Cash Benefits	Percent Reduction in Poverty Due to Government Cash Benefits
1949	44	41	7
1959	27	22	18
1969	18	12	33
1979	21	12	43
1983	24	15	38

Source: Christine Ross, Sheldon Danziger, and Eugene Smolensky, "The Level and Trend of Poverty in the United States, 1939–1979," *Demography* 24 (November 1987), 587–600; Sheldon Danziger, Robert Haveman, and Robert Plotnick, "Antipoverty Policy: Effects on the Poor and the Nonpoor," in Sheldon Danziger and Daniel Weinberg, eds., *Fighting Poverty: What Works and What Doesn't* (Cambridge, Mass: Harvard University Press, 1986). Estimates for 1949 and 1959 derived from Ross et al., adjusted by data in Danziger et al.

to market income. These show an even larger drop in after-transfer poverty, from 41 percent in 1949 to 22 percent in 1959, and to 12 percent in 1979—and then a drift back up to 15 percent in the Reagan years. In 1949, these programs reduced U.S. poverty by only 7 percent; by 1979 they accounted for a 43 percent reduction (column 3). Even after the retrenchment in social programs in the 1980s, the government redistribution system resulted in a reduction in poverty of nearly 40 percent.[10]

This powerful equalizing impact of the government's redistribution system can also be measured by the change in overall inequality. Using a formula known as the Gini coefficient, which measures the extent to which the overall income distribution deviates from the norm of perfect equality, government redistribution reduced overall inequality by 6.4 percent in 1950, 10 percent in 1965, and 16.5 percent in 1985.

These numbers justify a strong conclusion: the government redistribution system has been a powerful instrument for reducing inequality and poverty over the last twenty-five years. Because of this system, poverty has been reduced by about 40 percent, and overall inequality by 15–20 percent. Over the last third of a century, this system has been the nation's most powerful instrument to bring us together, to counter those forces reflected in the "new inequalities," that keep many of us outside the mainstream.[11]

While these effects of government policy represent an important national achievement, they do not tell the whole story. What the statistics do represent are massive reductions in destitution, hardship, and suffering; and sizable increases in literacy, nutrition, and health. Perhaps most important, the redistribution system has greatly reduced the uncertainty faced by all of the nation's citizens—uncertainty regarding what happens when a job is lost, when an accident occurs, when a spouse dies, when a family splits. These events spell pain and adversity, and they potentially affect all of us. With this system in place, the pain and adversity associated with these risks are far smaller than they would otherwise be; we are far less a "nation at risk."

Taxing the Rich and the Poor, 1950–1980

Federal taxes, like government spending, leave a wake of differential effects across the population and cause people to change position in income rank. Some with lower income pay few taxes. They may leapfrog over others with higher income but high tax burdens. More newsworthy is the case of the rich person who pays little or no taxes and hence moves still further ahead of others in the distribution.

Like federal spending, the pattern of taxes has also changed radically since the 1950s. Throughout the postwar period, the federal government has raised nearly all of its tax revenue from four tax sources: individual income tax, corporate income tax, payroll taxes (to support the Social Security system), and excise taxes.

The most prominent of these taxes—the personal income tax—is a progressive tax; it takes a bigger bite out of the incomes of the rich than of the poor, and as a result narrows the gap between them. Marginal income tax rates—those that affect the last dollars of people's income—have ranged up to 70 percent during recent decades; since the "Great Tax Reform of 1986" they peak at about 35 percent. Because of the income tax, the gap between rich and poor is narrowed.[12]

The tax on corporate income is also viewed as progressive, even though both economists and tax experts question who really bears the burden of this tax. Some experts believe it is wrapped into the prices which companies charge and hence is paid by consumers. An alternative view is that owners of corporations—stockholders, bondholders, and managers with profit-sharing plans—ultimately pay the tax. If the first view is accurate, the tax may or may not be a progressive one. It depends on who is buying what goods and on how much the goods cost. However, the tax is clearly a progressive one if it is paid by corporation owners, a group which falls into the nation's top income brackets.

The burden of the Social Security payroll tax is easier to identify. Employees (workers) directly pay about one-half of the tax through deductions from their earnings; the other half is paid by employers. Most economists judge that the employer contribution also ends up being borne by employees: because the tax is an expense associated with hiring a worker, the market works to reduce the level of money wages and the tax thus becomes part of the workers' compensation. The payroll tax takes a constant bite out of all workers' earnings up to a maximum level, after which there is no additional tax liability. As a result, the tax tends to be proportional up to a fairly high income level, but regressive beyond that level.

Finally, excise taxes are like sales taxes, but are levied on only certain goods—alcohol and tobacco are examples. Again, identifying who actually pays this tax is tricky. As a type of sales tax, it could be regressive. On the other hand, to the extent that the tax is levied on goods which are more heavily consumed by the rich than the poor, the tax would be a progressive tax. Most experts judge our current government excise taxes to be progressive, taking a larger bite of the income of the rich than of the poor.

These four kinds of taxes are the main federal revenue raisers, and they differ in their distributional effects.[13] The big story, however, is how the composition of these taxes has changed over the period from 1950 to 1985. Table 5.4 tells this story, as does Figure 5.2.

Table 5.4
Federal Taxes, by Source, 1950–1985

	1950	1960	1965	1970	1980	1985
Individual income tax	15.8	40.7	48.8	90.4	244.1	334.5
Corporate income tax	10.4	21.5	25.5	32.8	64.6	61.3
Social Security taxes	4.3	14.7	22.2	44.4	157.8	265.3
Excise taxes	7.6	11.7	14.6	15.7	24.3	36.0
Other	1.4	3.9	5.8	9.5	26.3	37.0
Total	39.5	92.5	116.9	192.8	517.1	734.1

Source: U.S. Office of Management and Budget, *Historical Tables: Budget of the United States Government,* 1987.

Figure 5.2
Percentage Composition of Federal Taxes, 1960–1980

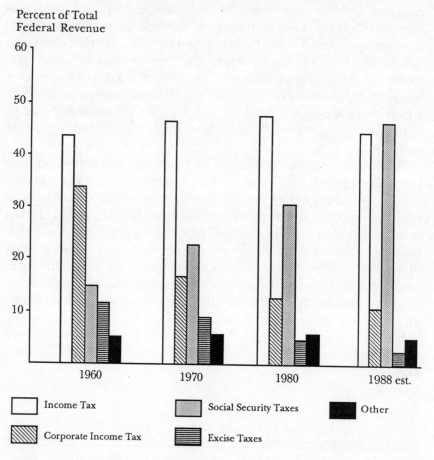

In 1960, the individual income tax accounted for about 44 percent of total government revenue, with the corporate tax accounting for another 24 percent. Payroll taxes stood at only 16 percent of the total, slightly more than the revenue raised by the excise taxes. By 1985, income tax accounted for nearly 50 percent of all revenue. The big changes, however, were for the payroll and corporate income taxes: payroll taxes accounted for well over 35 percent of total revenue raised, while the corporate tax shrank in relative importance as fast as the payroll tax increased. By 1985, the corporate tax accounted for only about 8 percent of total revenues, a far cry from its 1960 position. The Tax Reform Act of 1986 changed this situation somewhat, shifting some of the revenue raised from the personal income tax to the corporate tax.

While these patterns are decisive, their net effect on inequality is not clear. The income tax has increased, but it has become somewhat less progressive. Moreover, its growth has been dwarfed by that of the regressive Social Security payroll tax. Complicating the picture still further is the shrinking relative importance of the corporate tax.

Over the years, Joseph Pechman and his colleagues at the Brookings Institution have kept track of changes in the tax system and changes in taxpayers. Keeping score of these changes and their effects is tricky. The distribution of taxes among rich and poor depends on a variety of things: the characteristics of the taxes, the tax mixture in the overall system of taxation, the changing composition of income at various points in the distribution, assumptions about the various types of incomes and activities on which taxes fall, and the distribution of market income. All of these things change over time.

The most recent estimate of the effects of federal taxes on the rich and the poor is Pechman's *Who Paid the Taxes, 1966–85?*[14] Because of the substantial uncertainty about how the various taxes affect people with different income levels, Pechman played out the effect of a variety of possible "incidence assumptions" in his work. The two extreme sets of assumptions—the most progressive and the most regressive—form a boundary around the estimates. The most progressive set of assumptions indicates that people in the lowest deciles pay about 10–11 percent of their income to the federal government in taxes. This percentage rises to about 19–20 percent for those with the highest incomes. The least progressive assumptions give a more complicated picture: federal taxes appear generally progressive through the middle income range, but the system turns regressive at very high income levels and starts out regressive as well.[15]

Even though the progressive income tax has grown in importance since the 1960s, the entire system has become *less* progressive over the last two decades.[16] Two main reasons account for this: First, while the generally progressive corporate tax has faded in importance, the regressive payroll tax has grown rapidly. Second, the structure of the various taxes changed; in particular, the income tax became less progressive. The growth in special tax breaks reduced taxes for higher income people. More importantly, the "bracket creep" associated with the inflation of the 1970s pushed people into higher tax brackets and made increasing numbers of the poor liable for taxes.[17]

In spite of these changes, there is no doubt that the tax system has been an equalizer over the last thirty years, and still is today. By taking a bigger bite of the incomes of the rich than of the poor, federal taxes have reduced income gaps between them.[18] However, because the tax system is only mildly progressive, the amount of equalization that can be attributed to it is not enormous. Moreover, this equalizing impact appears to have decreased somewhat over time. Compared with the transfer system, the tax system is in the minor leagues when it comes to reducing inequality in America.

The Government and Inequality: A Bird's-Eye View

Each year, the government makes thousands of taxing, spending, and regulating decisions; moreover, it alters directions and decisions from year to year. People change their behavior—the amount they work and save, and where they live—in response to these decisions. As a result, it is not easy to uncover government's overall effect on poverty or inequality, and few researchers have attempted to estimate this effect in any comprehensive way. The best attempts have been by economists who focus on the "fisc"— the entire package of government taxes and expenditures. The questions they ask are: Does the fisc cause the income distribution in the United States to be more or less equal? Is government an equalizing institution or one that contributes to perpetuating or creating inequalities?[19]

From the separate discussions of transfers and taxes, it can be concluded that both sides of the government's budget tend to

Figure 5.3
Net Change in Income Due to Government Taxing and Payments

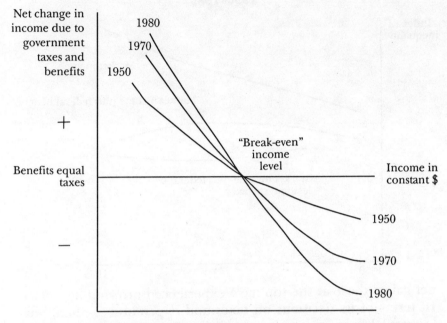

Source: Adapted from Morgan Reynolds and Eugene Smolensky, *Public Expenditures, Taxes and the Distribution of Income: The United States, 1950, 1961, 1970* (New York: Academic Press, 1977).

equalize incomes. The bulk of taxes comes from the top; expenditures favor the bottom.

This conclusion tells us nothing about the effect of this equalizing process on specific segments of the population. Figure 5.3 is one way of getting at this issue. The three lines in this figure characterize the results of studies for the years 1950 to 1980; it is a winners-vs.-losers figure.[20] Each line shows how people at different income levels gain or lose because of government taxing or spending policies in a particular year. Where the curve is above the horizontal line, people with incomes shown on the horizontal axis are net winners; where the curve dips below, people are on balance net losers.[21] All of the curves lie above the horizontal line for lower income people; they are net winners. The rich, who pay more taxes and get fewer benefits, are losers. Over time, those at the bottom of the distribution have increased their

Figure 5.4
Trends in Income Inequality Pre- and Post-Government, 1950–1985

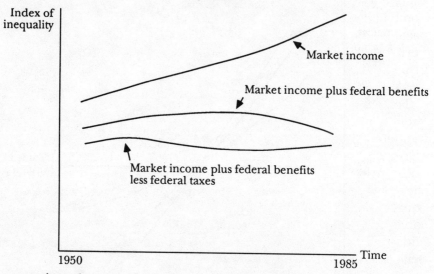

net gains; those at the top have experienced growing net losses. In terms of its decisions on taxes and expenditures, then, government has been a major equalizing force. And over time, its pro-poor impact has increased.

These bottom-line results, however, tell only about government efforts with regard to inequality. But inequality is not a monolith, and in fact, during the same period that these equalizing measures were at work, new inequalities had sprung up; the distribution of basic market incomes grew increasingly unequal over the period. Government efforts to bring people together were being undermined by countervailing forces—demographic changes, labor market changes, and economic changes—which made the benefits of government programs difficult to discern. Indeed, in some ways the programs actually fostered the new inequalities.

Figure 5.4 schematically summarizes the developments since 1950. The top line characterizes the trend in inequality of market incomes—inequality is high, and rising over time. The second line shows the inequality in the distribution of income defined as market income plus government benefits. It is fairly flat, but shows some slight downward trend, especially after about 1965. The gap between the top two curves has grown, reflecting the increasing effect of government transfers and social policies in combating market inequality. Finally, the bottom line represents income inequality after government benefits and taxes. The gap between it and the middle line shows the effect of the tax system. It too reduces inequality. But its equalizing impact is relatively weak and has diminished since the mid-1960s.

The bottom line of Figure 5.4, then, is the "bottom line." It shows where we are and where we have been in terms of income inequality over the past one-third of the century. In spite of massive increases in federal government taxes and spending, we are about as unequal in 1988 as we were in 1950. While the efforts of the government were effective in offsetting the increase in inequality generated by the market, they did not override the forces associated with "new inequalities." By 1988, those at the end of the income line had not moved closer to the middle, expensive efforts notwithstanding.

Chapter 6

Balancing Gains and Losses from Redistribution

Although the redistribution system has been relatively powerless to deal with many of the "new inequalities," it has nonetheless had a major impact on the old ones, and on the economy—affecting productivity and economic growth, family structure and human capital, migration and choices between work and leisure, saving and consumption. These resource allocation effects are part of the economist's "efficiency domain." They lead to the question: Has the nation's economic well-being improved or diminished because of these policies?[1] Here I will identify the principal channels through which redistribution measures can affect efficiency, and assess the claims which have been made about the magnitude of these effects.

The Costs of Redistribution

Taxes and transfers affect people's decisions about how much—and what type of—work to do.[2] Assume, for example, that an increase in income tax rates on high-income individuals is passed, designed to raise $1 billion to support increased welfare benefits for poor families. As a result of the higher tax rates, both the take-home income and the reward for working—or for working longer or harder—for high-income people is reduced.[3] Some will respond by curtailing their work effort. Some may choose not to enter the labor market in the first place—or to withdraw from it. For example, because of the decreased take-home pay, a wife in a high-income family may decide to work part-time instead of full-time, or even to quit her job. Some older workers may retire earlier than planned, or take more holidays, or give up the pursuit of new ventures. Or a schoolteacher, after comparing the after-tax income from teaching in a summer session to the value of leisure, may decide to spend the summer at a waterfront cabin. All of these reductions in labor supply may be the result of the tax increase. The $1 billion increase in welfare benefits also has an effect on the amount that recipients work. Some recipients may respond to the higher—or easier-to-obtain —benefits by working and earning less, or by stopping work altogether.

Other changes also may occur in response to increased taxes and benefits: Some taxpayers may seek unproductive shelter arrangements to avoid paying the higher taxes; some may save or invest less, recognizing that the lowered after-tax returns from these activities make them less worthwhile; some lower-income families may change their state of residence so as to become eligible for welfare benefits.

All of these changes involve a loss of potential productivity; to the extent that these losses are worth more than, say, the increases in leisure that accompany the reduced work time, the nation's economic well-being will be reduced. And this is the point: taxes and transfers contain incentives that induce uneconomic behavior; they tend to erode economic efficiency.

Here is the logic that underlies this conclusion: When a policy change results in less work effort, what is lost is the fruit of that lost labor, as valued by the worker's *gross wage*. What is gained is the increased leisure of the worker, which is valued at the *after-tax wage* (net wage). Because the gross wage exceeds the after-tax wage, there is a gap—a net loss to the economy, referred to as "deadweight loss." It represents well-being that the society could

Table 6.1
Efficiency Losses from Redistribution: Some Illustrations

Nature of Loss	Cause of Misallocation	Effects of Misallocation
1. Reduced supply of work	Income and payroll taxes. Welfare and Social Security transfers	Lower output and economic growth. Deadweight loss
2. Reduced supply of savings and investment	Corporate and property taxes. Social Security transfers	Lower productivity, output, and economic growth. Deadweight loss
3. Diversion of high-productivity capital into low-valued uses, and vice versa	Depreciation rules and special provisions of the corporate and personal income tax	Excessive production of some goods and services; insufficient production of others. Deadweight loss
4. Undesirable migration patterns	Relatively high transfer benefits in some states	Increase in urban ghetto problems. Increase in racial tensions
5. Marital break-up and births out of wedlock	Relatively attractive benefits associated with single parenthood	Increase in poverty and marital dissolution, the erosion of family values, and the creation of dependency
6. Diversion of investment from plant and equipment into unproductive activities	Special provisions in the tax law encouraging artificial devices to shelter income from taxation	Reduced productive potential of economy. Deadweight loss
7. Diversion of productive lawyer, accountant, and worker time into zero-sum unproductive uses	Special provisions in the tax law encouraging artificial devices to shelter income from taxation	Reduced productive potential of economy. Deadweight loss

8. Diversion of activities from formal markets to the unreported sector	High marginal income tax rates and rates-of-transfer benefit reduction	Erosion of social reporting system and protection afforded by antitrust, consumer, and safety legislation

have had, but does not have, because of distortions caused by taxes and transfers.[4]

The distortions caused by income redistribution measures (taxes and transfers) have several implications. First, because less labor is supplied, the total productivity of the economy is reduced; the nation's GNP is smaller than it otherwise would be; and economic growth is slowed. Second, when workers reduce their work effort, labor becomes more scarce, and the market reacts by increasing wages. With labor both scarcer and higher priced, businesses will use less of it, substituting land and capital, for example, for labor. In addition to the deadweight loss already noted, these changes also may cause efficiency losses.[5]

Table 6.1 shows the variety of potential efficiency losses that may be caused by redistribution—relating to labor supply, savings, investment, the capital market, and family size and structure. It catalogs the effects of all taxes and government benefits—especially those in which the amount of the benefit depends on how much a person or family works or earns.

While reduced or misallocated labor supply is the most frequently cited inefficiency caused by redistribution, the effects of taxes and transfers on savings and investment are also regularly the target of the business press and economists. The argument parallels the one for labor supply: Because corporate or property taxes reduce the returns from saving and investment, less of these activities take place than otherwise. Because new machinery, plant, and equipment are the driving forces in the growth process, economic progress is slowed. Productivity gains are lower than they could be as higher income people who do most of the saving divert their income away from productivity-enhancing saving and investment toward excessive consumption —yachts, cars, and vacations. The capital market is distorted; interest rates are unable to perform their allocative function.

This sort of inefficiency effect is attributed to government benefit programs as well as to corporate and property taxes. The common assertion that Social Security reduces private savings for retirement years is one example. Item 2 in the table illustrates this effect.

Item 3 captures a variety of other inefficiencies attributed to taxes and transfers. Among the most prominent are those associated with the rather arbitrary provisions in the corporate income tax for calculating depreciation expense and for assessing levies on income from various types of investment. As a result, certain investments—for example, oil drilling, apartment houses, and shopping centers—are made artificially attractive, while others that might be more productive and growth-inducing are sacrificed. Again, resource allocation is distorted. Output, growth, and productivity gains are lost, and deadweight losses are created. While these effects were reduced by the Great Tax Reform of 1986, they have surely not been eliminated.

Each of the distortions and inefficiencies attributed to redistribution occurs because market prices are altered by taxes and transfers—individuals are given incentives to make choices that deviate from those that would be made were market conditions maintained. Items 4 and 5 identify both incentives to migrate and to change family size and structure.

As another example, consider the special provisions in the tax law favoring the creation of shelters and other tax avoidance schemes (item 6). These provisions, which proliferated prior to the Great Tax Reform of 1986, include a wide variety of unproductive—indeed, counterproductive—activities. For example, by encouraging the formation of special tax avoidance arrangements, the tax law causes the diversion of savings and investment out of productive plant and equipment and into activities that look profitable only because of the tax law. Again, high-valued resources are diverted to low-valued uses, and deadweight losses are created. One important component of this diversion involves the time of accountants, lawyers, and taxpayers involved in ferreting out ways of avoiding taxes. The time of these professionals is used to promote zero-sum (often self-serving) interests with little if any social payoff (item 7).

One final distortion should be mentioned. Both sides of the

redistribution system—taxes and spending—encourage people into activities outside of the regular economy, some of them illegal (item 8). Drug trafficking, working for cash, and receiving payments in foreign accounts are all examples of activities where income is usually not reported. Individuals therefore either avoid paying taxes or avoid the transfer benefit reductions which accompany increased earnings. It is the redistribution system and the high penalties placed on earned income, according to this argument, that causes workers and small businesses to escape into the "underground economy," hence evading taxes or benefit losses. To the extent this occurs, the result is a loss of respect for social rules, a diversion of productive resources into evasive and counterproductive activities, and a breakdown in the social protection provided by antitrust, consumer, and safety legislation.

The Gains of Redistribution

The distinction was made earlier between the positive and negative effects of the redistribution system. The gains included such things as facilitating technological change, creating human capital, reducing insecurity and uncertainty, and increasing social cohesion and stability. They are long-term and often concern fundamental and difficult-to-predict changes in economic structure and dynamics. The gains and their sources are catalogued in Table 6.2. The losses concerned deviations from some efficient competitive economy. These are more easily quantifiable, and there are more data on them. The magnitude of the loss items in Table 6.1 is better documented than the gains in Table 6.2.

How Large Are the Gains and Losses?

While a large number of studies have attempted to measure the losses, they are not consistent; on any given loss item there is

Table 6.2
Efficiency Gains from Redistribution: Some Illustrations

Nature of Gain	Cause of Gain	Effects
1. Reduction in uncertainty	Welfare and Social Security transfers	Increase in individual well-being
2. Increase in human capital	Social programs in education, health, and nutrition	Higher productivity, output, and economic growth
3. Increase in economic stability	Countercyclical nature of taxes and transfers	Higher economic growth. Reduction in efficiency losses
4. Facilitate technological change	Safety net from social programs	Higher productivity and economic growth
5. Increase in social cohesion	Equalizing taxes and transfers	Increase in individual well-being

usually a wide range of estimates. The research results do not speak, as it were, with one voice. Depending on which interpretation one accepts, it is possible to conclude that the income distribution system is an albatross around the neck of the economy or that its effects are minimal. Like the losses, the quantitative estimates of the gains are not comprehensive. For many items, no reliable estimates exist.

The purpose here is to provide a balanced assessment of the magnitude of the effects of the public redistribution system. Before giving an overall assessment, it is useful to look at the evidence available on a few of the most studied effects. Because much of the research has been done by those who disagree with the basic purposes of the system, it is not surprising that some of the estimates are of the albatross-around-the-neck sort. Finding an objective appraisal is no easy task.

Labor Supply Effects

Since about 1980 the political debate has focused on the potentially adverse effects of income redistribution on work effort. The discussion lies at the core of Reaganomics and serves as the linchpin for supply-side economics thinking. The argument is straightforward: Taxes take a big bite out of everyone's paycheck; they depress the after-tax wage rate. People respond to this reduced financial reward by spending fewer hours on the job, and not working as hard. They strive less for promotions, search less for better jobs, and probably choose less training and education. Taxes sap motivation.

Income transfers—especially those in which benefits go up as a person's earnings fall or those which are available only to people with low earnings—are seen to have the same effect. They too depress the take-home wage and, by providing an alternative source of income, encourage people to rely on government benefits rather than their own efforts. Again, labor supply reductions, diminished initiative, and dependency are the result. While the tax system concentrates its incentive-eroding effects on higher income people facing higher marginal tax rates, the transfer system targets its disincentives on those with few skills.

To true supply-side believers, the poor performance of the United States economy in the 1970s can be blamed in large part on these labor supply effects of income redistribution policies. It is this judgment that served as the rationale for the huge Reagan tax cut and the retrenchment in social policy enacted shortly after he came into office.[6]

This simple logic is buttressed by a full arsenal of standard economic theory. Supply-siders can draw upon the "indifference curve analysis" taught in every university economics program to demonstrate the substitution and income effects that accompany taxes and transfers. They can point to a long shelf of research studies. Quantification of the labor response to taxes and transfers has become a mini-industry among economists, with each new data set and measurement method generating a new round of studies.[7] And while major inconsistencies exist among the studies, there are plenty of estimates by highly reputed scholars to bolster supply-side arguments.

Consider, for example, the effect of Social Security on retirement decisions. Professor Michael Boskin of Stanford University found that the Social Security system has a significant effect on the probability that older men will stop working and choose early retirement. Noting that the labor force participation rate of older men fell precipitously after 1970, at the same time that retirement benefits were increasing, he concluded that "the Social Security system has been the major factor in the explosion of earlier retirement."[8]

Professor Donald Parsons of Ohio State University undertook a similar study in regard to federal disability insurance benefits.[9] Again noting the sharp decline in the labor force participation of older but preretirement age men (forty-five to sixty-two), Parsons studied their response to increased disability benefits. He concluded that virtually *all* of their work reduction after 1950 was a response to the increased generosity and accessibility of disability transfers.[10]

One of the most widely cited of the studies measuring the labor supply effects of the redistribution system is by Professor Jerry Hausman of M.I.T., who focused on the effect of the tax system on work effort in the economy.[11] Hausman used advanced statistical techniques to detect the strength of the tax rate–labor supply relationship. He concluded that federal income and payroll taxes reduced by 8 percent—160 hours per year—the work effort of male family heads. The percentages were even greater for female heads and spouses. Indeed, Hausman concluded that with a mythical tax system that did not contain labor supply disincentives, female spouses would increase their labor supply by 18 percent.

These findings, seized upon by supply-side advocates, cite percentages that are much larger than economists a decade earlier would have predicted. They have, however, been followed up by subsequent work on the disincentive issue; these later studies, using improved methods and better data, have not found such large impacts.[12] While these studies have not overturned the gen-

eral point that the redistribution system has reduced labor supply, they support a far more moderate assessment of its effect. A
review of this work designed to "tease out" an overall assessment
concluded that the benefit programs probably reduced employment time by less than 5 percent and earnings by less than 4
percent.[13] The effect on labor supply of the increased taxes required to finance these programs could account for another 2
percent reduction in work effort. Adding this to the previous
estimate yields a 6 to 7 percent total reduction in work time.[14]
While a response of this magnitude is worthy of some concern, it
has little of the alarmist quality depicted by supply-siders.

Savings and Investment Effects

The impact of the income redistribution system on the level of
private savings and investment is as relevant as the labor supply
effects. Investment spending, after all, is the bedrock on which
economic growth rests, and private saving—by individuals and
corporations—finances this investment.

The theory and logic which motivate the mini-industry of
labor supply research are the same as those used to analyze the
response of savings and investment to taxes and transfers. And
the findings in the savings-investment area are at least as disparate as those measuring the labor supply effects of income
redistribution.

Consider first how savings and investment might respond to
transfer program benefits. In principle, all benefits from transfer
programs could affect savings. For example, welfare programs
protect people if they become poor; therefore one might conclude that saving for a rainy day no longer makes sense. A related argument applies in the case of Social Security programs: if
working age people conclude that their income in retirement
years will be supported by the government, their motivation to
save privately might be substantially reduced.[15]

Professor Martin Feldstein of Harvard University, formerly the
chairman of the President's Council of Economic Advisers, was

one of the first to study the savings effect of Social Security. He concluded in his 1974 study that the Social Security system reduced private saving (and hence investment) by over 35 percent.[16] As a result, GNP was about 15 percent below the level it would attain if the Social Security system were not in effect.

This astounding result had powerful political implications. Were it true, it would make a strong case for reducing—indeed, eliminating—this key element of the nation's redistribution system. As a result, numerous other scholars turned their computers to testing this Social Security–savings relationship. While their findings varied substantially, few found as strong a relationship as Feldstein. Moreover, in the course of this research, Feldstein's results were found to have been distorted by an error in the construction of his basic data. Correction of the error led researchers to the conclusion that no persistent relationship exists between Social Security transfers and private savings.[17] In the face of the numerous studies that have found some negative effect, this conclusion seems too optimistic. Rather, the research seems to suggest that the transfer side of the income redistribution system has reduced private savings somewhat, but its impact on investment spending and economic growth is not large. I would venture the conclusion that all transfer programs have depressed private saving by, at most, 20 percent, and the percentage could be as low as zero.[18]

The tax side of the income redistribution system is also suspected of depressing savings and investment. However, because different taxes have different savings effects, an overall appraisal is difficult. Most studies have focused on the effect of the corporate income tax—viewed as a tax on the return to capital investment.

One of the earliest studies of this relationship was by Professor Michael Boskin.[19] Boskin assumed a 50 percent tax rate on income from capital, a realistic assumption at the time he did his study. He asked what would happen to both investment and future consumption if that tax were eliminated and the same revenue raised without distorting the allocation of resources. His conclusion, which had a major effect on public discussion, was that the elimination of the corporate income tax would have a major positive effect on investment spending, capital accumulation, economic growth, and future consumption. Boskin placed the efficiency loss of the capital income at about 3.5 percent of the nation's final output.

As with Feldstein's Social Security–savings study, Boskin's also generated an outpouring of additional measurements. This subsequent work has weakened Boskin's linkage between capital taxes and investment and growth, but has not overturned it. Later studies indicate that abandoning the corporate income tax would bring an efficiency gain of 2–3 percent of GNP.[20]

The Underground Economy

In spite of numerous studies, there are no very accurate estimates of the size of the unreported (or underground) economy. Everyone agrees that this sector is substantial—at least 5 percent, perhaps as high as 15–20 percent of GNP—and growing.[21] While numerous causes for this have been identified, it is impossible to allocate the blame among them in any reliable or convincing way. Nevertheless, all observers believe that the redistribution system has played some role.

One simple example will show how the system can work to encourage a shift to the underground economy. Take a person who earns $20,000 per year working for a home redecorating company. The company must pay about 8 percent of this amount, or $1,600, to the government in the form of payroll taxes, plus another 15 percent, or $3,000, in other employment taxes or fringe benefits. Altogether, hiring the employee costs the firm about $25,000, of which the worker receives $20,000. Out of this gross pay, the worker must now cover income and payroll taxes, totaling about $5,000. Her take-home pay is $15,000. Hence, dollar outlays by the firm of $25,000 end up as $15,000 of disposable income to the worker. The $10,000 wedge between the two is largely due to the tax and benefit system.

Now assume that this worker decides to operate as a free-lance home decorator, making arrangements with clients to be paid only in cash, which will not be reported to the government. She would now work for, say, $18,000 per year rather than the

$25,000 of gross pay that was required in the formal economy. By switching from the reported to the unreported economy, then, both the worker (who takes home $18,000 rather than $15,000) and the customer (who pays $18,000 rather than $25,000) are better off. The government is the loser as the revenue that supports a variety of public programs and activities disappears. Efficiency losses may have an even larger effect as prices throughout the economy become distorted and even less reflective of social gains and losses.[22]

Incentives for operating clandestinely are implicit in the redistribution system. Moving into the underground economy, of course, involves extralegal activities and behavior—indeed, fraud—and this surely deters many people. Yet both the avoidance of high tax rates and the appeal of high transfer benefits are a powerful draw.

Growth in the unreported economy seriously affects the efficiency of the economic system. Society has set up a wide variety of arrangements to protect both consumers and suppliers operating in formal markets—safety practices, product standards, working conditions, and purchaser guarantees. These protections are not operative in underground markets. Moreover, the erosion of formal markets has its own dynamic. Because the revenue needs of government can be met only through the taxes imposed on reported market activities, the growth of the underground sector implies the need for higher tax rates on legitimate activities—resulting in still additional incentive for switching to the unreported sector. At a certain point the erosion of the open economy endangers the functioning of the public sector, the reliability of published statistical data, and the efficacy of private decisions. While some of the blame for this development must be laid at the doorstep of the nation's income redistribution system, no one is willing to venture a guess as to how much.

Effects on Family Structure

The 1980s have brought on a new form of criticism of the redistributive system, led primarily by the writings of George Gilder and Charles Murray.[23]

In their view, government benefits have encouraged the breakup of families and have contributed to the rapid increase in births out of wedlock. A weak and welfare-dependent population is said to be the result. The argument goes as follows: the incentives in the nation's welfare programs for marital dissolution, increased childbearing out of wedlock, and decreased rates of marriage or remarriage are side effects of well-intentioned efforts to target the benefits of these programs on individuals and families with unmet needs. For example, the AFDC program provides welfare support to individuals who are single parents, have eligible children (that is, beneath a certain age), and are poor. To obtain these benefits, all three conditions must be met. It then follows that the program provides incentives for individuals to become or to remain single, to have eligible children, and to become or remain sufficiently poor to qualify for aid.

However much it might seem the fantasy of some madcap economist to believe that people would get unmarried, have children, or resist remarriage only to qualify for government benefits, Charles Murray has pointed out that these family and childbearing patterns grew in intensity during the same period that welfare benefits were becoming more generous and easier to obtain. In his mind at least, the cause of the resulting increase in dependency is clearly attributed to that growth.

Earlier in the book I assessed the validity of this position in a discussion of the "new inequality" associated with mother-only families and arrived at a far more moderate position regarding the role of benefit programs. In this view, the welfare system cannot be totally exonerated, but its impact is far weaker than some have asserted. Professors William Julius Wilson and Kathleen Neckerman of the University of Chicago stated that:

> Research indicates that welfare receipts or benefit levels have no effects on the incidence of out of wedlock births. AFDC payments seem to have a substantial effect on living arrangements of single mothers, but only a modest impact on separation and divorce. [On] the extent to which welfare deters marriage or remarriage among single mothers . . . the evidence is inconclusive. [p.251][24]

Their conclusion is consistent with my reading of the evidence.[25] It implies that there are a number of more basic causes of these troubling changes in family patterns than welfare programs and benefits. Changes in the age structure of the population, the growing independence of women, the worsening joblessness of black males, and changes in attitudes toward marriage and parenthood have all played more substantial roles than the increased availability of welfare benefits. This is not to say, however, that the growth in transfers during the 1960s and 1970s—especially AFDC, food stamps, Medicaid—were completely unrelated to these effects.

Administration, Compliance, and Avoidance Effects

Good estimates of the costs of administering and complying with the income redistribution system are hard to come by. Experts agree that the costs of administering the income tax (per dollar of revenue) are low relative to other tax programs. Yet the aggregate of these costs, plus the costs borne by citizens in complying with the tax system, are far from trivial. For federal and state income taxes, a reasonable estimate is $30 billion per year. This works out to about $7 of administrative and compliance cost per $100 collected in revenue.[26]

The administrative and compliance costs of the transfer system are even higher. In terms of costs per dollar of benefits paid, the Social Security retirement and survivors program is the least costly; the benefit formula is clear, and people's earnings records and work status are fairly unambiguous.[27] For most other transfer programs, administrative costs per dollar of benefits are a good deal higher. Consider disability benefits through the Social Security system. Determination of individual eligibility requires more than earnings records and work status; it also involves physical and mental examinations to determine if health problems are sufficiently serious to qualify a person for benefits. And because such certification requires subjective judgments, reexaminations and appeals are often involved, and in some cases, ultimately, litigation.

Serious problems of compliance and administration (including benefit determination) also plague benefit programs such as unemployment and worker's compensation. And, as is widely recognized, income-conditioned welfare programs have special administrative difficulties of their own, largely in the area of benefit determination and verification of work and income status.

Professor Robert Lampman of the University of Wisconsin–Madison has estimated that about 10 percent of each dollar of spending on income redistribution programs is absorbed in administration, compliance, and collection costs. This figure is split about equally between the costs of raising the tax revenue and those required to provide the transfers.[28]

In addition to the administrative and compliance costs are the enormous time and resource expenditures that people make in order to take advantage of the special provisions—loopholes—in both tax and transfer programs. For example, until the Great Tax Reform of 1986, capital gains income was taxed at a much lower rate than earnings; taxpayers thus tried to shift their activities toward those that would generate capital gains. Such a shift is complicated and involves decisions on how much to work and what to work at, as well as decisions on the extent and nature of the investments one should pursue. Consultation with both lawyers and accountants is an integral part of these decisions on tax avoidance.[29]

Some corroborating evidence of the magnitude of this loss comes from a recent study by Lawrence Lindsey of the National Bureau of Economic Research.[30] Lindsey observed that a wide variety of tax avoidance behaviors are stimulated by high tax rates.[31] It follows, therefore, that lowering tax rates will lead to fewer of these activities as the gains to taxpayers decrease. Lindsey measured the magnitude of this response by exploiting data on tax revenues before and after the large Reagan tax rate cut of 1981. His findings are striking, although not undisputed. Overall, $15.5 billion of actual revenue over and above that expected with the new lower rates was collected—a 6 percent increase in tax revenue due to the reduction of tax-avoidance activities (or to other unidentified effects). Moreover, the pattern of this increase over the income distribution is remarkable. While overall tax revenues rose about 6 percent, revenues collected from the wealthiest taxpayers (those with more than $100,000 of income) rose by nearly 11 percent. Clearly, those people with the most to lose from taxation also exhibit the most skill at evading it.[32]

Human Investment Effects

One of the largest, and most quantifiable, positive effects of the income redistribution system is its contribution to the stock of human capital, and hence to the productivity of the work force. Numerous studies have established the link between public education, health care, nutrition, and housing programs and the productivity of workers as reflected in their wage rates and earnings. An important study by Edward Denison of the Brookings Institution suggests that more than 10 percent of economic growth in the postwar period is attributable to the increase in education over this period.[33] A good deal of this educational improvement is credited to public social welfare expenditures for education, a part of the nation's income redistribution system. Professor Lampman estimates that an amount equal to between 4 and 6 percent of the nation's GNP is properly attributed to the rapid increase in these public expenditures since 1950.[34]

But this figure is only the tip of the iceberg. While gains in education, health, and nutrition bring about increased earnings which are reflected in the Denison and Lampman figures, they also contribute directly to people's well-being in other ways. A study that Professor Barbara Wolfe and I did at the University of Wisconsin–Madison estimated that the value of nonmarket effects, for example, improved consumer and fertility choices, reduced criminal and antisocial behavior, are likely to be as large as the market effects described by Denison and Lampman.[35] It is reasonable to attribute an amount equal to about 10 percent of GNP to the human improvements brought about by the redistribution system.

Insecurity and Uncertainty Reduction Effects

In my judgment, the reduction of some of life's uncertainties is the most important gain from the income redistribution system; unfortunately, its value cannot be measured. How much is it worth to people to know that they are protected from destitution in the event of unemployment, or disability, or marital breakup, or death of a key family breadwinner? The answer is unknown. The following numbers, however, show the percentages of the relevant populations in 1985 that received benefits from public programs designed to protect against fate's arrow:

Disability	6 percent of working age population
Loss of family breadwinner	7 percent of two-parent families
Unemployment	7 percent of full-time employed persons

These percentages convey a rough sense of the likelihood that any one of us struck by one of these arrows would be protected by the social safety net. The amount that each of us would be willing to pay to be insured against the potential hardship which these events imply does not have to be large to add up to a sizable percentage of the nation's GNP.

Facilitation of Technological Change

Here again, we are in the realm of unmeasurables, but the softening of the resistance to economic growth afforded by the nation's redistribution system seems undeniable. To measure its value, we would need to know to what degree past and future economic growth has been (and will be) affected by the presence of the cushion afforded by the system, and for this, there is no hard evidence. According to Professor Moses Abramovitz of Stanford University, a renowned expert on technological change and the process of economic growth,

> The pace of growth in a country depends not only on its access to new technology, but on its ability to make and absorb the social adjustments required to exploit new products and processes.... The process includes the displacement and redistribution of populations among regions and from farm to city. It demands the abandonment of old industries and occupations.... [It implies] a great change in the structure of families and in their roles in caring for children, the sick, and the old. Because the required adaptations can and do alter the positions, prospects, and power of established groups, conflict and resistance are intrinsic to the growth process. To resolve such conflict and resistance in a way which preserves a large consensus for growth, yet does not impose a cost which retards growth unduly, a mechanism of conflict resolution is needed. The national sovereign state necessarily becomes the arbiter of group conflict and the mitigator of those negative effects of economic change which would otherwise induce resistance to growth. The enlargement of the government's economic role, including its support of income minima, health care, social insurance, and the other elements of the welfare state, was therefore—at least up to a point—not just a question of reducing irregularities of outcome and opportunity, though that is how people usually think of it. It was and is—up to a point—a part of the productivity growth process itself. [p. 2][36]

An outstanding example of this accommodating effect of transfers is the unemployment insurance program. The cushion that it provides to workers in case of layoffs and unemployment must reduce their resistance to the introduction of new technology. Simultaneously, by imposing some of the costs of unemployment on employers, any proposed new technology will be required to confront—and, indeed, cover—some of the special costs it creates.

Increase in Social Cohesion

Income redistribution alleviates hardship and helps bring us together as a people. The issue is whether the attainment of this objective is important to people: Do citizens generally—both rich and poor—value the reductions in disparities and the cohesiveness this affords? The answer has to do with feelings of altruism and charity, notoriously difficult phenomena to describe, let alone measure and evaluate. Who really knows why people give to charity or support public income redistribution—is it to "buy off" those who might otherwise resort to crime, violence, or social upheaval? Is it to reduce the pain of living in a society where one is daily exposed to the effects of destitution? Is it to buy personal satisfaction from knowing that someone in need has been helped? Is it to contribute toward attaining a social state that one believes constitutes the "good society"? Perhaps it is all of these things, and more.

That people do value such cohesion is known and accepted. For example, when the income of the nonpoor rises, society's evaluation of what constitutes a poverty income also rises. This linkage has been described as the "nonpoor's taste for equality," and estimates indicate that it is substantial. In public opinion polls and political activities, the nonpoor regularly assign high priority to poverty reduction, the elimination of hunger and homelessness, and the mitigation of prominent economic disparities among people.[37] That such feelings exist and that they are satisfied to some extent by the nation's income redistribution system is clear; the economic value placed on these accomplishments of the system is not. Would it add up to 1 percent of GNP, or 5 percent, or 10 percent? The first number is surely too low; the last may be high.

Striking a Balance: Expand, Contract, or Eliminate?

Many of the positive and negative effects of the nation's existing redistribution system have been identified and, where possible, valued. The gains are relatively familiar and experienced directly; each of us feels the security and cushion which the system provides and sees the contributions to our own human capital and our children's. Each of us feels better, knowing we live in a society which protects the weak and less able and moderates the extremes in income and economic power that accompany the operation of free markets.

The losses of the redistribution system are of a different sort. They stem from misallocated resources and efficiency losses, effects which can only be measured by comparing what is observed to what might have been.

This discussion naturally leads to the question of the "balance" between these gains and losses. At its simplest level, the question concerns the total impact of the redistribution system:

- Do the losses associated with the system exceed the gains; should the public redistribution system be retained or abolished?

In fact, this sort of question has little relevance to policy. Instead, it should be asked:

- At the margin, do the losses associated with expanding the income redistribution system exceed the gains; should the system be expanded or cut back?

Figure 6.1 will help in interpreting these "balancing" questions. On the horizontal axis, the size of the income redistribution system is plotted, measured as a percentage of the nation's GNP annually devoted to it. The vertical axis measures the gains and losses associated with varying the size of the system—the gains and losses catalogued in Tables 6.1 and 6.2. The TG curve plots the total gains associated with any given system size, and its shape indicates the presence of diminishing marginal returns. The TL curve plots the total losses, and its shape reflects increasing marginal losses. Both of these shapes reflect expected patterns.

Figure 6.1
Economic Gains and Losses from
Redistribution System

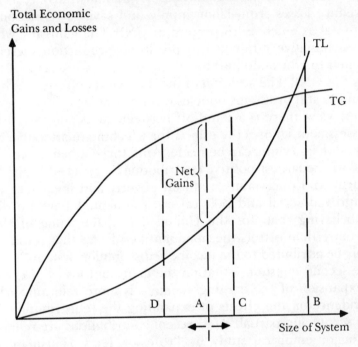

With reference to this diagram, the first question asks whether the amount of public income redistribution is at a position such as A, where total gains exceed losses; or at a position such as B, where the reverse is true. If the system is positioned at B, and the only options are whether or not to do away with the system entirely, abolition would be the superior option.[38]

The second question is more interesting: Given that the redistributive system is at A, where it is yielding net gains, should its size be increased or decreased? Here the question is a marginal one, and it concerns whether the *net* gains attributable to the welfare state could be increased by either expanding its size to, say, C—or reducing it to, say, D. As the figure is drawn, net gains could be had by reducing the size of the system—at the margin, an expansion would create more losses than gains.

With respect to the first question about aggregate gains-losses, it is evident that no clear answer is possible since several of the effects in Tables 6.1 and 6.2 are not quantifiable, although crudely estimated values can be placed next to some of them. Taken together, the quantifiable losses—administrative costs and the welfare losses from labor supply and savings reductions— might total as much as 10 percent of GNP. The gains for which some quantitative estimate was possible—production increases attributed to education and health measures—were set at 4 to 6 percent of GNP. The addition of the nonmarket effects of education and health programs doubles this percentage.

In my view, there is a stand-off between gains and losses. But this assessment ignores the effects for which no quantitative estimate, however crude, can be made. And, these, I believe, are the source of the largest positive contributions—reduced individual insecurity and uncertainty, reduced poverty and inequality, and an improved social and political environment. I have no difficulty believing that, for the United States, the value of these gains more than offsets the nonquantified losses that could reasonably be attributed to the income redistribution system.[39]

The second question—that on the gains and losses of continued expansion of the existing system—is more relevant. While the evidence on the effects of expanding the redistribution system is scanty and partial, a few recent contributions are relevant. In a major empirical study by Professor Jerry Hausman, the deadweight loss of the U.S. income tax was estimated to be over 20 percent of the revenue collected for husbands and over 50 percent for their wives.[40] Moreover, the loss associated with marginal expansion of the income tax is estimated to be well in excess of that figure.

Even more to the point is a study by Professors Edgar Browning and William Johnson.[41] They focused on the entire tax-transfer system, rather than just the taxation side, and researched the effects of expanding it so as to transfer additional income from the rich to the poor. Considering that both increased taxes and increased transfers would generate additional labor supply effects and deadweight losses, they concluded that the upper income groups bearing the costs of the taxes would sacrifice $350 for every $100 that the poor gained—a net dead-weight loss of $250. In Okun's terms, the leaks in the redistribution bucket are enormous—starting out with a bucket of $350 raised from the nonpoor, $250 is lost on the way to delivering it to the poor, a breathtaking figure. For several reasons, critics of this study have found this estimate to be substantially too high.[42] However, even if this were cut in half, it would still be troublesome. Would our society be willing to accept a loss of economic efficiency of $125—or even $100—in order to equalize the distribution of income by transferring $100 to the poor?[43] The answer is by no means clear.

Should we continue to expand the system, in its existing form, as we have over the past two decades? I have substantial doubts. In my view, we have about exhausted the poverty-inequality-insecurity reduction potential of the taxation-income transfer strategy—a conclusion reached by assessing practical matters and empirical relationships. At this point, additional gains in economic security, welfare, and equality appear too costly in terms of economic efficiency to warrant continued expansion—at the margin the losses may well exceed the gains. Professor William Baumol of Princeton characterized this conclusion in his theoretical treatise, *Superfairness:*

The main and most surprising result...so far is that with the methods of redistribution currently used...very large output losses are also likely to accompany any attempt to get anywhere *very close* to equality....[T]he methods we are currently using [in redistribution policy], namely a combination of the progressive income tax and transfers, may simply not be up to the task.[44]

PART IV

Toward Equality
with Efficiency

This section sketches out a program for restructuring the nation's redistribution system, a program designed to provide new and expanded access to opportunity and to increase the productivity, efficiency, and independence of the population. It is a strategy to promote "equality with efficiency."

The program sketched out is suggestive rather than definitive. It is intended to be a benchmark against which future proposals for reform might be measured. Many aspects are left out (for example, health care, policies for the disabled, elementary education, day care) in order to concentrate on the central features of the nation's social programs (cash and in-kind welfare programs, Social Security, subsidies for manpower training, and education).

Specifically, the objective of the redesigned system suggested here is to equalize opportunities, improve incentives, and in the process, to foster individual responsibility and accountability. Short-term needs will be met at the same time that long-term incentives for productivity are provided. It will be less expensive to administer than the present system. But because it is complex and will have to be phased in over time, the transition is likely to entail costs and confront obstacles. These are probably unavoidable, but almost certainly manageable. (See the Appendix to Chapter 7, "How Much Would All This Cost?")

In any case, much discussion needs to take place before a new way of doing the nation's inequality reduction business can be identified and put into place. I intend to provoke such a debate in order to focus attention on new initiatives and possibilities that can level the playing field while maintaining incentives for work, effort, independence, and productivity. Reduced inequality can go hand in hand with greater efficiency.

Chapter 7

Redesigning the Nation's Redistribution System: A Sketch

The preceding chapters documented the successes and short-comings of the nation's current income redistribution system—a complex melange of several hundred programs supported by annual expenditures of $500 billion. I have argued that simple expansion of the current set of programs which comprise the nation's tax and benefit system cannot further reduce poverty and inequality at reasonable economic welfare (efficiency) costs. In this sense, the system has exhausted its potential. This suggests the need for a new way of doing the nation's inequality reduction business. Only a break from the past can release the "Big Tradeoff–Leaky Bucket" hammerlock that hobbles the system. And there is reason to believe that such a break is possible.

What is required is a fresh approach to poverty and inequality reduction—a major restructuring of the nation's redistribution system. Transfer payments are necessary but not sufficient. New policies must be assembled that will expand access to opportunity and provide incentives to increase the productivity, efficiency, and independence of the population. Unlike our current mix of income support and education-training programs, these new measures must simultaneously promote both efficiency and equality.

This chapter sketches out such a new "equality with efficiency" strategy. It represents a radical departure from the current system, and as such is not feasible in the short run. It serves as a benchmark against which proposals for future reform should be compared, a standard by which they should be gauged. Moreover, because the changes are large and involve unexpected changes in prices and behavior, it is impossible to estimate accurately their budgetary costs. In this respect, the changes proposed are not unlike the Tax Reform Act of 1986, which was enacted to achieve a new, more efficient, and more equitable arrangement, without accurate estimates of its revenue increasing or decreasing effects. Hence, I only trace the outlines of the structure and suggest how it would look when put in place. I do, however, describe the components, how they are consistent with the overall strategy, and how they fit together to form a new system. In the Appendix to this chapter, I also attempt to measure "How Much Would All This Cost?" The sketch is designed as a prototype; it is not a full blueprint.

The policy measures that I describe do not form a comprehensive redesign of social policy. Reforms of the health care and elementary and secondary schooling systems are not discussed, nor are the important needs in the day care and preschool education areas. Policies toward the disabled and mentally ill—both social insurance and training—are left untouched. Those measures that I do propose constitute an alternative to the tax transfer system defined to include cash and in-kind welfare programs, the Social Security retirement program, and a wide range of subsidies for manpower training and higher education. It is this core of the nation's social policies that has been most studied, and about which enough is known to discern a new, more efficient, more equitable approach.

To put this new system in perspective, I will characterize the existing redistribution system and then point out the differences in objectives and approach between it and the proposed strategy.

The Nation's Redistribution System: A Characterization

The causes of inequality among people are systemic. They derive from, among other things, the diversity of individual talents and motivations (nature), individual upbringing (nurture), the condition of labor markets, the legacy of bequests, and inequalities of opportunity. The public redistribution system is not systemic; it is more like a "final stage" taking from some and giving to others. It does little to actually improve the opportunities available to people—the resources with which they start life. With the exception of some education, training, health care, affirmative action, and family support programs, the bulk of the tax and benefit system affects only economic outcomes. The basic structure of markets is largely left untouched, and income flows are claimed by those with title to them—labor suppliers or the suppliers of capital services. At that point government intervenes, often to take from the rich to help the poor, but by no means always.

An original and important intent of the system was to equalize opportunity. However, as it has evolved, transfers and taxes have come to occupy center stage—outcomes rather than opportunities have become the focus. Moreover, the rules by which this "taking and giving" system operate are complex. One explanation for the complexity might be that both the tax system (the "taking" mechanism) and the transfer system (the primary "giving" mechanism) are driven by several, often conflicting, motives. Analysts only dimly perceive the processes by which some are helped and others hurt. Because of inevitable side effects not originally foreseen, efforts designed to redistribute from A to B may end up aiding A at the expense of B. As a result of this complexity in giving and taking, "cross-hauling" is common; those who give often also get, and those who are the major beneficiaries of the system are also required to contribute to it.

Because of its final stage orientation, the current redistribution system (especially its "giving" component) focuses aid on those who are disadvantaged in some relevant dimension, either temporarily or more permanently. The disabled, the elderly, single parents, and some of the unemployed are its main targets. Food stamps and Medicaid go to the poor, and most training and employment assistance to those with few skills. Not all of the benefits flow to those at the bottom of the distribution, however. A high fraction of Social Security, veterans', and Medicare benefits, to say nothing of the benefits from special provisions in the tax law, accrue to people well up in the distribution.

By taxing and subsidizing, the system changes people's behavior, often in ways judged to be inefficient and socially undesirable. In the view of some, its most damning characteristic is that it undermines the independence of the individual; an outcome that is inconsistent with the traditional American vision that success depends upon individual work effort and initiative. In addition, the current income redistribution system is viewed as having high administrative costs. Collectively, these burdens erode the vitality and sap the growth potential of the economy.

If these arguments are correct, a simple characterization of the current redistribution system and its effects would read as follows:

- It is oriented to easing poverty and meeting short-term needs. Neither opportunities nor market arrangements are fundamentally altered. The starting line is left uneven.

- It is complex, resulting in confusion, cross-hauling of dollar flows, and contradictions.

- It often provides incentives for inefficient decisions, including reductions in labor supply and other behaviors that retard economic growth by diverting resources to low-productivity activities.

- For some, it has made dependence on the public sector an acceptable substitute for individual initiative and independence.

These are the negative aspects of the existing redistribution mechanism. It has also yielded important positive aspects—the reduction of poverty and inequality, the provision of economic security, increases in human capital, the maintenance of social cohesion. My objective has been to outline an alternative strategy that will maintain the positives while avoiding the negatives.

Toward Equality with Efficiency: Charting a New Approach

The objectives that guide the proposals that form this new strategy include the following:

- To bring those groups who have been left behind into the mainstream of the U.S. economy; *to reduce the "new inequalities"*;
- To achieve more equal outcomes in the long run by *equalizing opportunities*;
- To insure that the well-being of each citizen exceeds some *social minimum* level;
- To increase both *individual responsibility* and *individual accountability* for one's own well-being;
- To increase the *flexibility and performance of the labor market* by offsetting a variety of constraints and rigidities with which it is now burdened;
- To reduce the *disincentives for work, saving, and initiative* which now plague operation of the current system; and
- To *simplify* the current system, and to *reduce its administrative costs*.

No strategy can achieve all of these objectives simultaneously; compromises must be made. Is it possible to simplify the system and, at the same time, to mount an attack on the rigidities and constraints which now plague operation of the labor market? Is it possible to reduce the "new inequalities" while simultaneously increasing incentives to work? The strategy that I sketch out here deals with these conflicts.

The approach that I envision scales back Social Security retirement benefits for higher earners, some in-kind assistance such as food stamps and public housing, some public subsidies for higher education and student loans, and some traditional welfare programs. These reductions free up the budgetary resources to support a series of new policies—personal capital accounts for youths which could be used to purchase education, training, and health care services; an employment subsidy program focused on

153

workers with low education, training, and job prospects; and a child-support system to assist children in single-parent families. In addition, the hodgepodge of cash and in-kind benefit programs would be replaced with a unified and universal system integrated with the newly reformed personal income tax. Finally, there would be incentives for individuals to save during their working years so as to increase their own contribution toward retirement. As a corollary, the federal government would accept responsibility for guaranteeing a social minimum income for every citizen.

The following summarizes the core of this new approach to the nation's inequality reduction business:

A Universal Demogrant, Integrated with the Personal Income Tax

This program, a refundable tax credit, is the base of the new strategy. It provides a guaranteed income to all families. It is akin to the existing earned income tax credit (EITC), but provides support even in the absence of earnings.[1] The amount of support—the tax credit—depends on the size and composition of a household (or tax) unit, and varies according to income from other sources. It sets a social minimum income floor under all families; it will not eliminate poverty, but it will cut off the bottom tail of the income distribution.

A Standard Benefit Retirement Program plus Tax-Favored Private Annuities

Benefit levels in the Social Security retirement programs are reduced for workers who are high earners during their working years, but a standard, poverty line benefit is guaranteed for all. The system becomes more like an insurance system, with financing less closely tied to earnings.

The federal government also sponsors an information program to assist families to plan for their financial future, and provides tax-related incentives for individuals to privately purchase insurance or annuities yielding benefits in retirement years.

A Universal Child-Support System

To provide improved support for children living in one-parent families—a significant component of the new inequality—a universal child-support system is substituted for the current arrangement involving court-determined awards and Aid to Families with Dependent Children. The proposed system provides income support to all children living with one parent. Benefits are paid on the basis of a fixed national schedule; they are financed by additional withholdings from the incomes of absent parents, plus residual public spending. Absent parents are thereby assigned responsibility for the support of their children.

An Employment Subsidy for Disadvantaged Workers

To reduce the cost to employers of hiring labor relative to capital—and especially low-skill labor relative to high-skill labor—an employment subsidy is introduced. Both prongs of this program —the first modeled on the New Jobs Tax Credit Program of 1977–1978 and the second an employee-based wage subsidy focused on disadvantaged workers—offset constraints on labor demand from market rigidities, and increase the employment of less skilled workers. Business costs and prices would tend to fall while output would tend to increase. The credit would result in some reduction in corporate and personal income revenues.

A Universal Personal Capital Account for Youths

Each youth, upon turning eighteen, receives a personal capital account of, say, $20,000 provided by the government. The account would be interest earning, and could be drawn upon for approved purchases of education and training as well as for health care services.

The Components of the New Strategy and Their Rationale

The overhaul of the nation's redistribution system that I am proposing is built on several pillars; it is important to understand how they fit together and how they contribute to the stated objectives. This section attempts to put the program into perspective.

A Universal Tax Credit, Integrated with the Personal Income Tax

For two decades now, the main candidates for federal policy reform have been the personal income tax and the cash transfer system. President Carter labeled the first system a "disgrace," and the second a "mess." His sentiments are echoed by both earlier and later occupants of the Oval Office.

The Tax Reform Act of 1986 radically changed the personal income tax system. It corrected, at least partially, the major efficiency and equity problems primarily by reducing the differential tax treatment of income from various sources (for example, capital gains, earnings, real estate, investments). It also expanded the income base from which taxes can be raised by limiting exemptions, deductions, exclusions, and other special provisions. With lower tax rates, the incentives for "tax avoidance" (working less, investing less in productive capacity, diverting earned income to tax sheltered income) are reduced, as are the efficiency costs of the system. The Tax Reform Act of 1986 simplified the tax system, increased its equity, and improved resource allocation.

While the transfer side of the redistribution system has many of the same sort of problems that plagued the pre-1986 tax system, no similar reform has been enacted. No significant change in direction has occurred, in spite of numerous proposals put forth by every president since Lyndon Johnson, social activists, and economists.[2]

Each proposal sought simplification. At present, the programs are not well-integrated; hence, the rate at which benefits fall as other income rises—equivalent to a marginal tax rate—increases with multiple program participation. This lack of integration also creates serious inequities among and between recipients and equally poor nonrecipients. Further, the complicated rules concerning eligibility and dollar amounts make these programs difficult to understand, to gain access to, and to evaluate.

The reforms proposed have sought to reduce the disincentives to work and to save that accompany the transfer system by reducing the rate at which benefits fall when other income increases—the benefit reduction rates—and by proposing benefit levels that do not exceed the earnings possibilities of potential recipients. They also seek to increase the equity of the transfer system—equal benefits to equally poor people; no higher income for nonworking recipients than for nonrecipient workers; availability of benefits to all people with low incomes rather than just certain categories of poor people.

My proposal for greater simplification, efficiency, and equity involves a wholesale redesign of the present income support system. Many of its existing components would be phased out (Aid to Families with Dependent Children, Supplemental Security Income, food stamps, and a variety of housing support programs) and replaced by a single integrated safety net program. Because of this universal safety net, related programs providing income support—programs such as unemployment insurance, Social Security retirement, general assistance, and Medicare and Medicaid—will have to be revised to ensure that their benefit schedules mesh with the base level of support of the safety net program.

The new safety net is a credit income tax or demogrant program. A family's income would be defined comprehensively, much as in the newly reformed income tax. A tax credit would be awarded to each family or taxpaying unit according to how large it is and who lives in it (for example, how many adults and how many children). This credit would guarantee to families a minimum income set at one-half to two-thirds of the poverty level. Families with no other means of support would receive the full amount of the credit as a grant; those with some other income would receive smaller net payments; better-off families would receive no net payment at all. Such a plan can be fine-tuned by altering either the amount of the refundable credit (or the income guarantee) or the rate at which the available credit decreases as the amount of other income goes up. The program could be readily integrated with the income tax structure as it was overhauled in 1986, although marginal rates may have to be adjusted somewhat.[3]

A refundable income tax credit to provide a safety net of support to all citizens is not a new idea; similar proposals have come from both the so-called political left and right.[4] Those of both perspectives agree that the gains forthcoming from such a plan are major ones. The problem of "genuine" poverty would be reduced as the bottom tail of the income distribution would, in effect, be eliminated. The plan would decrease the work disincentive created by the existing high-benefit reduction rates; strip away the complexity of the melange of current programs; eliminate much of the stigma associated with public assistance programs as we know them; and increase equity. In such an integrated structure, incomes are taxed and support provided in a simple, open, universal, and just manner.

A STANDARD BENEFIT RETIREMENT PROGRAM AND TAX-FAVORED PRIVATE ANNUITIES

The largest element in the U.S. income transfer system is the Social Security system, in particular the Social Security retirement insurance program. Its primary objective is to cushion income losses to older individuals when they leave the labor force. In earlier times, individuals saved during their working years in order to provide for their retirement. In effect, the Social Security system has taken over this responsibility. It collects taxes from workers—a form of forced saving—and makes payments during retirement years.

The Social Security system is regularly at the center of the national debate over economic reform.[5] In a period of unprecedented federal deficits, many think that the generosity of public retirement benefits should be trimmed along with cuts in nearly all other government programs, especially since the system has been shown to induce workers to retire before the normal retirement age, to penalize their working (even part-time) after they do retire, and to pay significantly greater benefits to higher income workers than to low wage earners. Moreover, largely because of the growth of the system, the elderly as a group have achieved levels of well-being which are at least as high as those of the rest of the population. Yet the older population and representative organizations have fought to maintain benefit levels, and they have been successful.

Social Security is financed by the regressive payroll tax (one-half paid by workers with their contribution matched by employers), which takes a higher percentage bite out of the earnings of lower-wage workers than of higher earners. Many have argued for a fairer and less restrictive means of financing, but thus far the payroll tax has been maintained. In fact, very few fundamental changes in the financing of the Social Security retirement system have ever been legislated.[6]

My proposed change in the retirement benefits system is a far-reaching one. Its merits and demerits can be most clearly seen if the most critical features of the current system are understood:

- Nearly all of the nation's workers are now covered.

- High-income workers face a lower payroll tax burden than lower-income workers because payroll taxes are not collected on earnings above $43,800 per year.

- Full benefits begin at age sixty-five; reduced benefits are available upon retirement after age sixty-two.

- Restrictions limit the amount of earnings that recipients are permitted if they are to avoid losing benefits.

- Benefits are greater for those who worked more than for those who worked less, and greater for high wage earners than for low. But benefits replace more of the earnings of those with low earnings than high earnings. For the average earner, benefits replace about 45 percent of prior earnings.

- Benefits are largely paid out of the receipt of current payroll taxes; hence, the system is known as a pay-as-you-go system. It has little resemblance to an insurance program.

- The ratio of expected benefits to "contributions" is high for those retiring now because of the trends of benefit payments and payroll tax rates over time. When today's retiree was working, both payroll taxes and benefits were much lower in real terms than they are now.[7]

- The system provides additional benefits to a retired worker if he or she has a spouse or dependent children, even though these people may have contributed nothing to the system.

- The system provides benefits only to families that have a member who worked and paid payroll taxes. People who did not work or who worked in occupations not "covered," or were married to such nonbeneficiaries, often live in poverty.

There is no question that the Social Security system has successfully redistributed a large and growing amount of income from younger to older people, so that their spending power (relative to their needs) is now equal to or greater than that for most other groups in the society—including families with children.[8]

While this important accomplishment is its most visible effect, the rising tide of Social Security has not raised all boats. A sizable group of elderly people—for example, widows whose husbands worked at low-paying jobs, or were often unemployed, or whose jobs were not covered by Social Security—have been excluded from these gains. They live in poverty, removed from both the population as a whole and from other elderly people. The system has increased inequality among the elderly.

A third effect of the current Social Security system stems from its benefit levels, which have expanded at the same time that both private pensions have grown and the accumulated assets of the elderly have increased. As a result, a high proportion of Social Security payments go to people who are rather well-to-do.[9] (Such payments exceed the total volume of welfare expenditures to the poor.)

Another effect of the existing system is that it encourages workers to retire earlier than they otherwise would, in part because of the early retirement provision. This has increasingly dubious merits in light of the rapidly increasing life expectancy and improved health of older people.[10]

Finally, as a result of the complexity of the system, few people have a clear idea of how Social Security will affect them when they reach retirement age. Few can estimate their expected benefits with any accuracy at all. The uncertainty is compounded by taxation of benefits for those with other income, and by the question of whether the real value of benefits will grow or erode over the remainder of their working career. Under these circumstances, the system discourages people from rational savings decisions and careful plans for their own retirement.

The reform in the Social Security retirement system which I propose seeks to correct the drawbacks of the existing system and accomplish the following objectives:

- Guarantee all working citizens an above-poverty minimum income level in retirement years;
- Encourage individuals to provide for retirement income over this minimum, and assist them in these efforts;
- Diminish incentives for reduced work effort or early retirement; and
- Stimulate private savings.

These objectives reflect a set of value judgments that deserve to be made explicit. The first is that older citizens should not suffer poverty during their retirement years. (The existing system achieves this objective only partially, and then only in conjunction with the Supplemental Security Income (SSI) program, a welfare program.) Second, requiring citizens to make forced savings during their working years in order to secure public benefits which, in many cases, supplement large income flows from other sources in retirement years is unnecessary and in many ways undesirable for an affluent society. Those workers with sufficient resources to make a choice of how generously to provide for their retirement years should be encouraged to exercise that choice. This judgment reflects a preference for independence and individual accountability when there are no serious and adverse side effects. Third, assisting—indeed, subsidizing—people to save for retirement is justified on economic grounds. The options available for securing reliable retirement income are complex and not well understood, and there are social benefits from risk sharing. Without such governmental assistance, encouragement, and subsidization, some will make insufficient provision for retirement.[11] Finally, once society commits itself to providing a retirement safety net, funds should be raised in as efficient and equitable manner as possible—there is no reason for Social Security to be solely financed by the regressive payroll tax.

With these judgments and objectives as a backdrop, the alternative public retirement income system that I propose would have the following characteristics:

- Each worker would participate in the Social Security retirement program, in that he or she would pay the appropriate taxes while working and receive benefits when retired.

- A standard benefit level at or above the poverty line would be guaranteed.

- When a worker reaches the normal retirement age, he or she would be paid the standard benefit from the Social Security program, regardless of earnings or other income available.[12]

- Benefit receipts would be indexed to the price level and would be included in income for personal income tax purposes.

- Nonworkers, including the dependents of retired workers, would receive the refundable tax credit and no Social Security retirement payment. Survivors would be entitled to the larger standard poverty line benefit of the Social Security program.

- The financing of the program would be through some combination of general Treasury monies and a payroll tax redesigned to reduce its regressive character.

- The Social Security program would undertake a major and ongoing program of providing both information and counseling to encourage financial planning for retirement. Individuals would be provided regular statements of the benefit payments they would receive upon retirement. A major information and counseling program would be developed to assist people to plan for their retirement through the individual purchase of retirement annuities. The Social Security program would itself offer a variety of plans among which individuals could choose in purchasing individual retirement annuities in excess of social minimum benefits. (Private insurers and/or groups would be able to offer competing plans.)

- The federal government would offer tax deferments (or partial tax credits) on approved individual annuity investments to encourage working age individuals to participate in such retirement plans.[13]

- A transition would be provided for both older workers and those currently receiving benefits from existing Social Security programs. Existing retirees would continue to be covered by the old rules. A sliding, age-related, adjustment scale would be developed to ease the transition for older workers.

These Social Security reforms, in conjunction with the demogrant welded on to the reformed income tax, contribute in a major way to several of the objectives the new strategy is designed to achieve. Together, they would set an income floor under all citizens—a safety net for all working age citizens and older persons who have not worked, an above-poverty minimum for working citizens who have retired. Individuals would be encouraged to take increased responsibility for providing for their own retirement above the benefit guarantee and would be held accountable for the choices that they make. With a standard individualized benefit, the Social Security retirement program would become a simpler, less impenetrable arrangement than it is now. The "earnings test," which now constrains the incentive to work after retirement, would be removed. Finally, the proposed reform would encourage private saving, hence contributing to this national goal.[14]

A UNIVERSAL CHILD-SUPPORT SYSTEM

Children are the nation's most important asset. Future economic growth depends on the skills, training, education, and initiative that they bring to the production process. Yet, as noted earlier, the nation is not doing well by its children. Increasing numbers of them are growing up in homes with a single parent, homes that are faring badly in terms of economic well-being. Even the incomes of intact families with children have failed to grow as fast as the average income. And, as Professor Samuel Preston of the University of Pennsylvania has pointed out, children have lost out in the competition for federal support; other groups, especially the elderly, have made gains, while the benefits targeted to children have eroded.[15] As a result, their poverty rate has risen steadily, and the proportion of them living in mother-only homes has skyrocketed. This development is an important component of what I have called the "new inequality."

Being raised in a poor family has important short-term consequences, and even greater long-term implications. These adverse effects are magnified when the family is also headed by a single parent. The increased incidence of single-parent families does not portend well for our nation's economic future.[16] Current policies hardly seem up to the task posed by this "new inequality."

The child support system I am suggesting is targeted on those in mother-only families. Many of these mothers find it difficult to work because they have small children, and most have low education levels and low skills—low earnings capacity, in any case. Few would be able to earn enough to move their families out of poverty even if they were able to find a job.

The main source of income for those mother-only families who work little or not at all is the nation's welfare system, in particular the Aid to Families with Dependent Children (AFDC) program. But the support often does not go to the poorest families, or is meager, or creates a "welfare trap" for those who do receive benefits. (Since benefits fall by about one dollar for each additional dollar of income that the family receives, there is little incentive for single mothers to seek work.)

Payments from absent fathers (child support and alimony) are virtually the only other income source for mother-only families, but not all mothers are awarded such support, and many who are do not collect.[17] As with the welfare system, the system of court-based child support awards creates substantial inequities among otherwise similar families.

The capriciousness and meagerness of these sources of income have created a dependent population—dependent on the discretion of the courts, dependent on the whims of former spouses, dependent on the welfare system. Few who have studied this arrangement doubt that major steps need to be taken:

- To ensure an adequate level of support for all single-parent families;
- To increase the certainty of this support and simplify procedures for it;
- To establish the principle that absent parents are responsible for their children's well-being; and
- To create both incentives and opportunities for single parents to work.

If the support from an absent parent falls below a social minimum level, the difference would be made up with public transfers, according to the following plan:

- Parents who live apart from their children would be subject to a "child-support tax," the amount to be determined by a schedule based on their gross earnings and the number of children concerned.

- This tax would be withheld by an employer along with other tax withholding, thus ensuring payment.

- The tax payment made would go directly to the absent parent's children or their custodian.

- Public benefits would depend on payments from absent parents, the custodial parent's income and marital status, and the number of children. An implicit "take back" of public payments according to a schedule would depend on the income of the custodial parent, but with an eye to minimizing disincentives for working.

- The child-support system would be integrated with the refundable tax credit program.[18]

This system would replace both the current system of court-determined awards and the AFDC program. It would be simpler, integrated with the remainder of the tax and social welfare system, and it would be more equitable. Although benefits would vary, absent parents with the same income and number of children would be making the same payment;[19] furthermore, all children in single-parent families would be assured a minimum standard of living.

A major effect of this proposal is to shift responsibility from taxpayers to absent parents. It would also reduce the work disincentives which confront single parents in the existing welfare system, avoiding the "poverty trap."[20] The proposal would also eliminate the stigma many welfare mothers now experience, as well as the anxiety associated with dependence on the good faith of a former spouse. I would argue that providing both the inducements and the opportunities for single parents to become independent and self-sufficient is a legitimate public sector function. Through such a program, the nation could go far toward correcting the last decade's neglect of its children.

AN EMPLOYMENT SUBSIDY FOR DISADVANTAGED WORKERS

A major source of inequality in the United States is the differences among various groups in access to jobs, especially to good jobs with decent pay, stable employment, and a promising job ladder. Minorities, youths, disabled workers, single mothers—all characterized by low skill and education levels—face relatively bleak labor market opportunities.

This phenomenon is not a new one. The pattern was already present in the 1960s and led to the growth of multi-billion-dollar education and job-training programs in order to provide the target groups with labor market skills. Some employment gains did result, but they were not large and did not persist. In part because of this assessment, policy interest in the 1970s turned to direct job creation. A major public service employment effort, providing jobs to 750,000 workers at its peak, was in effect in the latter half of the 1970s, as were subsidies favoring the hiring of these workers. Nearly all of these measures were abandoned after 1980.[21]

The labor market problem that confronts disadvantaged workers is primarily a structural employment problem; joblessness for certain groups exists in spite of near full employment in the rest of the economy. The most basic reason for this is their inherent lack of skills and education—hiring them simply does not generate much additional output and profit for employers. This is compounded by the distortionary effects of the combination of minimum wage laws, union wage contracts, and the fringe benefits and payroll taxes that businesses are required to pay for every worker. These constraints contribute to the labor market disadvantage of the low-skilled.

But the costs imposed on society by this unemployment are enormous. The output not generated when able-bodied people fail to work is but the most obvious one. In addition, there is a long catalog of individual troubles that accompany the inability to find work—depression, family breakup, alcoholism, and drug abuse among them. These personal disasters often spill over into society more generally, showing up as welfare dependency and crime, among other things. The result is additional taxpayer costs for the treatment and control of these social maladies.

My proposal is to pick up on the promise of direct job creation and employment subsidy programs initiated in the 1970s. It is modeled on a modest effort that was in effect in 1977–1978 known as the New Jobs Tax Credit (NJTC). Although the NJTC was never enthusiastically embraced by the Treasury Department, which administered it but never publicized it, research evaluations indicate that it was successful in creating jobs for low-skill workers, and at a rather low cost to the Treasury.

The NJTC provided a tax credit equal to 50 percent of the first $6,000 of wages paid to the fifty workers hired in a firm above 102 percent of the previous year's employment level. The program did not distinguish among workers by their skill or unemployment status. However, the subsidy—and hence the incentive for private employers to hire low-wage workers—was a higher percentage of total wages for less skilled workers.[22]

Studies of employment effects of the NJTC indicate that up to 30 percent of the 1977–1978 employment growth in the studied industries was attributable to the NJTC—it was a potent job creation device.[23]

My labor market proposal is two-pronged, aimed both at disadvantaged workers and those who hire them. Its effect would be to alter the terms on which workers could be hired—in effect, to make hiring them a more profitable and attractive proposition than it is now.

The first prong of the proposal is the reestablishment of the NJTC, but with modifications learned from experience. For instance, the new NJTC should be viewed as a permanent program, not one which puts low-skill labor on "sale" for a temporary period. The government should enthusiastically support the plan, publicize it widely, and work with the business community to minimize misunderstandings and bureaucratic difficulties.[24]

The second prong of the proposal focuses on the low-skill workers themselves. An employee-based subsidy program would be instituted for disadvantaged workers and those with long-term and persistent unemployment problems.[25] Some portion of the wages of low-wage workers would be subsidized by the government, giving the worker a labor market advantage, and hence an incentive to seek work. As compared to the employer-based NJTC, workers are encouraged to exercise job-seeking initiative on their own behalf; it is a program oriented to the supply side of the labor market for low-skill workers.[26]

This new environment will improve the operation of the low-skill labor market by generating ongoing demand and supply-side pressure for the creation of jobs for marginal workers at reasonable cost. As such, it will equalize employment opportunities. By targeting the additional employment on segments of the labor market with slack, GNP could be increased without significant inflationary pressure. It will fundamentally alter the wage structure in private labor markets, raising the take-home pay of low-skilled workers relative to those with more secure positions in the labor market. The cost of an employment subsidy strategy would be substantially lower than providing equivalent jobs through public works or a general increase in spending. Most important, it would reduce inequality in employment and earnings in a way that encourages independence, work, and initiative.[27]

A Universal Personal Capital Account for Youths

The potentially most explosive element of the "new inequality" is the alienation of youths—especially minority youths—from the mainstream of economic life in the United States. My proposal seeks to bring them in in a way that stimulates independence and accountability, primarily by opening up employment opportunities. The ultimate goal is to assure that all youth have a reasonable—if not equal—base on which to build a career and on which to attain economic self-sufficiency.

The vision on which this proposal rests is substantially different from that which drives current policy. Current policy presumes that youth—especially those from lower-income families—will underinvest in their own education, qualifications, and skills. The remedy is often paternalistic. The current system subsidizes organizations rather than individuals. Funds are given to organizations—colleges, universities, training programs—to enable them to provide training and educational services to youths at low or no cost. These subsidized suppliers recruit participants as best they can; many of those who apply hear about the programs by chance. Because the system subsidizes organizations, individual choices are often made with partial or no information, and are all too often based upon biased and erroneous cost considerations.

The subsidy program through student loans or grants has a less paternalistic cast, but the funds can still be spent only in support of specific activities at the institutions that participate in the loan programs. Such subsidies complement the direct institutional subsidies. Hence, overall investment choice is still restricted since the youth cannot "shop" for the best option.

Many of these arrangements have been worthwhile, passing a benefit-cost test, but I would argue that they are basically unfair. Benefits are available only to those who apply for them, qualify, and participate; they are not available to all.

My proposal is for a universal capital grant of, say, $20,000 to be given to all youths at age eighteen, to be used for human capital investments of their choice.[28] Individuals possessing such an account will have the incentive to shop for and choose the activity they judge will best serve their needs. They could draw on this account at any time for approved purchases of education and medical care services (as well as some related living expenses and "incidental" costs), and an annual statement of the value of the account would be sent to each youth.[29] Assignment of the account to private creditors would be prohibited. The account would earn interest, and to the extent it was not drawn down prior to the normal age of retirement, it would be available to supplement other income sources at that time.

The proposal I have outlined here is meant to be the basis for a general reform of policy toward youth, and thus entails the modification and perhaps elimination of many existing programs.[30] A capital grant—constrained by guidelines for approved education and health care expenditures—encourages efficient choices by both increasing the range of choice and by requiring that the individual actually spend the money himself or herself, thereby spending it more prudently. It grants individuals the dignity of more freely planning their own lives, rather than being induced into certain activities through the incentives of existing institutionally-based and paternalistic subsidy schemes. It would go far toward reducing a major set of inequalities in U.S. society.

The large and growing gap among youths in terms of education, income, and employment would be significantly narrowed. Further, the growth in the gap between youths and the remainder of the population would be restrained, and perhaps reversed. Both of these differences—among youth, and between them and the rest of us—are important components of the "new inequality."

The proposal, obviously, does not solve all problems. A flexible labor market is required to absorb those with the skills which the capital account would have supported. The two-pronged employment subsidy program proposed above complements the personal capital account in this regard. And while the capital account proposal would contribute to reducing the concentration of unemployment among minority youth, it would not assure "equality of opportunity." Basic education and skill training should become universal because of the proposal, but the program does very little toward equalizing or improving the basic background conditions which are a root cause of the youth transition problem—poverty, family instability, and the absence of a community-school-home environment emphasizing personal responsibility and achievement. Four years of college will still be out of reach for many—although less so than before.

To be sure, implementation of the plan would probably cause a variety of short-run adjustments in various aspects of the economy. Educational institutions would be forced to rethink their financing and tuition policies, and would have to adjust to the inevitable competition from new suppliers of education/training services. The current mix of public and private, four-year and two-year, vocational and liberal arts institutions would undoubtedly be altered in response to the new patterns of education/ training demands. Government programs in the education/ training area would, likewise, have to confront the reallocation away from direct institutional grants and institutionally administered loans, and learn to deal with the new sources of supply. Certification of new suppliers (to ensure that they meet standards acceptable for personal capital-account spending) would be a complex task. And youths themselves must be assisted in evaluating the new options that will be available to them in order to choose wisely.[31]

A transition period is inevitable, during which mistakes will be made, money wasted. When the adjustment period has passed, however, the new system will yield a youth population more qualified to compete and succeed in the labor market, less unequal in resources and opportunities, and more responsible for their own status in life. The personal capital account, by increasing both the resources available for and the options open to youths, will directly attack the root causes of the dependency and low earnings of the most disadvantaged of this group. It will make starting lines even, foster individual responsibility and accountability, and open a window for economic success and a career which, for many, now seems closed. When it is linked with the other elements of the strategy sketched out here, a major step toward reducing inequality with efficiency will have been taken.

Appendix to Chapter 7

How Much Would All This Cost?

It would be irresponsible to propose a fundamental redirection of social policy such as that represented here without giving at least some "guesstimate" of what it would cost, yet there is no cost estimate that would be truly reliable. The proposed changes are designed to alter people's behavior—to increase work and independence, to stimulate private savings, to make more education and training available to groups that now have little access to either. It is difficult to quantify responses to these sorts of incentives. Moreover, the various programs suggested here can be designed at different levels of adequacy and generosity. While I have recommended a $20,000 youth capital account, a demogrant set at from one-half to two-thirds of the poverty line, and a poverty-line retirement benefit, I have left unspecified a large number of design and integration issues. Finally, since the various programs interact, the costs of the separate components would yield a larger figure than the entire package.

Nonetheless, it is possible to give some "ballpark" notion of what a new redistribution system is likely to cost the taxpayer, if the reader recognizes that the numbers are only crude, back-of-the-envelope calculations.

So how much would the entire package cost? Taking the conservative end of the estimates for the individual components, it would be about $15–20 billion per year. An upper figure would be in the neighborhood of $40 billion per year.

Were the entire set of programs to be enacted simultaneously and integrated appropriately, the net cost would be about 1 percent of the $1.2 trillion of projected total federal budget outlays in 1988. The following shows how these figures were arrived at.

As I have described the refundable tax credit or universal demogrant, it involves integrating basic income support into the existing federal personal income tax. Those at the bottom of the income distribution would be given a "refund" from the government, in excess of whatever taxes they might have paid (or have had withheld). This support level, which would by itself keep all families above one-half to two-thirds of the poverty line, would allow a variety of existing welfare and income transfer programs to be eliminated, thereby saving tax money.

A similar policy change was analyzed before the 1986 Tax Reform Act and this study can provide some idea of its cost.[32] The maximum tax credit level in this plan (using price levels and incomes for 1975) was set at about 75 percent of the poverty line (I have suggested from one-half to two-thirds), and most other welfare programs (for example, AFDC, food stamps, and Supplemental Security Income) were eliminated. All families that received the tax credit refund faced a marginal tax rate of 50 percent on income from all sources. All other taxpayers faced a marginal income tax rate of 23 percent on a comprehensive income base that eliminated all itemized deductions and made Social Security and unemployment compensation benefits taxable. With these provisions, the plan was self-financing and resulted in no increase in the net budget deficit. The total amount of income support to the lowest income households increased by about $16 billion, an amount made up by small increases in the taxes required of higher income taxpayers (resulting in a decrease in after-tax income of slightly more than 1 percent).

The 1988 equivalent of this $16 billion would be about $35 billion. However, because the maximum tax credit suggested here is one-half to two-thirds of the poverty line (rather than 75 percent), this drops to about $20–25 billion. And, as in the 1976 study, the net effect on the budget deficit would be zero if accompanied by a small upward adjustment in tax rates for those above the poverty line.[33]

The second component of my proposed plan involves substituting a standard retirement benefit equal to the poverty line for the disparate benefits—some far below the poverty line and some way above—paid by the existing Social Security retirement system. In 1988, about $190 billion of retirement benefits will be paid out by the system. Data for 1986 show that the average monthly payment to a retired worker was $488, to a spouse $252, to a widow or widower $444.[34] Were the proposed plan in effect in 1988, the single-person benefit rate would be about $6,000 per year (about $7,300 per year for a retired couple) and households would be expected to provide for retirement income above this amount through private pensions, savings, or annuities. By moving to a flat benefit plan, total government outlays will fall to about $130 billion per year, and if these benefits are taxable, the net costs to the government would fall to about $110 billion per year (taking into account that some Social Security retirement benefits are now taxable). This represents a reduction of $80 billion in net government spending.

This shift, however, could not be implemented immediately. Current retirees would experience no change in benefits at all; those now close to retirement would confront only small reductions in benefits through the introduction of a sliding scale; younger persons, far from retirement (those aged less than, say, forty years in 1988), would be brought into close conformity with the proposed system. The full expected reduction in government benefit payments would be experienced only after the year 2000.

This component of the proposed strategy also includes government provision of financial inducements (through subsidized retirement accounts for example) and information and counseling to assist individuals in assuming greater responsibility for their retirement years. The taxpayer costs of these elements depend on the level of the subsidy and the extent of the counseling. The loss of tax revenues from the Individual Retirement Account (IRA) provisions of the pre-1986 tax law, for example, was about $19 billion.

Using these estimates as a guide, a total reduction in government spending of about $10–20 billion might be reasonably expected within a few years after this component of the plan had been implemented.

The third element of the overall plan is the Universal Child Support System targeted on single-parent families. This program replaces both the current court-determined child-support system and the nation's welfare program for poor single-parent families. It shifts the responsibility for the support of children in single-parent families from taxpayers to absent parents.

A calculation has been made of the national budgetary cost of a child-support system such as that now being tested in the state of Wisconsin, which provides an assured benefit of $3,000 per year for the first child.[35] The researchers conclude that the level of child-support collections in 1983 would total about $30 billion (raised largely from absent parents), revenues that could be used to supplement the income of the custodial parent according to a specified benefit schedule. (When translated into 1988 dollars, this amounts to about $36 billion.) Because these benefits would largely replace welfare (AFDC) benefits, the researchers estimated that there would be no required increase in tax revenue beyond the levy imposed on absent parents for the support of their own children.[36]

A similar study for a less generous child-support system (about $1,200 per first child and lower support collections from absent parents) reported a similar conclusion, namely a very small residual net cost for the program.[37] If one regards the collections from absent parents not as a tax, but as a legitimate cost imposed upon parents for the support of their own children, it follows that the child-support system is a budgetary "wash." With the refundable tax credit in place, the net cost implications of the program proposed here would also be effectively zero.

The fourth component of the new system consists of the two-pronged employment subsidy for disadvantaged workers. The first prong of this incentive is the employer-based subsidy patterned on the New Jobs Tax Credit of 1977–1978. In the second year of this program, the subsidy was paid on nearly 1 percent of the labor force, at a cost to the federal government of about $2 billion (about $4 billion in 1988 dollars). It seems safe to presume that a similar (but improved and restructured) program supported by publicity and a commitment to reduce bureaucratic difficulties would entail a larger budgetary cost—perhaps as much as $5–10 billion.

The second prong of this employment incentive would be targeted directly on disadvantaged workers, and could take the form of a wage subsidy voucher giving disadvantaged workers a distinct labor market advantage. Its budgetary cost is dependent upon both the level of the subsidy and the definition of workers who will be eligible, neither of which has been specified in the program I have sketched out.

Some clues as to budgetary costs are available, however. In the 1980s, the Targeted Jobs Tax Credit has been in effect. This program has several features in common with that being suggested here, though it is perhaps more restricted in its coverage and limited in the extent of the subsidy offered than would be optimal. In a representative year, 1984, its cost was about $1 billion, the minimum of what might be expected.

Another clue is found in a careful simulation study of the costs and work effort effect of a wage subsidy provided to all heads of families with children who earned less than $4.40 per hour (in 1975 dollars).[38] The subsidy equaled 50 percent of the difference between the actual wage and the target figure of $4.40 per hour. In 1975 dollars, the net cost was estimated to be about $5.5 billion, which translates into about $12 billion in 1988. Because this simulation assumes that all low-wage workers who are family heads receive the subsidy, and because the subsidy rate is a rather high 50 percent of a rather high target wage (nearly $10 per hour in 1988), this would seem to be at the far upper limit of cost estimates.

A final clue is found in a very recent study of wage subsidies.[39] For a wage rate subsidy of 50 percent of the difference between $7.00 per hour and a worker's actual wage rate, and paid to the primary earner in families with children (in combination with the elimination of the Earned Income Tax Credit in the current tax law and the reduction in welfare benefits associated with the increased earnings of subsidized workers), a small *reduction* in net government expenditures was estimated.

Assuming that the wage subsidy prong of the labor market strategy would cost $5 billion, a reasonable estimate of the total cost of the labor market component of the strategy proposed here would be in the range of $10–15 billion.

The final component of the overall proposal is the Universal Capital Account for Youth. Its costs are most difficult to estimate as it represents a basic restructuring of the market for higher education and training services. A simple calculation of the annual budget cost would multiply the $20,000 figure by the number of youths turning eighteen in a representative year, but this would yield a grossly exaggerated estimate of $38 billion. For one thing, youths holding a capital account do not draw it down fully in a single year; a more typical case would be where a youth would draw upon the account over a five- or even ten-year period during which additions to human capital (education or training) are being sought. In fact, because unused funds earn interest, some share of the accounts would remain unused until the holder reached retirement age. Moreover, such a calculation would not reflect the fact that withdrawals from the account are taxable as income (making the net cost to the government significantly less than the gross withdrawals from the account) nor would it reflect the fact that a wide variety of existing higher education subsidies and reduced tuitions would be eliminated by the personal capital account.

A simple calculation that adjusts in a reasonable way for these kinds of considerations indicates the net budgetary cost of the capital account to be about $10 to $15 billion in the first years of the plan, rising to about $20 to $25 billion after a period of five to ten years.

The lower bound of the summed estimates for all of the components is about $15–20 billion per year; an upper bound is about $40 billion. Were the several components to be introduced in an integrated and coordinated fashion, a reasonable best guess would be about $20 billion per year—a 1.5 percent increase in federal outlays.

But even this estimate is likely to be substantially too high. The purpose of the approach proposed here is to stimulate increased saving, work effort, and independence in order to bring about improved economic performance. The resulting increase in income and tax revenue would reduce net budgetary costs still further. I would argue that an effectively implemented "equality with efficiency" program could be financed with a 1 percent increase in federal government expenditures.

Chapter 8

Conclusion: Mission Accomplished?

This book is about the economic differences among us and the recent growth of new inequalities. And it is about the role of the nation's redistribution system in altering these inequalities. While some have laid the responsibility for these new inequalities at the doorstep of this large and complex system, the facts belie the claim. Even though some reductions in work, saving, and initiative (and some dependency) are due to the disincentives to work created by that system (receiving more income through welfare payments than through an entry-level job, for example), many of our recent problems are the result of much broader developments: a decade of lagging economic growth, a baby-boom generation needing to be absorbed by the labor market, the increased commitment of women to work and career, increased dissolution of marriage and out-of-wedlock childbearing, an evolving technological structure with new and more disparate employment demands, and the erosion of community, diversity, and family support in inner city areas.

Those who helped create the existing redistribution system could not have foreseen the extent to which it would be overtaken by these developments. Clearly, the programs and policies now in place bring benefits to many; I have argued, however, that the existing strategy has exhausted its ability to stem the disequalizing pressures at reasonable social and taxpayer costs. Even if it were politically feasible, further expansion of the current redistribution system would yield only modest benefits in terms of reducing poverty and inequality, increasing individual security, and promoting growth of our human capital. More important, general expansion of these programs without restructuring would be accompanied by still greater disincentives, rising dependency, and a further expansion of the unreported economy. Such expansion would further aggravate the Big Tradeoff between equality and efficiency, with no assurance that the gains would exceed the losses. The growth of the holes in Okun's "Leaky Bucket" preclude expansion of our presently structured redistribution strategy.

This melancholy assessment indicates the need for a new way of doing the nation's redistribution business, a new way of moderating the economic inequality produced by the market, a way to break out of the Big Tradeoff–Leaky Bucket straitjacket. The new strategy that I have sketched out is designed to remove the reasons for dependency and low earnings by increasing both the opportunities and the motivation for the nation's poor to become productive members of society.

The capacity of this proposed approach to reduce inequality and increase efficiency should be measured against the objectives that guided its design. Will it, in other words, achieve its goals? Will a comparison of its gains and costs—in terms of both efficiency and equality—justify placing it on the nation's social policy agenda?

Reducing the "New Inequalities"

The first objective is to find a way to reduce the problems facing those at the bottom of the economic ladder—especially single-parent families and black and minority youths. The proposed child-support system and youth capital account are aimed directly at the problems faced by these groups. Children in single-parent households will be assured a minimum income; unemployed youths will be given access to the resources they need to gain the training and education necessary for labor market success. The universal refundable tax credit guarantees all individuals a social minimum standard of living, thus eliminating the very bottom of the income distribution. The strategy will bring back into the mainstream those groups that have recently pulled away.

Drawing an Even Starting Line

The second objective is to equalize outcomes by guaranteeing greater access to opportunities—to create an even starting line. Although the existing system alters outcomes because it is rooted in the government's tax and benefits mechanism, it does not get to the heart of the problem of unequal opportunity. The two-pronged employment subsidy proposal would fundamentally change the effective wage structure in the economy, and it would do so in a way that would simultaneously increase the earnings and employment of low-skilled workers. The result would be that those without jobs would have a far better chance of getting them—employment opportunities would open up. Moreover, the capital account for youths, which makes access to human capital resources available to all, also evens the starting line. Similarly, the child-support system would improve the standard of living of children in mother-only families, improving their chances for employment, careers, and economic success.

Providing a Safety Net

The design of the strategy would ensure that all citizens have a social minimum safety net placed under them—the third goal. The refundable tax credit explicitly provides this for all citizens, although it will not remove all citizens from what is officially defined as poverty. For children in single-parent families, the national minimum built into the child-support program would secure a guaranteed level of well-being. For workers in their retirement years, the revised Social Security system would assure an escape from poverty.

Promoting Individual Responsibility

Perhaps the major accomplishment of the plan will be that it sends out a clear message that individuals must take the responsibility for choices made, that people will be held accountable for their actions and decisions. This objective is built into the fundamental change proposed for the Social Security system: that the choices people make during their working years will have a major effect on their standard of living during their retirement years. While they are guaranteed a minimum level of support in retirement, consumption beyond that is dependent on how long they choose to work, and how much they choose to save.

The child-support system sends out the same message to parents who choose to live apart from their children—that decision no longer absolves them from the obligations they incurred by their decision to have children. The same accountability will be expected of the fathers of children born out of wedlock. The mothers of these children will have to identify the fathers as part of the "contract" to receive benefits—and the fathers will then have the statutory support payments withheld from their salaries. While this kind of enforcement is not easy, recent experiments suggest that it is feasible at reasonable cost. (This arrangement is currently employed in the child-support system adopted by the state of Wisconsin—a system with many of the same characteristics as that sketched out earlier.)

Finally, the capital account for youths represents a revolution in the way the nation provides for the development, training, and education of young people beyond high school. It also represents a big unknown, because we have never attempted a program that allows individuals to, in effect, have a drawing account at their disposal. The bookkeeping requirements are simpler than for Social Security, and well within the competence of computer technology. While costly, the program will allow reductions in a number of other public programs such as education loans, public training programs, grants and subsidies to educational institutions, and Medicaid. The unknown is the difficulty of establishing a vigorous monitoring procedure to insure that withdrawals are effectively used to achieve the purposes for which the accounts are designed. (The nation's experience with the GI Bill and recent job training and employment subsidy arrangements indicates that strict monitoring is necessary if the programs are to effectively carry out their missions.) The account needs to be structured in a way that youths will be obliged to use it wisely. The objective is to replace ongoing income transfers with the access to resources that can promote future success and to do so while fostering individual responsibility and accountability.

Improving the Labor Market

Achievement of the fifth objective—improving the performance of the labor market for low-skill workers—is the explicit target of the employment subsidy program. By increasing the demand for the services of those groups that now experience scandalously high unemployment rates, a giant step will have been made toward correcting the most important shortfall in labor market performance. This program is designed to neutralize the numerous constraints that now impede the efficient functioning and flexibility of the labor market.

Plugging the "Leaky Bucket"

The final two objectives are efficiency goals. A primary drawback of the existing redistribution system is that it generates efficiency

costs in the process of securing reductions in inequality and insecurity. These costs stem from the disincentives built into the system that reduce the motivation to work, to save, or to exercise
much initiative. In addition, the system is complex and administratively awkward. I have suggested that at the margin, these
costs are high, especially when measured against the benefits. To
simply expand the current system in the face of more effective
and efficient options is hard to justify. And the appeal to outright
"retrenchment" no longer musters support.

My proposed strategy trims down and simplifies the methods
used to attempt to reduce inequality. Instead of several badly
integrated and complex cash and in-kind benefit programs, it
has a single tax credit tied to the personal income tax—an administratively efficient component of the existing tax transfer
system. The proposed Social Security system is a far less complicated arrangement than now exists, with a standard individualized benefit and a more direct financing arrangement. The
child-support system also has a single national benefit structure
and a financing mechanism that works through the federal income tax. The two new programs—the employment subsidies
and the capital account for youths—will require new administrative arrangements. The labor market efforts have already been
tried in various forms, and the administrative arrangements that
are most effective in achieving its goals have been studied. And
the capital account for youths offers a way of substituting a
straightforward program for the numerous categorical and
administratively complex arrangements that now exist.

Creating Incentives

My proposed system would go a long way toward increasing individual incentives to succeed. The tax credit and the child-support
system will encourage mothers, especially single mothers, to
work. The individualized Social Security system does far less to
encourage early retirement than the current arrangement, and it
emphasizes the importance of private savings. It transfers back to

individuals responsibility for providing for their retirement years. The highlights of the new approach in terms of fostering work, initiative, and independence are the employment subsidies and the capital account for youth. Both of these programs aim at low-skilled citizens and are designed to give them the resources and training necessary for success in pursuing careers.

Caveats and Concerns

Three caveats to this otherwise optimistic assessment need to be mentioned. First, what would be the cost of this new system to the taxpayer? There is no definitive answer to this basic question. The changes proposed are fundamental ones; they are designed to alter people's behavior and performance in a variety of ways. Work and initiative will increase and with it the performance of the economy. The nation's savings rate should rise, easing the financing of new investment. These changes will generate new federal revenue, but how much cannot be known with accuracy. In addition, large savings in public expenditures on existing pro- grams—AFDC, food stamps, housing, Supplemental Security In- come, and especially Social Security—will be achieved. Some increases in private responsibility and expenditures will be re- quired.

At the same time, the initiatives proposed have taxpayer costs. The refundable tax credit would result in a net loss of revenue to the Treasury, but how much depends on the level of the credit and on reductions in existing welfare programs. A revenue loss would also result from the two-pronged employment subsidy program if it is tied to the tax system, as was the New Jobs Tax Credit of the 1970s. However, jobs would be created by these efforts—people would increase the amount they work, and the income generated by these initiatives would help offset the reve- nue losses. On the other hand, by reducing Social Security bene- fits for higher earners and transferring some of the responsibility for retirement income to individuals, substantial expenditure savings would result. The child-support system should involve little if any increase in net public spending as it would shift the responsibility for the care of children from taxpayers generally to their parents, especially absent parents. The big unknown cost factor is the capital account for youths, but even here expenditures may be far less than anticipated. Annual federal expenditures need cover only annual withdrawals; there is no need to finance the entire account immediately. In addition, part of these costs will be offset by the elimination of a variety of existing public programs that now support or provide education and training beyond the high school level and for which the capital account will substitute. My best guess is that the system proposed will require an overall but insubstantial increase in federal public spending—between 1 and 2 percent. (In the Appendix to Chapter 7, I try to answer the question of how much all this will cost, presenting the rationale for this estimate.)

A second caveat concerns evaluation. All new policies or policy reforms require detailed designs and rigorous evaluations prior to adoption. The new strategy proposed here is no exception. This discussion of it provides neither. The purpose of this book is to do what needs doing prior to design work or evaluation studies; it is to lay on the table a new vision, a new approach to reducing inequality and poverty. It is to provoke discussion and debate, to broaden horizons and possibilities. However, while it contains no detailed designs or rigorous evaluations, the reorientation that I have proposed rests on far more than dreams or hopes. Two decades of research on poverty and inequality, stimulated by the War on Poverty, have focused on the nation's existing policy strategy, its impacts, and alternatives to it. This mini-industry of studies, demonstrations, experiments, simulations, and designs forms the knowledge base on which this proposed strategy rests, and it is what gives it credibility. Indeed, it was my effort to tease a coordinated policy approach out of this body of knowledge and findings that guided the new strategy for reducing poverty and inequality proposed in this book.

And the final caveat. While the proposed system targets some of the most troublesome of the nation's social problems, it deals with others only tangentially. The deep-seated problems of the underclass in some of our inner cities, especially those problems that stem from the prevailing values and mores prevalent in these communities, remain to be confronted—both by these communities and by the society at large. This proposal is only a first step toward correcting some of the frustrations and feelings of helplessness that have fostered the growth of this culture. It does not solve the nation's health care problems, although it would give youths the resources with which to obtain health care. The large segment of the population without health insurance— up to 40 million people—would remain uncovered, although this number could be reduced if the new strategy results in increased incomes and resources to families unable to purchase insurance.

Similarly, the proposed new system says nothing about the quality of the nation's educational system, the need for or strategies of compensatory or preschool education, the public responsibility for providing child care services to families in which all adults work or wish to work, the access of the disabled to rehabilitation services, the services and facilities that ought to be provided for the treatment of the mentally retarded, the advisability of mandating work or training for those who receive public benefits, or the desirability of allowing the enormous differences in wealth which now exist to stand. These problems are complex and intertwined. Unlike the problems of poverty and inequality dealt with in this book, there has been far less thought and study given to the policy options available or their effectiveness.

It is too early to know if the nation is now ready to deal with the inequality problems highlighted in this book—the large numbers of low-income and dependent individuals, youths without jobs or futures, and the increasing numbers of poor single mothers and children. But there is increasing evidence that policymakers recognize that the focus of the 1980s on increased economic growth and productivity has, through neglect, exacerbated these social sores. It has left us with pulled-apart populations—the new unequals—and fundamental and growing inequalities of opportunity. The fact that simple expansion of our current strategy carries with it serious efficiency costs implies the need for a new way of doing the nation's inequality reduction business. A new program to achieve equality with efficiency is within reach and can serve as the basis for the inevitable swing in political concerns, the shift from "capitalism" to "democracy," in McClosky and Zaller's terms. The important new insight of this book, I believe, is that these two central objectives—less poverty and inequality, more efficiency—are reconcilable after all. By focusing on opportunities rather than outcomes, and by attending to both incentives and accountability, government policy can support the operation of a more productive and less unequal society and economy.

Changes in Well-Being and Inequality, 1960–1985: Trends in Disparities

Ross E. Finnie

This Appendix provides the factual details concerning the contours of inequality and poverty in the United States since the 1960s. As such, it is a supplement to Chapters 2 and 3. The post-1960 period is the focus of discussion because the current U.S. situation can best be understood by tracing the changes that began with the years of government activism that were heralded by Lyndon Johnson's declaration of "unconditional War on Poverty" (in his State of the Union message, January 1964). The 1960 and 1980 decennial censuses are the major sources of information, since they provide more data than are available in non-census years. The record is updated to the mid-1980s by integrating with these data the findings of other researchers, who use a variety of data sources, plus tabulations from Current Population Survey data.

The text, structured around tables and graphs presenting the important facts of inequality and poverty, offers explanations of, and reasons for, the patterns in each graph and table. The textual narrative is thus the mortar that cements the statistical and graphic blocks together to enhance our understanding of the broad structure of inequality and poverty in the United States. Comparisons along racial/ethnic groups are, of necessity, largely restricted to blacks and whites, due to an inability to identify Hispanics in earlier census data. Where more recent data permit such identification, results are reported.

Because the labor market is the foundation on which the structure of U.S. inequality rests, it is the starting point of our analysis.

NOTE: THE DESCRIPTION OF EACH TABLE FOLLOWS THE TABLE AND IS
SET IN ITALIC TYPE.

Table A.1
Relative Average Earnings Across Race and Gender, 1960 and 1980
(White Men as Reference Group)

	1960	1980
Full-Time, Full-Year Workers Only		
All Age Groups		
White men	1.00	1.00
White women	.56	.56
Black men	.56	.71
Black women	.36	.52
Individuals Aged 35–44		
White men	1.00	1.00
White women	.53	.51
Black men	.57	.70
Black women	.34	.49
All Workers		
All Age Groups		
White men	1.00	1.00
White women	.45	.46
Black men	.53	.68
Black women	.27	.47
Individuals Aged 35–44		
White men	1.00	1.00
White women	.39	.40
Black men	.53	.67
Black women	.26	.44

Notes: "Average" refers to arithmetic means in this and subsequent tables, unless otherwise indicated. Earnings include wage, salary, and self-employment income; other published figures are often based on wage and salary income only. Both measures are interesting, but the measure used here probably reflects a broader indicator of differences in earnings opportunities. Self-employment income is more important for white men, thus scaling the relative earnings of others down commensurately. Hispanics are excluded from all tables unless otherwise indicated. This is regrettable, but a necessary omission in that identification of Hispanics was not provided for in the 1960 Census, thus precluding any analysis in the changing patterns of inequality for this group.

Source: Special tabulations by the author from Census of Population public-use computer tapes, 1960 and 1980.

Earnings differences across race and gender groups are enormous. The top half of the table looks at full-time, full-year workers only, while the bottom half looks at all those with any earnings at all. The first panel in each half looks at workers of all ages; the lower panels control for differences associated with age by looking only at "prime-aged" earners. In all cases the differences remain very great in 1980, but there is strong evidence of significant catching up by blacks, while white women appear to have made negligible progress. Earnings differences among all workers are wider than those for full-time, full-year workers as shown, reflecting both market opportunities and individuals' labor supply decisions. Looking at the latter group only presents a more unambiguous measure of earnings opportunities.

It is worth noting that as income levels rise, a given ratio represents an increasing absolute dollar difference in incomes. Throughout these tables, a mix of these measures will be presented in an effort to provide sufficient information with brevity.

---

1. LABOR MARKET AND EARNINGS DIFFERENCES ACROSS GENDER AND RACIAL GROUPS

Table A.1 contains a simple comparison of the earnings of white and black men and women in 1960 and 1980. White women who were full-time, full-year workers earned only a little more than half as much as white men in 1980, a situation that had remained virtually unchanged since 1960. On the other hand, in 1980 black men and women still lagged behind white men, but had made significant progress—even though their gains only brought black women close to the level of white women (at a level still far below white men), and black men still earned only 71 percent of what white men earned.

The more recent data presented in Table A.2, though not directly comparable to the decennial census data of Table A.1, suggest that women have made some progress of late, while black men have slipped back a little through the 1980s. Large differences in earnings are seen to remain.

Figures A.1 and A.2 add another dimension by tracing the "age-earnings profiles" of black and white men and women in 1960 and 1980. The profiles reveal roughly the same patterns as seen in Table A.1: white men continue to fare much better than others; there has been limited progress among white women, more progress among black men and women.

Education is strongly associated with labor market earnings, although there is considerable disagreement among economists as to why this is so: It may reflect productivity differences; "signaling" (a sorting of workers of differing abilities); the class divisions of society; or some other set of relationships. Regardless of the reasons, education and

Table A.2
Relative Median Weekly Earnings of Full-time Wage and Salary Workers by Race and Gender, 1980 and 1986
(White Men as Reference Group)

	1980	*1986*
White men	1.00	1.00
White women	.63	.67
Black men	.76	.73
Black women	.58	.61

Notes: Based on usual weekly earnings and representing annual averages of quarterly data as collected by the U.S. Bureau of Labor Statistics. Figures are thus not directly comparable to figures based on the 1960 and 1980 Census of Population, which appear elsewhere in this Appendix, but should provide a good indication of recent broad trends in earnings.

Source: Employment and Earnings, Vol. 34, No. 1 (January 1987), p. 54, Bureau of Labor Statistics.

Recent shifts in relative earnings suggest that women have made some progress against men, but black men have slipped back relative to white men. The progress of women reflects their increasing commitment to the labor force, and the first significant commensurate movements in labor market earnings. For black men, the depression of the early 1980s hit very hard, especially for younger and less educated ones, and their recovery has been incomplete; the future looks uncertain for black men.

Figure A.1
Age-Earnings Profiles for Full-Time, Full-Year Workers
by Race and Gender, 1980, in 1980 Dollars

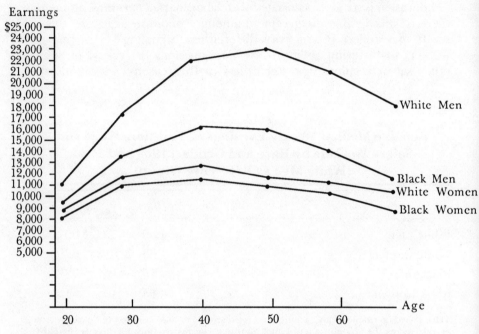

Source: Special tabulations by the author from 1980 Census of Population public-use computer tapes.

Notes: Full-time, full-year means at least forty-eight weeks worked in the year, and at least thirty-five hours "usually worked" per week. This definition applies throughout the other tables and figures as well. Earnings include all wage, salary, and self-employment income.

Figure A.2
Age-Earnings Profiles for Full-Time, Full-Year Workers
by Race and Gender, 1960, in 1980 Dollars

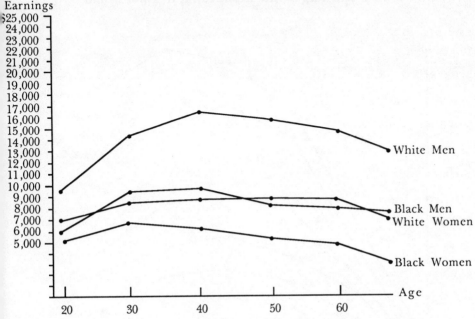

Source: Special tabulations by the author from 1960 Census of Population public-use computer tapes.

Notes: Full-time, full-year means at least forty-eight weeks worked in the year, and at least thirty-five hours "usually worked" per week. This definition applies throughout the other tables and figures as well. Earnings include all wage, salary, and self-employment income.

Figure A.3
Age-Earnings Profiles by Educational Level for Full-Time,
Full-Year Working White Men, 1980, in 1980 Dollars

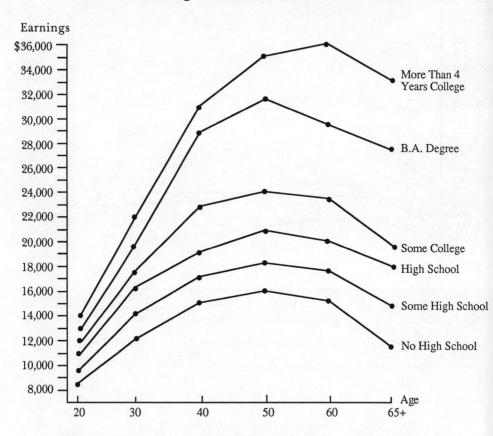

Source: Special tabulations by the author from 1980 Census of Population public-use computer tapes.

Notes: Full-time, full-year means at least forty-eight weeks worked in the year, and at least thirty-five hours "usually worked" per week. This definition applies throughout the other tables and figures as well. Earnings include all wage, salary, and self-employment income.

Figure A.4
1960 Age-Earnings Profiles for Full-Time, Full-Year Workers
by Race and Gender for Selected Educational Levels
(1980 $US)

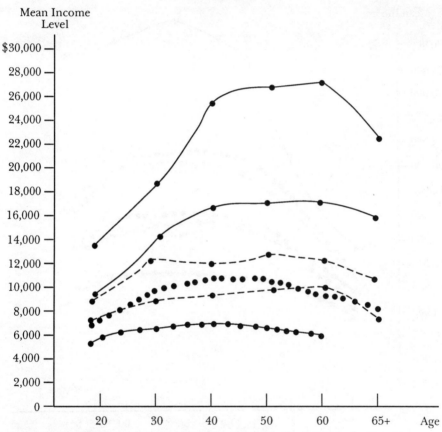

Notes: Full-time, full-year means at least forty-eight weeks worked in the year, and at least thirty-five hours "usually worked" per week. This definition applies throughout the other tables and figures as well. Earnings include all wage, salary, and self-employment income.
——— White men, high school (lower line) and B.A. degree (higher line)
– – – White women, high school (lower line) and B.A. degree (higher line)
● ● ● Black men, high school only
●●● Black women, high school only

Source: Special tabulations by the author from 1960 Census of Population public-use computer tapes.

Figure A.5
1980 Age-Earnings Profiles for Full-Time, Full-Year Workers by Race and Gender for Selected Educational Levels
(1980 $US)

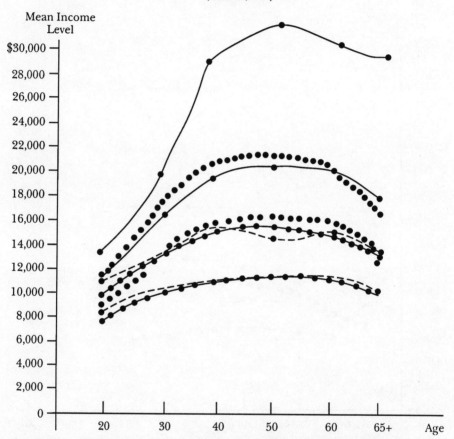

Notes: Full-time, full-year means at least forty-eight weeks worked in the year, and at least thirty-five hours "usually worked" per week. This definition applies throughout the other tables and figures as well. Earnings include all wage, salary, and self-employment income.

——— White men, high school (lower line) and B.A. degree (higher line)
– – – White women, high school (lower line) and B.A. degree (higher line)
● ● ● Black men, high school (lower line) and B.A. degree (higher line)
●—●—● Black women, higher school (lower line) and B.A. degree (higher line)

Source: Special tabulations by the author from 1980 Census of Population public-use computer tapes.

earnings are strongly related, as shown for white men in Figure A.3. The age-earnings profiles for those with less education are much flatter than, and lie far below, those of more educated men. Whether or not this represents a "problem" of inequality depends on one's judgment of how much these education-earnings differences reflect differences in opportunities as opposed to differences in choices made. Educational attainment is in fact "inherited" to a significant degree, in that children's educational levels are significantly affected by parental education, income, and other characteristics, so the resulting differences in earnings can thus be viewed as problems of inequality of opportunity, at least for the white men as illustrated so far.

Figures A.4 and A.5 broaden the education view by comparing age-earnings profiles across racial and gender groups for selected levels of education in 1960 and 1980.[1] Table A.3 augments Figures A.4 and A.5 by showing the earnings ratios of white women, black men, and black women relative to white men, for all educational levels. The ratios are restricted to those aged forty-five to fifty-four to control for age effects.

The age-earnings profiles of white and black women shown in Figures A.4 and A.5 were fairly similar by 1980, both in level and shape, in turn resembling those of less educated white men, and all much lower and flatter than white men with higher levels of education. The figures also reveal the widening of these earnings differences over a lifetime as well: white men pull further ahead, leaving black and white women even more distantly behind. Table A.3 shows that these cross-gender earnings differences exist among more educated women as well as less educated ones: clearly, education is not a panacea for overcoming low relative female earnings.[2] Since black women have reached the earnings levels of white women, their disadvantage now appears to be primarily due to gender rather than race. Perhaps the flatness of these women's profiles (Figures A.4 and A.5) is their most revealing aspect: both black and white women appear to remain in limited job situations, enjoying little of the career and earnings advancement that comes with age, experience, and job tenure for white men.

A more detailed look at black men, on the other hand, suggests dramatic earnings progress from 1960 to 1980. Table A.3 shows that annual earnings of black middle-aged employed men rose from under two-fifths to over three-quarters of white men's earnings at each educational level. Their increased educational attainment boosted overall mean earnings as well. That is, each education earnings profile shifted up, and more black men were on the higher education profiles. Figures A.4 and A.5 further suggest that the age earnings profiles of black men have also taken on more of the "hump" shape that characterizes the

Table A.3
Earnings Ratios Among Gender, Race, and Educational Groups Relative to White Men: Comparisons of Those Aged Forty-five to Fifty-four, 1960 and 1980*

Group	1960	1980
White Women		
No high school	.58	.51
Some high school	.55	.53
High school completed	.56	.54
Some college	.49	.54
College degree	.49	.44
Graduate degree	.52	.53
Total	.54	.50
Black Men		
No high school	.38	.76
Some high school	.39	.78
High school completed	.39	.77
Some college	—	.75
College degree	—	.76
Graduate degree	—	.80
Total	.31	.67
Black Women		
No high school	.34	.50
Some high school	.35	.48
High school completed	.40	.50
Some college	.36	.52
College degree	—	.46
Graduate degree	—	.53
Total	.31	.45

Notes: These values are the mean earnings of the group divided by the mean earnings of similar white men. All values are based on at least fifty observations and are for full-time, full-year workers only. Missing values are due to insufficient observations.

Source: Special tabulations by the author from Census of Population public-use computer tapes, 1960 and 1980.

Earnings differences by educational level are shown for 1960 and 1980. The ratios indicate that, controlling for education and age, which are two important determinants of earnings, (a) white women earned around one-half as much as white men in 1980, largely unchanged since 1960, (b) black men narrowed much of the gap with white men from 1960 to 1980, as their relative earnings almost doubled, to around 75 percent, (c) black women narrowed some of the gap from 1960 to 1980, but only to the level of white women, leaving them with about one-half the earnings of white men. While many factors help explain these differentials, much of the disparity is due to reduced labor market opportunities: Blacks and women on average get worse jobs, receive lower pay, and enjoy fewer possibilities of career advancement, even when they have the same amount of education as white men.

---

profiles of white men, indicating that at least some black men are entering labor markets traditionally closed to them.

It is important to realize, however, that at the same time that average earnings of black men are rising, greater numbers of black men and women, primarily youths, are actually doing worse than before. While earnings statistics generally show improvement, there are many non-earners who are not represented in these statistics, and they appear to constitute a growing subpopulation.

Table A.4 provides a first view of this "pulling apart," as it shows increasingly higher unemployment rates among black and white men of various ages; Table A.5 shows increasingly lower employment rates, by educational level, for men of two specific age groups. These two tables demonstrate that: unemployment among black men is much greater at younger ages, and the situation has sharply worsened since 1960; more education is associated with much higher work rates; all unemployment rates rose, and work rates fell, from 1960 to 1980, but deterioration was much greater for the already disadvantaged—blacks relative to whites, youth relative to the prime-aged, those with less education relative to those with more.

The conclusion is that higher average earnings have been accompanied by rising nonemployment rates. This apparent divergence has been greatest among blacks, whose earnings have risen more but whose work rates have fallen most sharply. Some are catching up while others are falling further behind than ever. This is an important dimension of the structure of inequality in the United States in the 1980s.

To summarize this section, earnings vary greatly across gender-race groups. White men continue to do the best by far; black men have

Table A.4
Unemployment Rates for Men, by Age and Race,
1960 and 1980

Age	Black			White		
	1960	1980	Percent Increase	1960	1980	Percent Increase
16–64	8.9	12.6	36	4.5	5.8	29
36–45	7.8	8.5	8	3.2	3.7	16
16–24	13.4	22.0	64	8.5	10.9	28

Note: See also Table A.22.

Source: Smith and Welch, op. cit., p. 108.

Rising unemployment rates are shown in Table A.4, with a situation especially critical for young black men, of whom almost one-quarter were officially listed as unemployed in 1980; since then conditions have deteriorated even further (see Table A.22). Black unemployment rates are, at all age levels, more than double those of whites, and their rates of increase from 1960 to 1980 are also greater. These numbers must be contrasted to the improved earnings of employed workers: there is a sizable group of men who are doing worse, even as many others are earning considerably more than before. Labor market opportunities and outcomes thus appear to be pulling apart in a dramatic way, both within and across age and racial groups. (See Table A.22 for more data on unemployment, by gender, race, and age for the period 1972–1985.)

made much progress but still lag behind and have slipped back a little since 1980; white women did not enjoy any relative earnings growth, on average, between 1960 and 1980, but then moved forward through the 1980s; black women have approximately caught up to white women. Education is a strong determinant of earnings for all groups, but gender-race earnings differences hold even when education is controlled for; the same is true for age as well. Finally, while average earnings of black men have risen, so too have their nonemployment rates, suggesting a disturbing divergence of labor market outcomes.

Appendix: Changes in Well-Being and Inequality

Table A.5
Percentage of Men Who Worked at Least One Week in Preceding Year, by Educational Level and Race, 1960 and 1980

| | Black | | White | |
Educational Level	1960	1980	1960	1980
Age 36–45				
0–7 years	89.8	74.5	91.2	78.5
8–11 years	91.4	81.9	97.0	92.4
12 years	93.8	87.2	98.5	96.3
13–15 years	95.0	90.4	98.4	96.7
16+ years	98.8	93.4	99.1	98.4
All educational levels	91.4	85.1	97.1	95.6
Age 46–54				
0–7 years	88.0	66.7	90.1	75.9
8–11 years	90.6	76.4	95.5	87.7
12 years	93.3	83.4	96.9	93.0
13–15 years	92.3	86.2	96.9	93.5
16+ years	97.7	91.9	98.0	96.5
All educational levels	89.4	77.9	95.0	91.2

Note: See also Table A.23.

Source: Smith and Welch, op. cit., p. 80.

Differences in labor force activity between black and white men are shown in Table A.5. At higher levels of education, both blacks and whites are more likely to have worked in the past year, and black unemployment rates are closer to those of whites. Note that these rates deteriorated uniformly from 1960 to 1980, suggesting that a sizable group is not sharing in the higher earnings of workers, shown previously. This falling behind is greater for blacks, and all men with less education. As some are doing better, many are doing much worse than before. (See Table A.23 for activity rates of young men and women.)

201

Table A.6
Measures of Educational Attainment, by Race and Gender, 1960 and 1980

Age	1960			1980		
	White	*Black*	*Difference*	*White*	*Black*	*Difference*
Men: average years of education, by age						
26–35	11.5	9.0	2.5	13.6	12.2	1.4
36–45	10.9	7.8	3.1	13.0	11.3	1.7
45–55	10.0	6.5	3.5	12.2	9.9	2.3
55–64	9.1	5.5	3.6	11.5	8.5	3.0
16–65 Total	10.7	8.0	2.7	12.5	11.0	1.5
Black Women: percent with at least some college education						
Aged 25–34	13			39		
All ages	10			31		

Source: Special tabulations by the author from Census of Population public-use computer tapes, 1960 and 1980.

The educational attainment of blacks has been catching up to that of whites. The top panel shows that mean years of education for black men has grown closer to that of white men, especially among younger cohorts. The bottom panel shows a remarkable rise in the percentage of black women who have attended college. This progress is probably the most important factor in the rise of the earnings of blacks relative to whites over recent decades.

2. UNDERSTANDING THE TREND OF INEQUALITY BETWEEN BLACKS AND WHITES IN THE LABOR MARKET

This section explores explanations for the facts presented above concerning earnings differences between blacks and whites. (Gender differences are discussed below.) The principal factors affecting the evolving patterns include the amount and quality of education, general economic growth, shifts in industrial structure, regional economic disparities and migration patterns, and affirmative action and related legislation.

Many economists have concluded that most of the reduction in the black-white earnings gap in the 1960s and 1970s is attributable to more and better education for blacks, narrowing the gap in three ways: (1) each black education–earnings profile has shifted up, toward the comparable white profile; (2) more blacks are now represented in the higher education–earnings profiles, as shown in Table A.6; (3) the higher profiles are where black-white differences are smallest. Some researchers estimate that changes in these quality-quantity schooling factors account for from 50 to 80 percent of the diminution of the male black-white earnings gap.[3,4]

Economic growth is probably the second major factor in reduction of the black-white earnings gap.[5] From the boom following World War II through the mid-1970s, fairly steady economic expansion opened up employment opportunities. The jobs taken by blacks were also increasingly better ones, requiring more skill, education, and training; offering higher earnings and greater security; and providing greater career advancement. On the other hand, a faltering economy since 1973 has affected blacks more than whites, as hard times have always been more difficult for blacks. This helps explain the increasing divergence in black fortunes: Those who have made their way into the economic mainstream are still doing relatively well, while those at the edge (especially the less educated and youths, among others) are doing worse. Strong and steady economic growth would appear to be critical to future advancement of blacks.

The great South-to-North migration of blacks was another major factor in narrowing racial earnings differences, at least into the 1970s. For several decades blacks moved from low-paying agricultural jobs, largely sharecropping cotton, to the growing economies of the North where pay was higher and black-white earnings differences were smaller.[6] There is, however, bitter irony in the fact that for the last decade and a half the northern economies have been weakening, particularly in areas especially important to blacks (that is, manufacturing industries and central city locations). While blacks with marketable skills and good jobs in some healthy local or regional economies are still enjoying earnings growth, those left in depressed areas are doing much worse.[7] Locational and migrational factors have thus played an important role both in the long-run narrowing of black-white earnings differentials and in the recent divergence of black labor market fortunes.

Civil rights legislation, and affirmative action in particular, has also probably played a significant role in narrowing the black-white earnings gap, even though some economists are skeptical, arguing that long-run gains cannot be legislated, but must instead be grounded in more strictly economic factors (such as education and economic growth). A study of the evidence suggests that such legislation has probably had the following effects: greater employment for blacks in the firms covered, representing in part a net increase in jobs, but in part only a shifting of black workers from one job to another; a short-run increase in the wages of young blacks with jobs; some long-run earnings increases, enjoyed principally by college-educated black workers; and a reduction in discriminatory attitudes, which has helped blacks generally.[8] Legislation has thus helped black workers by increasing the earnings of some and making better jobs available. Meanwhile, others were probably helped little, perhaps even hurt. These programs are therefore also responsible for some of the divergence among blacks that has been recently recorded.[9]

3. EARNINGS DISADVANTAGES FACED BY WOMEN

Why do women earn so much less than men? Is their earnings gap a result of "choice" or unequal opportunity? This section gives the subject a general review and concludes that women continue to perform a balancing act—in terms of career investment, marriage, and family responsibility, and work outside the home—which leaves them at a disadvantage in the labor market. Lower earnings are the result.

Women have historically specialized in home production and were, at most, secondary workers. While men prepared themselves for work in the labor market and made decisions which would maximize their success there, women made choices which reflected the primary nature of their nonmarket functions and the secondary nature of labor market considerations. Women traded labor market preparation and possibilities for success there for the primary role of homemaker. If women did work outside the home initially, their "career" usually ended with marriage or childbearing, perhaps to be taken up again years later. Their education, training, credentials, and skill development were consistent with this labor market interruption. Marriages were traditionally characterized by specialization: the man was the labor market specialist, the woman a homemaker.[10]

In the last quarter century this "equilibrium" began to give way, and the process accelerated after the mid-1960s. Patterns of labor force behavior, marital status, and childbearing all changed, reflecting the interdependence of these choices. Women became increasingly "serious" labor force participants, shifting from their traditional domain, the home and family, to compete in the labor market. But despite this reorientation women have continued to carry the major responsibilities in the home, and so their labor market chances remain compromised.

These enduring labor market disadvantages in turn still lead many women to turn from maximum preparation for the labor market, since the rewards of such preparation are incomplete, thereby reinforcing their disadvantages. (For example, the level and type of education women obtain will reflect their dual role, while men are more likely to specialize in education with steady and large labor market returns.) The continuing dual nature of women's roles, home versus the labor market, thus means that it remains difficult for women to compete as equals with men; hence, they continue to earn less. More specific factors can be cited to account for the male-female earnings gap, such as differences in education, experience, occupation choice, and so on, but they are also all related to this "compromise dilemma."[11]

Although some analysts have suggested that if individual women want to break out of these compromises and disadvantages they are free to do so, such freedom seems limited. "Free" choice is not quite accurate; it may be possible to "break out," but breaking out of traditional societal roles is in fact difficult. The labor market itself carries expectations that work against "career women," who often find it difficult to be taken seriously as such and who do not receive the opportunities they deserve as a result. Finally, for married women, equalizing career and home responsibilities requires a similarly oriented spouse; it is not clear how many such men exist.

In conclusion, a principal reason why women earn so much less than men is that they do not typically "specialize" in the labor market as men do. Their upbringings, education, and other preparations leave them with compromised opportunities in the labor market. Their actual working years reflect these earlier compromises and the acting out of a dual home-market role. While individual choice determines much, social forces, stereotyping and discrimination, and labor market structures and rigidities make it difficult for women to really enjoy the labor market opportunities men enjoy as a matter of course. Large earnings differences are understood better in this light of fundamental divergence of opportunities.

4. INEQUALITY ACROSS FAMILIES

We now turn from the earnings differences of individuals to consider inequality in income among families. This involves consideration of labor market earnings, plus other income sources, in conjunction with family structure.

Table A.7 compares income across race and family type in 1960 and 1980 (see also Figure 3.2 in Chapter 3); Table A.8 shows the income differences as ratios and updates the figures to 1985 with CPS data.

Table A.7
Family Income and Race, 1960 and 1980, in 1980 Dollars

	Total Income		Absolute Change	Percent Change	Per Capita Income		Absolute Change	Percent Change
	1960	1980	1960–1980	1960–1980	1960	1980	1960–1980	1960–1980
White Families								
Two-parent	$17,800	$25,800	$8,000	+45.0	$4,200	$6,400	$2,200	+52.0
Mother-only	8,500	11,600	3,100	+37.0	2,700	3,900	1,200	+44.0
Black Families								
Two-parent	11,300	20,000	8,700	+77.0	2,300	4,600	2,300	+100.0
Mother-only	5,800	8,600	2,800	+48.3	1,400	2,500	1,100	+79.0

Notes: Calculations are for all families with children. Per capita incomes are family income divided by the number of people in the family. Income includes all sources of income.

Source: Special tabulations by the author from Census of Population public-use computer tapes, 1960 and 1980.

Family income, shown in Table A.7, increased in absolute terms for all groups from 1960 to 1980, but percentage and absolute changes were much larger for two-parent relative to one-parent families, causing the latter to fall increasingly farther behind. On the other hand, within family types, blacks had larger percentage increases than whites, even though they registered only about the same absolute dollar increases relative to whites. (Table A.8 summarizes these relative income standings.) These patterns largely reflect differences in labor market earnings, but are also affected by other sources of income and how these interact with family structures.

Over this period all family types enjoyed substantial increases in average real incomes (Table A.7). Decreases in family size from 1960 to 1980 caused per capita incomes to rise more than total incomes, especially for black families.[12] Third, black two-parent families enjoyed the highest rates of income growth, thus raising their relative income ratios substantially (Table A.7, columns 4 and 8, Table A.8, row 2); on the other hand, their absolute income growth was only slightly higher than that of whites (Table A.7, columns 3 and 7). Two-parent families, both black and white, moved further ahead of mother-only families by every measure.

Table A.8
Family Incomes by Race and Structure as a Percentage of Income of Two-Parent White Families, 1960, 1980, and 1985

	Total Income			Per Capita Income		
	1960	*1980*	*1985*	*1960*	*1980*	*1985*
White Families						
Mother-only	48	45	43	64	61	—
Black Families						
Two-parent	63	78	77	55	72	—
Mother-only	33	33	32	33	39	—

Notes: Calculations are for all families with children. The values are the mean incomes of the indicated family type divided by the mean income of similar white two-parent families.

Source: Special tabulations by the author from Census of Population public-use computer tapes, for 1960 and 1980 (see Table A.7). 1985 figures are derived from the Census Bureau's Current Population Survey (see source note, Table A.10).

Income inequality across families is increasingly related to the difference between two-parent and one-parent families, rather than to differences of race alone. Through the 1980s, the average income of white mother-only families was below half the level of two-parent white families; for black mother-only families the income ratio stood at only one-third (Table A.8, columns 2, 3, and 5). These figures represent enormous differences in economic well-being among parents and their dependent children.

Table A.9 shows that education narrows family income differences somewhat, especially in terms of per capita income (row 1 versus 2, and 3 versus 4). But even though more education would clearly raise incomes of mother-only families, a large income gap still exists among those with more education. The distribution of education itself works against mother-only families (data not shown).

With the aid of calculations made by Sheldon Danziger and Peter Gottschalk, it is possible to consider the ebb and flow of family income from 1960 to 1985.[13] Table A.10 and Figure 3.3 in Chapter 3 show family income by race and family type for the period 1959–85. The subperiod from 1959 to 1967 was advantageous for all the family groups, but especially for two-parent families of both races. Then, while

Table A.9
Family Incomes as a Percentage of Two-Parent White Families, by Selected Educational Levels of the Family Head, 1960 and 1980

	White Mother-Only		Black Two-Parent		Black Mother-Only	
	1960	1980	1960	1980	1960	1980
Total Family Income						
Some high school	48	44	76	85	38	35
College degree	53	50	72	84	45	44
Per Capita Family Income						
Some high school	62	57	66	77	40	38
College degree	80	72	71	85	59	63

Notes: Calculations are for all families with children. The percentages for "total" do not always equal those of Table A.8 owing to rounding.

Source: Special tabulations by the author from Census of Population public-use computer tapes, 1960 and 1980.

Relative family income reflects the education of the family head, as illustrated here. Note that black families of both types have incomes considerably lower than those of white two-parent families, even holding education constant. Income differences are, however, generally smaller at higher education levels. The equalizing effect of education is much greater for per capita income than total income, which indicates that education is related to family size as well as income. The distribution of education also works against mother-only families: their overall mean incomes are lower due to their having less education on average, as well as having lower incomes at each given education level.

two-parent families maintained their rate of income growth from 1967 to 1973, average incomes of mother-only families flattened out. From 1973 to 1979 families experienced virtually no income growth, and from 1979 to 1985 real incomes actually declined. Over the entire period, all family types enjoyed income growth, but the increases were concentrated in the earlier years. Black two-parent families advanced

Table A.10
Total Family Incomes of Families with Children, Selected Years, 1959–1985, in 1984 Dollars

	1959	1967	1973	1979	1985	1985 Value Divided by 1959 Value	1959–1984 Absolute Increase
All Two-Parent Families							
White	24,308	30,963	36,276	35,976	35,717	1.47	11,668
Black	14,689	21,121	27,040	28,645	28,416	1.93	13,956
All Mother-Only Families							
White	10,749	15,836	15,853,	16,016	15,061	1.40	5,267
Black	6,769	10,819	11,619	11,710	11,280	1.67	4,941

Note: Data are for all families with children. The figures in this table are in 1984 dollars, while in the previous tables they are in 1980 dollars.

Source: The 1967–1985 numbers are derived from Sheldon Danziger and Peter Gottschalk, "How Have Families with Children Been Faring?" Institute for Research on Poverty Discussion Paper 801–86, January 1986, updated to 1985 with data from the Current Population Survey. (The 1979 values agree with the Census data presented in Table A.7, indicating that the two sources can be used to construct a constant series.) The 1959 values are from the decennial Census.

Mean incomes of families with children increased steadily up to 1973 for both black and white two-parent families, but then remained stagnant. For mother-only families, incomes leveled off earlier, sometime after 1967. These income figures reflect changes in individual earnings as well as in other income sources, government transfers in particular. They also reflect labor force participation patterns, including the rising number of working mothers.

---

relative to whites throughout by any measure (last 2 columns), but black and white mother-only families fell increasingly behind after 1967, again in terms of both rates and absolute dollar amounts of growth.

The data presented thus far have focused exclusively on average income of family groups. Table A.11 shows the distribution of income among all families with children from 1967 to 1985. In every case, the income share of the bottom quintile (the lowest 20 percent) declined

Table A.11
Percentage of Aggregate Income Received by Quintiles of Families with Children, 1967–1985

	1967	1973	1979	1985	1985 Value Divided by 1967 Value
All Families with Children					
Bottom quintile	6.6	5.8	5.2	4.2	.64
Middle 60 percent	54.9	54.9	55.4	53.7	.98
Top quintile	38.5	38.3	39.4	42.2	1.10
White Families with Children					
Bottom quintile	7.3	6.5	5.9	4.7	.64
Middle 60 percent	54.8	55.0	55.9	53.9	.98
Top quintile	37.8	38.5	38.2	41.3	1.09
Black Families with Children					
Bottom quintile	5.3	4.8	4.1	3.5	.66
Middle 60 percent	52.4	52.0	51.3	49.9	.95
Top quintile	42.4	43.2	44.63	46.7	1.10

Note: Figures do not necessarily sum to 100.0 due to rounding.

Source: Derived from Sheldon Danziger and Peter Gottschalk, "How Have Families with Children Been Faring?" Institute for Research on Poverty, January 1986, p. 17, and subsequent update for 1985. Calculations are the responsibility of the author.

Increasing inequality of family income is seen in the declining shares of total income going to those at the bottom of the distribution and the increased shares for those at the top. This is true for all families (top panel) as well as black and white families (bottom panels). The distribution of well-being among families with children is becoming increasingly unequal.

---

continually over the period, while the top quintile gained throughout. Poor families got relatively poorer, rich ones richer. Further, these absolute dollar shifts represent very large percentage losses for the low-income families at the bottom, but only small percentage income gains for

Table A.12
Incidence of Poverty Among Persons Living in Families with Children, 1967–1985 (in percent)

	1967	*1973*	*1979*	*1985*
All Families with Children	13.5	11.4	12.7	16.7
White	9.4	7.9	9.2	13.2
Black	41.9	34.4	33.3	35.7
All Two-Parent Families with Children	9.9	6.5	7.0	9.9
White	7.7	5.2	6.1	9.0
Black	31.3	18.7	15.5	14.8
All Mother-Only Families with Children	47.2	45.9	42.4	47.3
White	34.2	36.2	32.9	40.0
Black	67.6	61.1	57.1	59.7

Source: Sheldon Danziger and Peter Gottschalk, "How Have Families with Children Been Faring?" Institute for Research on Poverty, January 1986, p. 24, updated to 1985.

The incidence of poverty from 1967 to 1985 among persons in families with children declined for the most part in earlier years and rose in later ones. The entire period witnessed economic deterioration among all race and family types except, conspicuously, black two-parent families. (It should be noted that the 1985 figures reflect improvement over the highest poverty rates, reached in 1983.) Mother-only families continue to experience poverty at many times the rates of two-parent families. These numbers reinforce the theme that family income differences are increasingly issues of family structure rather than race.

---

those at the top: the losses hurt the losers more than the gains helped the winners.

Table A.12 concentrates on families at the bottom of the income distribution by showing poverty rates by race and family type from 1967 to

Table A.13
Percentage of Persons, Children Under Eighteen, and Children Under Six Who Were Poor, 1959–1985

	1959	1967	1973	1979	1985
All Persons in Poverty	22.2	14.2	11.1	11.7	14.0
Children Under 18 in Poverty	27.0	16.3	14.2	16.0	20.1
Children Under 6 in Poverty	n.a.	15.3	15.7	17.8	22.6

n.a. = not available.

Source: Gordon Fisher, "Developments in Money Income and Poverty in 1985 and Earlier Years," unpublished mimeo., 1986.

> *The incidence of poverty among all children has risen about 50 percent since the early 1970s. Almost one-quarter of younger children were poor in 1985, when the poverty rates of children were approximately double those of the rest of the population (implied by the numbers in Table A.13 with population weights from standard population data sources).*

1985. Figure A.6 graphs these trends. The earlier years were generally better than the later ones, the exception being the important gains made by two-parent black families. Black poverty rates overall are much higher than those of whites, but within each family type racial differences narrowed, while differences across family types widened; mother-only families experienced poverty at rates many times higher than those of two-parent families. Figure A.7 and Table A.13 focus on the deteriorating situation of children. By 1985 the poverty rate for children was about double that of the adult population, and one child in five was poor, a rate more than 50 percent higher than in 1967.

5. UNDERSTANDING INEQUALITY AND FAMILY STRUCTURE

Two-parent black families have made substantial progress primarily because of the significant increases in the labor market opportunities and earnings of black men and women, as previously shown. Moreover,

Figure A.6
Incidence of Poverty Among Persons Living in Families
with Children, 1967–1985*

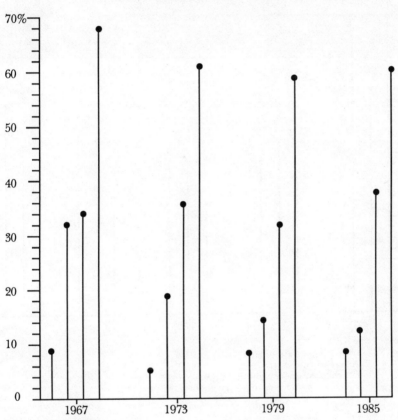

Source: Table A.12

Note: *Each year's graphs are ordered:
White two-parent
Black two-parent
White mother-only
Black mother-only

Figure A.7
Percentage of Persons, of Children Under Eighteen, and
Children Under Six in Poverty, 1959–1985*

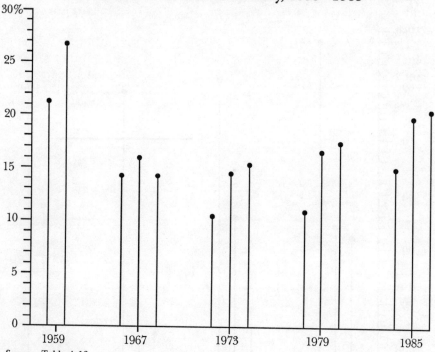

Source: Table A.13.
Notes: *Each year's graphs are ordered:
     All persons in poverty
     All children under eighteen in poverty
     All children under six in poverty (not available for 1959)

those earnings data actually understate the gains of married black men: Table A.14 shows that they have much higher earnings than unmarried black men, and that this difference widened from 1960 to 1980. Indeed, married black men had larger earnings increases over this period than any other group. On the other hand, these data also reflect an important statistical artifact: Fewer black men were married in 1980, and since marriage is correlated with earnings capacity, the married group includes an increasingly select sample of earners.

The relatively high labor force participation rates of black women, plus their increased earnings over recent decades, are another important factor in the rise of two-parent black family incomes.[14] Table A.15 shows the rising contribution of black wives to family income: By 1985, their earnings provided almost one-third of all family income.

Table A.14
Earnings of Married Versus Single Men, 1960 and 1980, in 1980 Dollars

	White Men		Change	Black Men		Change
	1960	*1980*	*1960–1980*	*1960*	*1980*	*1960–1980*
All Ages						
Married	13,900	18,000	4,100	7,500	13,100	5,600
Single	6,800	8,400	1,600	4,600	6,900	2,300
Aged 35–44						
Married	16,000	21,800	5,800	8,500	15,000	6,500
Single	10,500	16,000	5,500	6,700	10,900	4,200

Source: Special tabulations by the author from Census of Population public-use computer tapes, 1960 and 1980.

Marital status and earnings of men are strongly related, as shown here by the much higher earnings of married men relative to single men. This is true of both white and black men and of other age groups not shown. Average earnings increased more for married black men than for any of the other three groups from 1960 to 1980, reflecting both improvements in labor market opportunities and the characteristics of men in that group.

Table A.15
The Importance of Wives' Earnings, 1967 and 1985

	White		Black	
	1967	*1985*	*1967*	*1985*
Percentage of Two-Parent Families with a Working Wife	43.5	69.9	61.5	74.0
Percentage of Family Income Represented by the Wife's Earnings*	10.6	18.7	19.4	30.4

Note: *Values are averaged over all working and nonworking wives.

Source: Sheldon Danziger and Peter Gottschalk, "How Have Families with Children Been Faring?" Institute for Research on Poverty, January 1986, updated to 1985.

Earnings of wives comprise an increasingly greater portion of family earnings. This is true for both races, but black wives have always worked more and contributed more. Their increased relative earnings, as seen in earlier tables, have played an important role in the significant income gains of black two-parent families.

The major factors behind the pulling apart of mother-only and two-parent families are more diverse than the black-white patterns just discussed. They include continued low earnings capacity for single mothers; uneven and meager child support from absent fathers; and insufficient and declining government assistance.

Mother-only families generally have only a single potential primary earner; in two-parent families both parents can, and in the majority of cases do, work (Table A.15). Therefore, even were men and women to earn similar amounts, mother-only families would have only about one-half the earnings capacity of two-parent families. Because women in fact earn only a little more than one-half of what men earn, as we have seen above (see Tables A.1, A.2, and A.3), the earnings capacity of mother-only families really averages only about one-third that of two-parent families. This large differential lies at the heart of the poor economic position of mother-only families. Reinforcing this differential is the fact that single mothers tend to have less education, and consequently still lower earnings capacities, than other women, and must of course provide care for their children.

One outcome of these labor market disadvantages of single mothers

Table A.16
The Incidence of Low Weekly Earnings of Heads of Families, 1967–1985 (in percent)

Heads of Family Type	1967	1973	1979	1985	1973–1985 Increase
All Families with Children	20.8	21.5	23.8	29.1	+40
White	17.1	17.7	19.6	24.9	+44
Black	48.3	45.6	46.9	49.2	+13
All Two-Parent Families with Children	14.3	12.7	14.1	18.6	+53
White	12.4	11.4	12.6	16.8	+55
Black	n.a.	19.2	22.2	31.9	+57
All Mother-Only Families with Children	71.7	68.9	61.9	64.1	−5
White	64.8	63.8	56.7	60.7	−4
Black	83.9	78.4	71.7	70.6	−9

Notes: Defined as less than $204/week in 1984 dollars, which means they could not earn the poverty level if they worked 52 weeks. n.a. = not available.

Source: Sheldon Danziger and Peter Gottschalk, "How Have Families with Children Been Faring?" Institute for Research on Poverty, January 1986, p. 28, updated to 1985.

The incidence of low earnings among family heads has in-creased in recent years. The rates for mother-only families were relatively steady, but at extremely high levels: About two-thirds of such families, both black and white, could not work their way out of poverty in 1985. Low earnings are also a major cause of the poverty of two-parent families. These figures account in large part for the poverty of children and increasing inequality of well-being and opportunity across families.

---

is reflected in Table A.16, which displays the incidence of "low weekly earnings" (that is, below the poverty level, and really a measure of "earnings capacity" as the data are presented) by race and family type for the period 1967–1985. For white mother-only families the rate in 1985 was 61 percent, for blacks 71 percent (last 2 rows). Very high rates

Table A.17
Child-Support Receipts in Absent-Father Families, 1985

Race of Mother	Percent Awarded Support	Percent of Those with Awards Receiving Full Amount of Award	Percent of Those with Awards Receiving Any Support	Mean Level of Support Received 1985	Mean Total Income of Recipient Families 1985
White	70.6	—	74.6	$2,294	$15,052
Black	36.3	—	72.0	1,754	13,297
Hispanic	42.1	—	68.1	2,011	11,505
All	61.3	48.2	74.0	2,215	14,776

Source: "Child Support and Alimony, 1985," Current Population Reports, Series P-23, No. 152, August 1987, U.S. Bureau of the Census. Dollar figures are in 1985 dollars.

Child support received by absent-father families varies greatly. Even when awards are determined, a majority are not paid in full and about one-quarter are totally reneged upon. Mean award levels are low and represent quite small fractions of total family income, and are a major factor in the very high poverty rates and low income levels of mother-only families.

such as these persisted over the entire 1967–1985 period. Clearly, a majority of women who head families simply cannot earn their way out of poverty.

The second principal factor behind the low economic position of mother-only families is that child-support payments by absent parents are a meager and unreliable source of income for such families. Table A.17 shows how little child support is received by mother-only families, and reflects the following statistics:

- Only about 53 percent of white fathers and 26 percent of black fathers pay any child support at all;

- Of those who pay, average amounts in 1985 were $2,294 for whites, $1,754 for blacks;

- This amounted to 15 percent of family income for white mother-only families, 13 percent for blacks;
- Only about 60 percent of children in single-parent families get any court-determined child award at all, and less than one-half of awards made are paid in full.
- Of this 60 percent entitled to an award, 30 percent receive nothing at all.[15]

Court awards, as well as being quite low and ineffectively enforced, also vary tremendously across similar situations, depending on the proclivities of the court and judge involved. This ineffective and varying child-support system contributes in a major way to the large gaps in income and well-being between mother-only and two-parent families.[16]

The third factor underlying the difficult circumstances of mother-only families is the declining real value of public transfers to them. After an increase in assistance from the mid-1960s up to about 1973, support waned, and then plunged in the early 1980s, during the Reagan years.

The rise and fall of government assistance to children has been extensively researched, and only the broad facts are presented here.[17] The principal support program has been Aid to Families with Dependent Children (AFDC) and, increasingly, food stamps plus Medicaid. Table A.18 shows data from the Congressional Research Service documenting the early increases and later declines in AFDC payments to actual recipients (rows 1 and 2), and breadth of coverage of those in need (rows 3–5). Table A.19 shows roughly the same trends for total cash transfers, further documenting the increasing ineffectiveness of these transfers in lifting families out of poverty.[18] (See also Table A.26 and the related discussion.)

In conclusion, two-parent black families have done well principally because of their improved labor market opportunities. Mother-only families are, on the other hand, hampered in three ways: low earnings capacity, uneven and meager support from absent fathers, and declining government support.

6. THE RISING NUMBER OF MOTHER-ONLY FAMILIES

The dramatic rise in the number of mother-only families is shown in Table A.20. From 1967 to 1984 they grew from about 10 percent of all families to 21 percent, including more than one-half of all black families. This section summarizes the research that has explored this shift.

Table A.18
AFDC and Poor Families, 1960–1983

	1960	1967	1973	1979	1983	Ratio of 1983 Level to Peak-Year Level*
Monthly payments per recipient family (in 1983 $)	$356	$463	$428	$360	$312	.65
Monthly payments per recipient (in 1983 $)	$93	$112	$123	$123	$107	.81
Thousands of poor families with children under 18 years	5,328	3,586	3,520	3,955	5,849	1.66
Percentage of poor families receiving AFDC benefits	14.8	33.9	89.4	88.7	62.9	.70
Thousands of poor families not receiving AFDC**	4,539	2,370	373	447	2,169	5.82

Notes: *Peak year not necessarily shown; **author's calculations; compared to trough years in rows 3 and 5.

Source: Congressional Research Service and Congressional Budget Office, *Children in Poverty,* prepared for the House Committee on Ways and Means, 1985.

Income support for low-income children rose significantly through the late 1960s, then fell from the early 1970s through the early 1980s. Table A.18 shows that fewer poor actually received support (rows 3–5) and less support went to each recipient (rows 1 and 2). Table A.19 shows the trends for all cash transfers, rather than AFDC alone. Mother-only families have been especially affected, as their pretransfer poverty rates were higher to begin with (see earlier tables), and fewer are being helped out of poverty by government transfers. (See also Table A.26.)

Most researchers attribute this growth to economic factors.[19] For whites, the secular rise in the labor force participation rates of women in general, and wives and mothers in particular, has generated a new level of economic independence which has made separation and divorce more financially viable than in the past. White two-parent families may therefore be separating where in the past it would have been economically impossible to do so.[20]

The primary factor for blacks, on the other hand, is judged to be a diminution of the "marriage pool" of black men, encouraging black women to have children out of wedlock, which is now the principal source of black mother-only families.[21] This decline in eligible husbands/fathers is ascribed to the growing numbers of young black men

Table A.19
Total Cash Assistance to Poor Families, 1967–1984

	1967	1973	1979	1984	1984/ Peak Year*
Average Cash Transfers Received by Pretransfer Poor Families (1984 $)					
Two-parent families	$1,832	$4,024	$3,776	$2,946	.73
Mother-only families	3,908	5,217	4,056	3,276	.63
Elderly head	4,756	6,484	6,926	7,322	1.00
Percentage of Families Lifted out of Poverty by Cash Transfers					
Two-parent families					
White	15.6	27.9	26.9	19.1	.68
Black	8.7	17.4	25.1	18.2	.73
Mother-only families					
White	25.1	29.1	23.6	14.0	.48
Black	11.2	18.0	16.5	9.9	.55

Note: *Author's calculations; peak year not necessarily shown.

Source: Sheldon Danziger and Peter Gottschalk, "How Have Families with Children Been Faring?" Institute for Research on Poverty, January 1986, pp. 31, 41.

Table A.20
Proportion of Families Which Are Mother-Only Families, by
Race, 1967–1984

	1967	1973	1979	1984	1967–1984 Percent Change
All Families with Children	10.4	14.6	19.1	21.3	+105
White Families with Children	7.8	11.0	14.7	16.5	+112
Black Families with Children	30.8	39.7	47.9	51.8	+68

Source: Sheldon Danziger and Peter Gottschalk, "How Have Families with Children Been Faring?" Institute for Research on Poverty, January 1986, p. 10.

Family composition has shifted dramatically. The proportion of mother-only families doubled from 1967 to 1984, when they represented more than one family in five. The rate of increase has been greatest for whites, but the level was three times as high for blacks as whites in 1984, for whom one family in two was headed by a single mother.

who are unemployed, underemployed, or who otherwise have low earnings or have dropped out of the labor market altogether.[22]

Unemployment and reduced economic circumstances also play a direct role in explaining the dissolution of marriages, owing to the stresses they create. Social norms have probably played a role as well, although the evidence available suggests that social attitudes toward family structure and single parenthood tend to follow, rather than lead, changes in behavior.[23]

Finally, one view is that the availability of welfare has been important in the increasing numbers of mother-only families. Charles Murray is perhaps the chief recent advocate of the position that welfare, especially for mother-only families, encourages young single women to bear children out of wedlock and become welfare dependent.[24] The burden of research fails to support this view of the welfare system, however. The welfare system does, on the other hand, apparently affect living arrangements, increasing the tendency for single mothers to form their own households rather than live with their parents or remarry.[25]

7. THE DECLINING LABOR MARKET FORTUNES OF YOUTH

Recent age cohorts of youths have seen diminished labor market opportunities as compared to earlier generations, especially for minorities and those with less education. This section presents data on these declining fortunes, and outlines the principal factors behind them.[26]

For several reasons, earnings data, such as those presented in Figures A.1–A.5, are somewhat difficult to assess for youth. Many young people are still in school, and their earnings experiences are difficult to interpret in terms of labor market opportunities; on the other hand, looking only at earnings of those not in school involves selection bias, and will also not reflect general opportunities or outcomes. Moreover, earnings of part-time versus full-time workers are also difficult to assess, especially if long-run prospects are different for these groups, as is probably true. And finally, if age-earnings profiles are shifting up, but more so for older workers (See Figures A.1–A.5), should we infer that young people of today will not enjoy earnings improvement in later years?

Youth earnings evidence will thus be considered along with unemployment and "activity rate" (referring to work and schooling) data to present a more complete picture of the general fortunes of youth. Table A.21, along with Figures A.1 and A.2 show that the earnings of youth have indeed fallen relative to older workers. A dramatic rise in youth unemployment rates is shown in Tables A.4 and A.22, especially for black youths, whose rates are almost triple those of whites.[27] Table A.23 shows "activity rates" for white and black youths in 1980: a full one-quarter of black men aged eighteen to twenty-four were neither employed nor in school, and the situation has certainly worsened since that time. For young black women the "inactivity rate" is one-third, although it drops to about one-fifth when parenthood is taken into account. Inactivity rates for white youths are lower, but at 10 percent (aged eighteen to twenty-four) still appear to bode ill for the future. In sum, earnings data, in combination with unemployment and activity rates, all point to declining fortunes for recent youth cohorts, especially blacks.

One reason for this is the general slowdown of the U.S. economy since 1973, which has impaired the entrance of youth into the labor

Table A.21
Relative Median Weekly Earnings of Youths Versus Older Workers, by Gender, for Full-Time Wage and Salary Workers, 1980 and 1985

	1980	1985
Median earnings of males aged 16–24 years relative to men aged 25 and older	.61	.54
Median earnings of females aged 16–24 years relative to men aged 25 and over	.79	.71

Notes: Based on usual weekly earnings, and representing annual average of quarterly data as collected by the U.S. Bureau of Labor Statistics. Data are not available by race for youth workers. Figures are not directly comparable to those derived from the 1960 and 1980 Census of Population, which appear elsewhere in this Appendix, but should be a good indicator of the direction and magnitude of recent trends in earnings.

Source: 1987 Statistical Abstract of the United States, op. cit., p. 402.

market.[28] Black youths were affected most, because they remain relatively concentrated in the declining northern central cities, and may be subject to discriminatory hiring practices.[29] Further, as the structure of the U.S. economy shifted from manufacturing toward both the high-technology and service sectors, young workers were most affected by the resulting "transitional" unemployment. Many others have found only low-paying jobs with little promise of advancement in the expanding sectors, even as others with better education have secured good, high-paying, career-advancing jobs. Due to their mobility, youths are overrepresented in these expanding, but divergent, sectors and underrepresented in traditional middle-class jobs, which helps explain the pulling apart of fortunes within recent youth cohorts which has been illustrated.[30]

A third factor stems from the overrepresentation of youth, especially minorities, in the military forces. The cutback in military personnel since the Vietnam War has thus diminished labor market opportunities. In fact some researchers find this factor to have affected employment opportunities as much as the well-publicized "baby-boom effect" (see below).[31]

The minimum wage has been cited as a cause of youth unemploy-

Table A.22
Unemployment Rates by Race, Gender, and Age, 1972–1985

	1972	1980	1983	1985
All civilians	5.6	7.1	9.6	7.2
All men	5.0	6.9	9.9	7.0
All women	6.6	7.4	9.2	7.4
All whites	5.1	6.3	8.4	6.2
All blacks	10.4	14.3	19.5	15.1
Young white and black men				
16–19	15.9	15.9	23.3	19.5
20–24	9.3	8.7	15.9	11.4
Young white and black women				
16–19	16.7	16.4	21.3	17.6
20–24	9.4	9.6	12.9	10.7
Young white men and women				
16–19	14.2	14.0	19.3	15.7
20–24	8.4	7.6	12.1	9.2
Young black men and women				
16–19	35.4	36.5	48.5	40.2
20–24	16.3	20.6	31.4	24.5

Notes: Rates are for the civilian labor force. Figures are annual averages of monthly unemployment figures collected by the U.S. Bureau of Labor Statistics. Figures are thus not directly comparable to figures based on the decennial Census of Population presented elsewhere, but are instead intended to reflect broad recent trends.

Source: 1987 Statistical Abstract of the United States, op. cit., p. 390.

Youths experienced increasing hardship in the labor market in more recent years, as shown by the lower relative earnings in Table A.21, and the high and rising unemployment rates in Table A.22. The earnings drop is quite precipitous for such a short period of time, while the unemployment rates are a stark reflection of dismal employment opportunities. The unemployment rates of young blacks are most distressing, peaking at almost 50 percent in 1983 for men and women combined; almost unbelievably, rates for young black men alone would be even considerably higher than these.

Table A.23
Activity Rates for Young Men and Women, 1980 (in percent)

	Aged 16–17	Aged 18–24
Men		
Enrolled in School or Employed		
White	95	89
Black	91	75
Enrolled in School, Employed, or Unemployed		
White	96	96
Black	93	86
Women		
Enrolled in School or Employed		
White	95	88
Black	91	67
Enrolled in School, Employed, or Unemployed		
White	96	92
Black	92	86
Enrolled in School, Employed, Unemployed, Married, or Parent		
White	96	94
Black	93	86
Enrolled in School, Employed, Married, or Parent		
White	95	91
Black	92	81

Note: Values represent the percentage of youths in the population who were engaged in one of the indicated activities.

Source: Special tabulations by the author from Census of Population public-use computer tapes, 1980.

"Activity" rates for youths were in some cases at alarmingly low levels in 1980. One-quarter of black men aged eighteen to twenty-four were neither in school nor working. One-third of black women were "inactive," although some had parental responsibilities. Activity rates for whites were much higher, but still suggest that a core group of youths was engaged in no apparently productive activity.

---

ment, on the theory that it effectively prices them out of the market, but many studies suggest that its negative effect cannot be very large, especially since the real minimum wage has been falling throughout the period that youth problems have worsened.

Indeed, an alternative view is that the decline in the minimum wage has hurt youths, perhaps both in terms of earnings and employment. The real earnings of employed young people at or slightly above the legislated minimum have of course dropped. Further, as wages decline, working becomes less attractive; youths become unemployed, drop out of the labor force, cease making career investments (for example, attending school) and perhaps opt for crime and other "underground" activities. This side of the minimum-wage issue has not been thoroughly investigated.[32]

Another general factor is the population bulge produced by the post-war baby boom. As the supply of entry-level workers increased, the labor market responded with lower wages and higher unemployment. Empirical studies suggest that the earnings effect has been greater than the unemployment effect. This demographic factor has indisputably worked against recent cohorts of youth, yet the period of greatest labor market entry has passed and there has been no marked improvement, suggesting that the passing of the population bulge will probably not be equally matched by improved youth labor market fortunes.[33]

Two other demographic changes have also been at work: the increased labor force participation of women, and the entrance of immigrant workers. Both are alleged to have contributed to "job crowding," which has hurt other entry-level workers, including youths. The limited economic research in this area suggests that both wages and employment of youth have been adversely affected, especially among those with the least amounts of education and training.[34] These factors are likely to increasingly affect youth employment prospects into the future.

A final consideration is family background and socioeconomic environment. Factors such as family income, parental education and occupation, family structure, and other aspects of the home environment, plus such influences as role models, peer groups, and cultural environment, all affect life chances and outcomes for youth.[35] As family income inequality has diverged, so too have the opportunities for youth which are associated with these socioeconomic factors.

8. THE ELDERLY: BETTER ON AVERAGE, SOME LEFT BEHIND

The elderly population has enjoyed a dramatic improvement in average well-being over the last quarter century, largely due to government income support programs; at the same time, certain groups among the elderly still remain mired in, or near, poverty.

Table A.24 shows the rise in relative average well-being of the elderly as measured in terms of relative median income between 1966 and 1981 (row 1). Although the ratio in 1981 stood nominally at two-thirds that of nonelderly families, after adjusting income to take into account family size, tax advantages, capital assets, owned housing, and other factors that, for the most part, favor the elderly, they were estimated to be at least as well off as the nonelderly population in 1980 and have since almost certainly pulled ahead (data not shown).[36]

On the other hand, Tables A.24 and A.25 also show that elderly blacks and nonmarried white women have fared much less well: Their poverty levels were much higher than those of white men and married white women in 1981 (rows 4 and 5) and the income data in Table A.25 affirm growing inequality according to race and marital status.

The improved average well-being of the elderly is largely attributable to the growth in government benefits targeted on them. Table A.26 documents the rise in real government spending on Medicare and Social Security, the two principal benefit programs for the elderly (rows 4 and 5). From 1967 to 1985 real Social Security benefits approximately tripled while Medicare spending went up almost sevenfold (columns 5 and 6). Together, these two programs accounted for over one-quarter of all federal spending in 1985; in comparison, AFDC, the principal cash program for needy children, took up less than 1 percent (column 7).[37]

But while government income support programs have tilted toward the elderly as a group, they also remain heavily weighted toward those elderly who had high labor market earnings in preretirement years. This generates the pattern of inequality across gender and race that has been shown above. From the earnings data shown in previous sections, it follows that the relative positions for the elderly which we see now are likely to persist into the future, except for some probable advances by married black couples.[38]

It is important to ask why government support for the elderly con-

Table A.24
Relative Incomes and Poverty Rates of the Elderly, 1966, 1981, and 1985

	1966	*1981*	*1985*
Ratio of Median Income of Families with Elderly Heads to All Families	.49	.64	n.a.
Ratio of Poverty Incidence			
All elderly to all persons	1.94	1.09	.92
White elderly to all persons	1.80	.94	.76
Black elderly to all persons	3.75	2.79	(2.13)*
Female elderly to all persons	3.01	1.96	n.a.

Notes: *Black and Hispanic combined; the black rate would be higher than this, the Hispanic lower.
n.a. = not available.

Sources: Columns 1 and 2 from Sheldon Danziger, Jacques van der Gaag, Eugene Smolensky, and Michael Taussig, "Implications of the Relative Economic Status of the Elderly for Transfer Policy," in *Retirement and Economic Behavior*, H. Aaron and G. Burtless, eds., The Brookings Institution, 1984; special tabulations of Current Population Survey data performed by the author for column 3.

Households headed by the elderly have enjoyed increased relative average incomes and much lower poverty rates over recent years, as shown in rows 1 and 2. On the other hand, rows 3 through 5 show that well-being varies across race and gender: Elderly blacks and single white women in 1981 had poverty rates much larger than those of white men, largely due to the linkage of elderly incomes to labor market earnings, especially through private pensions and the Social Security program. Measured increases in average well-being of all elderly taken together thus veil the low economic position still suffered by many elderly persons, especially women and minorities.

tinues to grow while assistance to other "dependent" groups, especially families with children, has fallen, although it should also be noted that relative incomes of the elderly in fact fell significantly between World War II and the early 1960s, and it is of course natural, and laudable

Table A.25
Incomes of Families with Elderly Heads, by Race and Marital Status, 1960 and 1980, in 1980 Dollars

	White			Black		
	1960	*1980*	*1960–1980 Increase*	*1960*	*1980*	*1960–1980 Increase*
Married Couples	11,900	17,200	5,300	6,400	12,000	5,600
Widowed, Separated, Divorced						
Men	7,800	10,200	2,400	3,900	6,000	2,100
Women	5,800	8,100	2,300	3,600	5,900	2,300
Never Married						
Men	5,900	9,600	3,700	3,700	5,200	1,500
Women	6,700	9,900	3,200	3,400	6,200	2,800

Source: Special tabulations by the author from Census of Population public-use computer tapes, 1960 and 1980.

Income inequality among the elderly groups is illustrated by the disadvantaged position of blacks relative to whites, women to men, single persons to married couples. These relative patterns remained largely unchanged from 1960 to 1980, except that married couples pulled even further ahead. The structure of inequality among the elderly reflects differences in earnings in preretirement years; both government transfers and private income are related to earlier labor market experiences.

for a society to be concerned about the well-being of its elderly members.[39,40]

Samuel Preston, a demographer at the University of Pennsylvania, argues that the elderly have gained much political support, which has translated into dollars, in contrast to the political powerlessness of other dependent groups, especially needy children.[41] He makes several points. First, the elderly themselves comprise a large block of voters who turn out at elections. Second, those under sixty-five see an advantage in supporting programs for the elderly, thinking of their own fu-

Table A.26
Federal Spending on Medicare, Social Security, AFDC, and Defense, Selected Years, 1967–1985, in Millions of 1985 Dollars

Program	1967	1973	1979	1985	Percentage Change, 1967– 1985	Percentage Change, 1973– 1985	Percentage of Total Federal Outlays in 1985
AFDC*	$8,103	$13,706	$9,233	$8,625	6%	−37%	0.9%
AFDC* plus Food Stamps**	8,443	18,815	19,140	20,326	+141	+8	2.1
AFDC plus Food Stamps and Medicaid**	11,783	28,964	36,132	41,719	+254	+44	4.3
Medicare	9,448	20,924	40,894	69,649	+637	+233	7.4
Social Security	63,420	111,507	148,988	186,432	+194	+67	19.7
Defense	262,090	195,231	177,417	252,748	−4	+29	26.7

Notes: *Actually the category is "Assistance Programs," but this is almost entirely AFDC.
**Food stamps and Medicaid are available to the poor, including single persons and the elderly.

Source: Gene Falk, "1987 Budget Perspectives: Federal Spending for the Human Resource Programs," Congressional Research Service, February 1986, pp. 11, 15, 55, 59, 81, 85.

Federal spending on income support has shifted dramatically since 1967, especially since 1973. The programs targeted on children, shown in the upper portions of the table, were constant or declined after early increases, at the same time that the target population (poor families with children) grew. On the other hand, programs assisting the elderly grew throughout the 1967–1984 period. Programs targeted on families with children represent a small proportion of total federal outlays (last column); spending on behalf of the elderly is many times greater. These priorities are important elements in the structure of inequality. Defense spending is shown for comparison only; note that defense spending was thirty times greater than expenditures on AFDC in 1985, and six times greater than AFDC, Medicaid, and food stamps.

ture. Third, those with elderly parents have a stake in government support for them. Fourth, fewer adults are having children, and many who do, no longer live with them nor provide support, thus eroding the political bloc which might naturally vote pro-children. And finally, an increasing percentage of today's children are minorities: their parents have weaker political power, and racial attitudes might affect social priorities. Preston concludes that the shift of political forces in favor of the elderly is a trend likely to continue in the future.

In summary, the elderly have made significant economic gains relative to other groups since the 1960s, but the government support which has accomplished this has favored white men over elderly women and minorities. Without policy changes, these trends are likely to endure, and to lift the remaining elderly up into the economic mainstream will require income support which is less dependent on labor market earnings than current programs.

9. CONCLUSION AND SUMMARY

This Appendix has outlined some of the important contours of inequality of opportunity and well-being in the United States and their evolution over the past quarter-century. Group differences, across gender, race, marital status, and age were concentrated on, as these intergroup inequalities represent important social problems around which public policy will continue to be debated and programs implemented.

The findings of this Appendix may now be summarized.

A. *Labor Market Inequalities*
- Earnings data show that men earn much more than women, and whites earn more than blacks, even when age and education are held constant.
- Age-earnings profiles are considerably flatter and lower for women and blacks, indicating increasingly divergent opportunities and outcomes over career lives.
- Black men and women made significant progress between 1960 and 1980, but slipped back a little through the early 1980s.
- White women made virtually no gains up to 1980, but caught up somewhat from 1980 to 1985.

B. *Black Men and Women*
- Greater quantity and quality of education has been a prime factor in the significant progress of black men and women.

- The recession of the 1980s has hurt blacks disproportionately, as they are still less ensconced in good, secure jobs than whites, and they are overrepresented in the sectors and northern central cities which have been hurt most. Continued economic growth seems crucial to the possibility of renewed progress for blacks.

- Migration patterns, affirmative action and other legislation, and changing racial attitudes are other factors which have affected black-white earnings differences.

- Black women have almost entirely caught up to white women in terms of earnings; their principal disadvantage now appears to be gender rather than race.

- Simultaneous with higher earnings of black workers, there are also lower employment rates: while many blacks are doing better, many others have been excluded from the progress, especially younger and less educated blacks.

C. *Black and White Women*
- Although gender earnings differences can be explained to a significant degree by objective differences in occupation, work experience, education and training, and so on, the gender gap is largely the result of women not specializing in the labor market to the degree men do.

- This reflects the dual roles of homemaker, wife, and mother versus wage earner, which the majority of women still must attempt to balance.

- Labor market job opportunities partially reflect employers' expectations and prejudices, thus making it difficult for individual women to freely and equally specialize in the labor market. The playing field remains uneven; large earnings differences endure.

D. *Inequality Across Families*
- Differences in economic well-being are increasingly across family types rather than race: mother-only families are falling even further behind two-parent families, while black families have almost caught up to white ones of the same types.

- Black two-parent families represent a dramatic success story from 1960 to the present, especially those with more educated family heads.

E. *The Mother-Only Families Crisis*
- Mother-only families have earnings capacity which is 50 percent that of two-parent families at best, and effectively much lower due to their gender disadvantage in the labor market, overrepresentation at lower levels of education, and unshared family responsibilities.
- The current child-support system provides very uneven and meager assistance to mother-only families.
- Public support has never been adequate to lift most mother-only families even just out of poverty, and has become increasingly narrow in coverage and stingy in payments to recipients since the early 1970s.

F. *Rising Numbers of Mother-Only Families*
- The last quarter century has witnessed a dramatic rise in the number of mother-only families; the trend is not likely to abate.
- For whites, one reason is the increasing economic independence of women, who now participate in the labor market at historically peak rates. This makes separation more economically viable, even though their earnings remain much lower than men's.
- For blacks, "the declining marriage pool" is seen as the principal factor. High unemployment, incarceration, and homicide rates are indicators of the diminishing numbers of "eligible" young black men. Black women are thus forced to form families on their own or to forego the family experience.
- Welfare is almost certainly a minor factor in the formation of mother-only families, although it probably does affect living arrangements and remarriage rates.

G. *The Special Problems of Youths*
- Earnings, employment, unemployment, and "activity" data all suggest declining labor market opportunities for many current youths.
- Minority and less educated youths are suffering the most.
- Some factors are probably once-and-for-all, such as the labor market bulge of the baby boom and the reduction in the military.
- Other factors seem more long-run in nature, and bode ill for the future: slow economic growth, structural shifts of the economy, and competition from women and immigrants.

H. *Mixed Fortunes for the Elderly*
- The elderly have made great progress, on average, from 1960 to the present.
- Well-being in old age is highly correlated with earlier labor market outcomes, however, leaving white men far ahead of nonmarried white women and minorities; the still-needy elderly should not be overlooked.
- Government policy is a prime factor in these new patterns of well-being of the elderly, and reflects the successes society can enjoy with a committed and sustained pledge of support to a group perceived as needy and deserving of support.

Notes

Introduction

1. In *An American Ethos* (Cambridge, MA: Harvard University Press, 1985), Herbert McClosky and John Zaller have characterized the cycles as a result of the inevitable tension between capitalism and democracy:

> Among the most important choices Americans face...are those between the competing values of capitalism and democracy. Asked to decide between preserving a laissez-faire economy and enacting measures that promise greater social and economic equality, conservatives emphasize capitalist values while liberals emphasize democratic values.... The nation has seemed, at least, in this century, to swing from periods in which the values of capitalism are emphasized to other periods in which democratic values are stressed. The 1920s and 1950s, for example, were decades in which business values were dominant and matters of social and political equality excited relatively little public interest. During the decade of the 1930s, by contrast, unrestrained capitalism was on the defensive as Franklin D. Roosevelt and the New Deal pressed for greater popular control of the economy and a more equal distribution of the nation's wealth. Capitalism was again on the defensive in the 1960s and early 1970s, as public concern for democratic values...and racial and sexual equality assumed a dominant position in the nation's politics. The early 1980s seemed to herald another swing toward capitalism.

2. "Poverty in America," *Public Opinion* (June/July 1985), p. 26.

3. Robert Reischauer, "Welfare Reform: Will Consensus Be Enough?" *The Brookings Review* 5, no. 3, Summer 1987, pp. 3–8.

4. See *NGA Welfare Reform Policy*, National Governors' Association, Adopted February 24, 1987; "One Child in Four," Part I of *Investing in Poor Families and Their Children: A Matter of Commitment*, Report by the American Public Welfare Association and the National Council of State Human Services Administrators, November 1986; *A Social Contract: Rethinking the Nature and Purpose of Public Assistance*, Report submitted to Governor Mario Cuomo by the Task Force on Poverty and Welfare, December 1986; *Ladders out of Poverty*, A Report of the Project on the Welfare of Families, co-chaired by Bruce Babbitt and Arthur Flemming, December 1986; and *A Community of Self-Reliance: The New Consensus*

on Family and Welfare, Report of the Working Seminar on Family and American Welfare Policy, Marquette University and the American Enterprise Institute, March 1987.

5. For a recent attempt to stand back and appraise the successes and failures of the War on Poverty–Great Society initiative, see Sheldon Danziger and Daniel Weinberg, eds., *Fighting Poverty: What Works and What Doesn't* (Cambridge, MA: Harvard University Press, 1986).

6. Robert Nozick, *Anarchy, State, and Utopia* (New York: Basic Books, 1974).

7. George Gilder, *Wealth and Poverty* (New York: Basic Books, 1981).

8. Charles Murray, *Losing Ground: American Social Policy, 1950–1980* (New York: Basic Books, 1984). See also Lawrence Mead, *Beyond Entitlement: The Social Obligations of Citizenship* (New York: Free Press/Macmillan, 1986).

9. The "Big Tradeoff" doctrine as it applies to issues of antipoverty and inequality reduction policy was most clearly articulated in Arthur Okun, *Equality and Efficiency: The Big Tradeoff* (Washington, DC: The Brookings Institution, 1975).

10. This stagnation of the 1970s is seen by some as lying at the heart of several of the nation's current problems and demographic trends. See Frank Levy, *Dollars and Dreams* (New York: Russell Sage Foundation, 1987); and Richard Easterlin, *Birth and Fortune: The Impact of Numbers on Personal Welfare,* 2d ed. (Chicago: University of Chicago Press, 1987).

11. See U.S. Congressional Budget Office, "Major Legislative Changes in Human Resources Programs since January 1981," Staff Memorandum, August 1983. These programs include Social Security, veterans' benefits, AFDC, SSI, food stamps, medical services, nutrition, housing, education, training, and social services. See also Chapter 6.

12. A detailed discussion and critique of the retrenchment in social policy during the Reagan presidency is found in John Palmer and Isabel Sawhill, eds., *The Reagan Experiment: An Examination of Economic and Social Policies Under the Reagan Administration* (Washington, DC: Urban Institute Press, 1982). See also John Palmer and Isabel Sawhill, eds., *The Reagan Record: An Assessment of America's Changing Domestic Priorities* (Cambridge, MA: Ballinger, 1984), and D. Lee Bawden, ed., *The Social Contract Revisited: Aims and Outcomes of President Reagan's Social Welfare Policy* (Washington, DC: Urban Institute Press, 1984). For an account of the relation between changing social policy and social science research, see Robert H. Haveman, *Poverty Policy and Poverty Research: The Great Society and the Social Sciences* (Madison: University of Wisconsin Press, 1987).

13. Sheldon Danziger, Robert Haveman, and Robert Plotnick, "How Income Transfer Programs Affect Work, Savings, and the Income Distribution: A Critical Review," *Journal of Economic Literature* 19 (1981), pp. 975–1028.

14. This concentrated inner-city poverty problem has been referred to as the "underclass problem." Since 1970, it has at least doubled. See the discussion of this dependent population and its growth in Isabel Sawhill, ed., *Challenge to Leadership: Economic and Social Issues for the Next Decade* (Washington, DC: Urban Institute Press, 1988).

15. See Robert Plotnick and Felicity Skidmore, *Progress Against Poverty: A Review of the 1964–1974 Decade* (New York: Academic Press, 1975), and Robert Haveman, ed., *A Decade of Federal Antipoverty Programs: Achievements, Failures, and Lessons* (New York: Academic Press, 1977).

16. The adjusted poverty rate takes into account in-kind benefits in addition to cash income in comparing the resources available to a family with the official needs standard. The first study to propose such an adjustment is Timothy Smeeding, "Measuring the Economic Welfare of Low Income Households and the Effectiveness of Cash and Noncash Transfer Programs," Ph.D. dissertation, University of Wisconsin, Madison, 1975.

17. Robert Lampman, "What Does It Do for the Poor? A New Test for National Policy," in Eli Ginzberg and Robert Solow, eds., *The Great Society* (New York: Basic Books, 1974).

18. The U.S. Census Bureau report, *Money Income and Poverty Status of Families and Persons in the United States: 1986,* July 1987, shows that the 1986 official poverty rate is significantly higher than that in 1980 (by about 3 million people) and in 1977 (by about 8 million people). It also demonstrates that in 1986 the gap between the richest 20 percent of families and the poorest 20 percent reached its widest level since the Census Bureau began collecting these data in 1947.

Chapter 1

1. Among the primary countries in the OECD (the Organization for Economic Cooperation and Development) the United States ranks in the top tier in terms of overall inequality. A comparison of these countries is shown in Table 1. These data are by and large for the early 1970s, the last period for which such a comparative study, using comparable definitions and concepts, has been done. (A study with less consistency in definitions and concepts done for the late 1970s and 1980s shows about the same pattern, though the United States has become more unequal relative to those countries with which we compare ourselves. See United Nations, *National Accounts Statistics: Compendium of Income Distribution Statistics,* Statistical Papers, Series M, no. 79 [New York: United Nations, 1985].) The table shows the share of the total after-tax income that is held by each decile (each 10 percent) of the nation's population when the families are ranked from poorest to richest. Therefore, the number for the first decile of families in Australia (2.1) indicates that the poorest 10 percent of the population receive only 2.1 percent of the total after-tax, or disposable, income generated in Australia. In reading this table, it is helpful to keep an eye on the shares for the top couple and the bottom couple deciles. These numbers will give the picture of how the richest and the poorest people in the countries are faring. The larger the numbers for the top deciles and the smaller the numbers for the bottom deciles, the more unequally incomes are distributed.

As compared to the average for these countries, the U.S. income distribution is quite unequal. For example, while the average share of income held by the poorest two deciles in the list is nearly 6 percent, *the poorest 20 percent of the people in the United States hold but 4.5 percent of its income.* At the rich end of the distribu-

Table 1
Size Distribution of Post-Tax Income (decile shares)

Country	Year	1	2	3	4	5	6	7	8	9	10
Australia	1966–1967	2.1	4.5	6.2	7.3	8.3	9.5	10.9	12.5	15.1	23.7
Canada	1969	1.5	3.5	5.1	6.7	8.2	9.7	11.2	13.1	15.9	25.1
France	1970	1.4	2.9	4.2	5.6	7.4	8.9	9.7	13.0	16.5	30.4
Germany	1973	2.8	3.7	4.6	5.7	6.8	8.2	9.8	12.1	15.8	30.3
Italy	1969	1.7	3.4	4.7	5.8	7.0	9.2	9.8	11.9	15.6	30.9
Japan	1969	3.0	4.9	6.1	7.0	7.9	8.9	9.9	11.3	13.8	27.2
Netherlands	1967	2.6	3.9	5.2	6.4	7.6	8.8	10.3	12.4	15.2	27.7
Norway	1970	2.3	4.0	5.6	7.3	8.6	10.2	11.7	13.0	15.1	22.2
Spain	1973–1974	2.1	3.9	5.3	6.5	7.8	9.1	10.6	12.5	15.6	26.7
Sweden	1972	2.2	4.4	5.9	7.2	8.5	10.0	11.5	13.3	15.7	21.3
U.K.	1973	2.5	3.8	5.5	7.1	8.5	9.9	11.1	12.8	15.2	23.5
U.S.	1972	1.5	3.0	4.5	6.2	7.8	9.5	11.3	13.4	16.3	26.6

Source: Malcolm Sawyer, *Income Distribution in OECD Countries*, OECD Economic Outlook —Occasional Studies (Paris: Organization for Economic Cooperation and Development, 1976).

tion, the share of total income held by the richest 20 percent in the United States is greater than for the average of these countries. Figure 1 is taken from the same study and brings home the degree of inequality among the countries by focusing on the share of income held by the poorest 20 percent in each. By this standard, the United States and France stand apart from the rest—the inequality in the distribution of income is the greatest in these countries.

More recent data (1975–1981) indicate that the United States has a higher poverty rate than any other country on which comparable data exist, except for Australia. A 12.7 percent figure for the United States is to be compared with an 11.7 percent rate in the United Kingdom and rates ranging from 5.6 to 7.4 percent for Canada, West Germany, Norway, Sweden, and Switzerland. See Timothy Smeeding, Barbara Boyle Torrey, and Martin Rein, "Patterns of Income and Poverty: The Economic Status of the Young and the Old in Eight Countries," in John Palmer, Timothy Smeeding, and Barbara Boyle Torrey, eds., *The Vulnerables: America's Young and Old in the Industrial World* (Washington, DC: Urban Institute Press, 1988).

Figure 1
Shares of Lowest Two Deciles in Post-Tax
Household Income Distribution

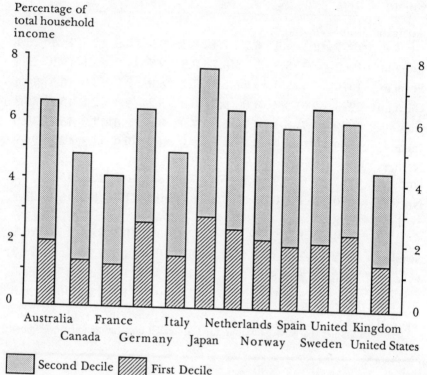

Percentage of
total household
income

Source: Malcolm Sawyer, *Income Distribution in OECD Countries,* OECD Economic Outlook—
Occasional Studies (Paris: Organization for Economic Cooperation and Development, 1976).

2. Lester Thurow has referred to this as a "surge in inequality." See Lester Thurow, "A Surge in Inequality," *Scientific American* 236, no. 5 (May 1987): 30–37.

3. This discussion of "equality of results" and "equality of opportunities"—as well as much of the subsequent discussion—casts us into the unavoidable complexities of the term *equality* that have been emphasized by Douglas Rae, in *Equalities* (Cambridge, MA: Harvard University Press, 1981). The lesson of this volume is that equality has so many distinctions and dimensions—treating individuals or blocs equally?; treating equally in what dimensions (or domains)?; seeking equality of results or equality of opportunity?; equality of the means of, or the prospects for, success?; providing people equal lots, or lots of equal

value?—that anyone venturing into the territory takes a substantial risk of being "simple-minded." The issue is too important, however, not to take the risk.

4. Arthur Okun in *Equality and Efficiency: The Big Tradeoff* (Washington, DC: The Brookings Institution, 1975), chapter 3, states this case as well as it can be. "I am confident that greater equality of opportunity would produce greater equality of income. To be sure, that is not a logical necessity, and one can imagine contrary examples.... But those are unrealistic suppositions. Quite apart from its effect on the equality of income and on efficiency, equality of opportunity is a value in itself. It [is] desirable to have fairer races. I am also confident that greater equality of opportunity would produce greater social mobility from generation to generation. If the impact of family advantages is reduced, so must be the dependence of the incomes of sons and daughters on those of their parents" (pp. 83–85).

This view is closest to Rae's notion of equalizing means, in the belief that reducing differences in people's access to resources will also reduce the differences in their "prospects" and their outcomes. The strategy which I will advance is a combination of, again in Rae's terms, "compensatory inequalities" and "redistribution of domains." What is sought is an efficient reduction of unwanted economic differences among people, and not "global equality" in the Marxian sense.

This position does not rest on any set of inviolable general ethical principles; it is what James Fishkin, in *Beyond Subjective Morality* (New Haven and London: Yale University Press, 1984), has termed "intuitionism." Such a position requires a careful weighing of moral factors which often conflict, in a case-by-case evaluation. It is similar to the philosophical position adopted by Okun, ibid.

5. However, recent research does indicate that some high-risk pregnancy and early infant care programs are able to reduce infant mortality rates and the probability of low-weight births.

6. See Robert Haveman and Barbara Wolfe, "Schooling and Economic Well-Being: The Role of Non-market Effects," *Journal of Human Resources* 19 (1984): 377–408.

7. In Western Europe, however, the growth of the underground economy appears to have been more rapid than for the United States, and the narrowed wage structure may have been one of the causes of this development.

8. Some of these transfers, however, do contribute to the reduction of inequality of opportunity as well. The benefits paid to the survivors of those covered by Social Security are an example.

9. However, it may be claimed with some legitimacy that equalizing *results* for parents is one way of improving *opportunities* for many children.

10. This is in fact the prescription of Jeremy Bentham and the utilitarians more than a century ago. See Bentham, *The Principles of Morals and Legislation*, 1789. These conditions are a simple version of those outlined by Rae, op. cit., as being necessary to justify complete equality.

11. This criticism was raised early on by the French philosopher, Bertrand de Jouvenel, in *The Ethics of Redistribution* (Cambridge, England: Cambridge University Press, 1951). As de Jouvenel put it, "History shows us that each succes-

sive enlargement of the opportunities to consume was linked with unequal distribution of means to consume." He was one of the original supply-siders.

12. Henry Wallich in *The Cost of Freedom* (New York: Harper & Row, 1960) stated the natural response to this argument: "If man is the master of his fate, why should he not correct the consequences of biological inequality if he finds them unattractive? [Why not go] some way in evening up what nature made uneven?"

13. Robert Nozick, Murray Rothbard, and Milton Friedman—prominent scholars all—have argued the libertarian position, citing this sanctity as a form of "constitution" that binds us together. See Robert Nozick, *Anarchy, State, and Utopia* (New York: Basic Books, 1974); Murray Rothbard, *Left and Right* (San Francisco: Cato Institute, 1979); Milton Friedman, *Capitalism and Freedom* (Chicago: University of Chicago Press, 1962).

14. As Rae, op. cit., has pointed out, libertarians such as Nozick do not oppose equality but rather wish to limit the domain of equality to rights in processes and certain civil and political rights. As he stated: "Market liberals (corresponding roughly to American conservatives) are not so much *anti*egalitarian as they are narrowly egalitarian" (p. 47).

15. R. H. Tawney, *Equality*, 4th ed. (London: Allen and Unwin, 1952).

16. John Rawls, *A Theory of Justice* (Cambridge, MA: Harvard University Press, 1971).

17. By focusing on the economic efficiency effects of redistribution policy, I am neglecting the losses of freedom and liberty which are so heavily emphasized by some observers. These effects cannot be valued in any conventional sense, but they are surely relevant in any deliberation over redistribution policy.

18. Arthur Okun, *Equality and Efficiency: The Big Tradeoff* (Washington, DC: The Brookings Institution, 1975).

19. This "Big Tradeoff" idea can be captured in a gains-losses framework when thinking about a nation's redistribution efforts (see Figure 2). Consider a nation's income redistribution system, one which seeks to attain some desired level of inequality—presumably, a level smaller than that generated by the market economy. As the system expands, both gains and losses rise, but at different rates. The figure shows these gain and loss relationships as the TG and TL curves. Consider the situation if the size of this system is (measured as a percentage of GNP), say, at point A. There are net gains at this point, but further expansion—say, from A to B—is problematic. The increase in losses from any expansion is likely to exceed additional gains, and *net gains* would shrink. The fact that such an expansion would create more losses than gains is the essence of exhaustion.

This notion of exhaustion rests on the shapes of the TG and TL curves, which are drawn in conventional fashion in Figure 2. The upward sloping TL curve embodies a kind of law of increasing costs: The first doses of redistribution will generate small losses, but the losses associated with continued expansion of the system are increasingly serious. The flattening out of the TG curve represents a different set of responses. As the redistribution system grows in size, the big and easy-to-reap gains in equality reduction, poverty reduction,

Figure 2
Economic Gains and Losses from
Redistribution System

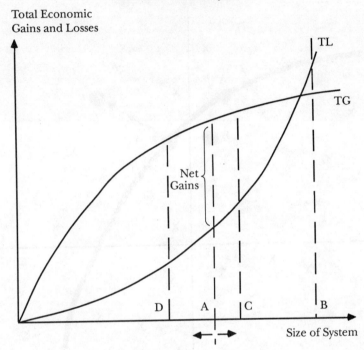

and uncertainty reduction will already have been obtained. Further expansion of this system will encounter diminishing returns.

Figure 3 pulls this gains-losses framework together in a single picture. It provides a useful way of thinking about this "Big Tradeoff" perspective. Again, begin with a rational world with full information. The horizontal axis measures the efficiency effects of a policy (or a group of policies) such as a redistribution system. Envision the value which people place on having Social Security, food stamps, and Medicare-Medicaid being measured on this axis. If the policy lies to the right of the vertical line, the net benefits that are generated are positive— they pass a benefit-cost test. If net costs are created, the policy lies to the left. The vertical axis itself measures the equalization impact of policies, say, some measure of the degree to which they benefit poor people. If the policies are equalizing, or pro-poor, they are located above the horizontal line; if disequalizing, or pro-rich, they are below the line.

If the redistribution system is strongly equalizing (see Chapter 6), it is properly placed in the top half of the diagram. If net efficiency gains are attributable to the system (see Chapter 7), it should be placed to the right of the vertical axis. A position such as point A—located to the right of the vertical line and above the horizontal line—would characterize such a system. A more negative assess-

Figure 3
The Equality-Efficiency Tradeoff

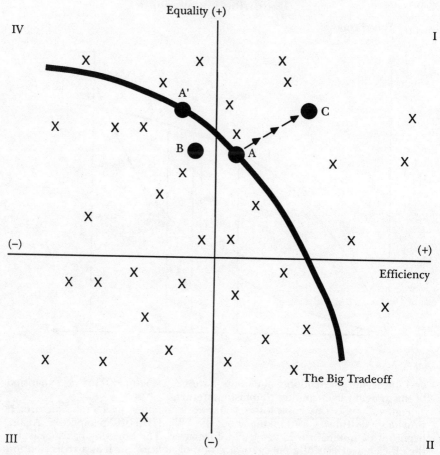

ment of the efficiency effects—such as Charles Murray's appraisal of the existing system in his *Losing Ground*—might place the policy at a point such as B.
Either assessment requires a good dose of judgment on the size of those effects
which cannot be (or at least have not been) measured.

Given the prospect of a fixed amount of equalization, one would prefer a
policy or set of policies further to the right. For example, both A and B reflect
the same level of equalization, but A simultaneously yields net efficiency gains
along with reductions in inequality.

Assume now that with full information on efficiency and equity effects and a
rational decision process, redistribution policy was deliberately located at A.
What would be the effect of expanding the system but leaving its *basic structure*

unchanged? This is the issue of balance at the margin, and it is here that one must compare the benefits from increased efforts with the losses that these efforts carry with them. Beginning at A, then, an expansion of the system—say, an increase in welfare benefits—is likely to yield some additional reduction in poverty and inequality for us, but at an increase in efficiency costs. For example, if welfare benefits are increased from $150 per month to $350 per month, an individual is likely to reduce his or her work effort. A movement from point A to point A' is a likely outcome.

Such movement is precisely what Okun's "Big Tradeoff" is all about. If today we are at point A, a contraction of policy would move us downward and to the right. We would choose more inequality and poverty in the interests of efficiency and economic growth. (Cutting welfare and transfer programs to free resources to promote investment spending by business might be an example.) An expansion of policy, on the other hand, would result in a slide upward and to the left—equality would be promoted and some efficiency sacrificed. The message of the "Big Tradeoff" is clear: Additional redistribution reduces net efficiency gains (or generates net losses), and the more redistribution that is attempted, the greater the efficiency losses. The tradeoff curve in the figure shows these equality gain-efficiency cost options. But remember, this curve was traced out by assuming rational decisions and full information.

20. To see that these conditions lead to a tradeoff relationship, consider the following simple and contrived example. At the beginning of the republic, a beneficent dictator establishes that the objective of government is to maximize the well-being of his or her people. This "social well-being" is defined so as to enable all options to be assessed in terms of their positive or negative contribution to this objective. The size of the society's economic pie is surely one important component of social well-being; the larger the pie, the greater social welfare. The contribution of the economic pie to social welfare is the "efficiency component." But social welfare also has an "equity component." Total social welfare cannot be at its maximum, if, alongside a large economic pie, destitution, malnutrition, and poverty characterize the lives of some citizens. The dictator recognizes that social well-being has both an "efficiency component" and an "equity component."

Now, with full information, the dictator knows just how much a given increase in the size of the economic pie contributes to social welfare, and how much of a contribution to economic well-being is provided by a given reduction in destitution. Such perfect information also allows him or her to know the interaction between the efficiency and equity components of social welfare—if reducing poverty causes the poor to work less hard, thereby reducing the size of the economic pie, this is known to the dictator.

Armed with this maximum social well-being objective and full information, the dictator, from the dawn of the republic onward, chooses rationally among the available options so as to maximize the well-being of his or her people. Having so chosen, he or she can sit back and observe—and take pride in—this constellation of optimum public policies. The economic pie will not be as large as it could be; the correct amount of sacrifice in the size of the pie will have been made in the interests of reducing destitution among the poorest citizens. Pursuit of equity will fall short of full equality; the correct deviation from equality will have been chosen in the interest of maintaining a large and growing economic pie. In terms of Figure 3, some point—like A—has been rationally and optimally chosen. It represents the best position available to society in terms of both equality and efficiency.

In this artificial world, an equality-efficiency tradeoff will confront the decision maker. Starting at A, further reductions in inequality will, in fact, reduce economic growth and the size of the economic pie. The pursuit of efficiency will generate increased destitution and increased poverty. It is not possible to make a change that will simultaneously secure both more efficiency and more equality. This is the hammerlock of the "Big Tradeoff."

21. This view of the government decision process is consistent with the writings of Nobel Laureate James Buchanan, and the "public choice" perspective which has grown up around them. See James Buchanan and Gordon Tullock, *The Calculus of Consent* (Ann Arbor, MI: University of Michigan Press, 1962); and Dennis Mueller, "Public Choice: A Survey," *Journal of Economic Literature* 14, no. 2 (June 1976).

22. Figure 3 is helpful in depicting this alternative view. The field of x's drawn on the diagram represents the set of policies actually in effect. Some may lie on or close to Okun's tradeoff curve, but many will not. As with the x's, public policy measures are strewn across the equality-efficiency landscape. Some policies in place may simultaneously secure equality and efficiency, and they would be in region I. The Head Start program is a likely example. Others may sacrifice both equality and efficiency, and they would be in region III. Federal water resources programs subsidizing irrigation come to mind. Still others will emphasize efficiency while sacrificing equality (region II) and vice versa (region IV).

This figure now contains two different views of what is possible in framing government policy toward poverty and inequality. Okun's view presupposes an immutable tradeoff, with the problem for policymakers being to find that point on the curve which best fits society's current preferences regarding equality and efficiency. The alternative view is represented by the x's on the diagram; it emphasizes a quite different framework and approach. If both efficiency and equality are valued, the first step is to identify policies that simultaneously promote both. If, in fact, such policy options are available (region I), they should be pursued, while policies that reduce efficiency and equality (region III) are abandoned. More generally, policy should be shifted toward the northeast—toward region I and away from region III. Shifting to an alternative mix of policies containing greater contributions to both equality and efficiency than the existing strategy can be envisioned as moving along the arrows to point C in the figure.

This perspective leads to the conclusion that the belief in an inescapable tradeoff is simply wrong. The "Big Tradeoff" view would advise a *retrenchment* of redistribution policy if the efficiency "leaks" are judged to be too high. An expansion is suggested if additional spending on the policy has net benefits. The alternative view, as represented by the x's, argues for a *reorientation* of policy—a substitution of measures that will secure inequality reduction simultaneously with efficiency for those that score poorly on both accounts.

23. If we stick with the simple diagram in Figure 2, the essence of this alternative approach can be clearly seen. Figure 4 reproduces Figure 2, but it has two new dashed curves, TG' and TL', drawn in. The shift of TG to TG' (and

Figure 4
Economic Gains and Losses from
Redistribution System

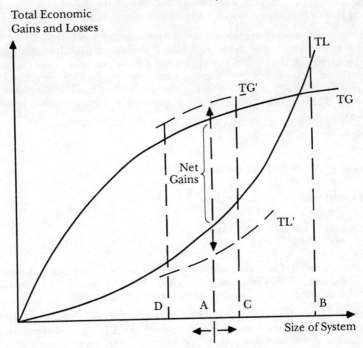

Total Economic
Gains and Losses

TL

TG'

TG

Net
Gains

TL'

D   A   C   B

Size of System

TL to TL') is what the alternative view is all about. Given the current size of redistribution efforts—say, at point A—can the structure of the system or its financing be fundamentally changed so that the gains from the effort are increased while the losses are reduced? Can we by redirecting policy shift up the gains curve or shift down the losses curve? If this can be accomplished, we are pursuing equality with efficiency.

24. William Baumol, *Superfairness* (Cambridge, MA: MIT Press, 1986).

25. The discussion in this section is heavily influenced by Robert Lampman, *Social Welfare Spending: Accounting for Changes from 1950 to 1978* (New York: Academic Press, 1984). See also Robert Haveman, *Does the Welfare State Increase Economic Welfare: Reflections on Observed Positives and Hidden Negatives,* Tinbergen Lecture, Erasmus University (Rotterdam: Stenfert-Kroese, 1985).

26. Two classic studies of the relationship between "human capital" and market wages are Gary Becker, *Human Capital* (New York: Columbia University Press, 1964) and Jacob Mincer, *Schooling, Experience, and Earnings* (New York: National Bureau of Economic Research, 1974).

Chapter 2

1. Data from "Changes in the Money Income of the Aged and Nonaged," *Studies in Income Distribution,* Social Security Administration, 1986.

2. This trend toward increasing inequality has been referred to by some observers as the "decline of the middle class." Professors Blackburn and Bloom defined groups that they called the upper, the middle, and the lower classes and calculated the income share of these groups over time (McKinley Blackburn and David Bloom, "What Is Happening to the Middle Class?" *Demography,* January 1985). Their figures give some substance to this characterization of what is happening.

	1969	*1983*
Percentage of families in upper class ($42,000+, 1985$)	8.2	12.8
Percentage of families in middle class ($11,000–41,000, 1985$)	62.4	55.9
Percentage of families in lower class ($0–11,000, 1985$)	29.4	31.3

3. Data are from *The Concentration of Wealth in the United States,* Joint Economic Committee, U.S. Congress, July, 1986, Tables 4 and 5 (as corrected by the Federal Reserve Board, Division of Research and Statistics).

4. See Lawrence M. Friedman, "The Social and Political Context of the War on Poverty: An Overview," in Robert Haveman, ed., *A Decade of Federal Antipoverty Programs: Achievements, Failures, and Lessons* (New York: Academic Press, 1977).

5. In 1965, the incidence of official poverty among the aged was about 28 percent, compared to an overall rate of about 16 percent. See Robert D. Plotnick and Felicity Skidmore, *Progress Against Poverty: A Review of the 1964–1974 Decade* (New York: Academic Press, 1975).

6. Haveman, op. cit., reviews these early developments of the War on Poverty.

7. Income includes all reported census categories of income. The data are based on tabulations by the author from the 1960 Census of Population; the 1985 estimates are based on tabulations from the 1986 Current Population Survey.

8. Calculated from data in U.S. Census Bureau, Current Population Reports, series P-60, No. 68 and subsequent poverty reports.

9. From Gene Falk, "1987 Budget Perspectives: Federal Spending for the Human Resource Programs," Congressional Research Service, February 1986.

10. The 1967 data are from Sheldon Danziger and Peter Gottschalk, "How Have Families with Children Been Faring?" Institute for Research on Poverty

Discussion Paper 801-86, University of Wisconsin–Madison, 1986; the 1985 estimates are based on tabulations from the 1986 Current Population Survey.

11. For 1960, earnings include wage, salary, and self-employment income of full-time, full-year workers. They are based on tabulations by the author from the 1960 Census of Population. For 1986, the data are for usual weekly median earnings of full-time wage and salary workers. They are from *Employment and Earnings* 34, no. 1, p. 54, Bureau of Labor Statistics. The 1960 and 1985 data are not precisely comparable but are sufficiently similar to evoke meaningful comparison. See the Appendix.

12. There is evidence that some of this progress has eroded since 1980. The U.S. Bureau of Labor Statistics reports that the ratio of the median full-time weekly wages of black men to those of white men fell from 76.2 in 1980 to 72.9 in 1985.

13. Income includes all reported census categories of income. The data are based on special tabulations by the author from the 1960 Census of Population and the 1986 Current Population Survey.

14. The 1967 data are from Sheldon Danziger and Peter Gottschalk, "How Have Families with Children Been Faring?" op. cit.; the 1985 estimates are based on tabulations from the 1986 Current Population Survey.

15. Moreover, these comparisons do not reflect the increase in the number of mother-only relative to intact black families or the erosion of black male earnings at the bottom of the distribution. These shifts are discussed below.

16. James P. Smith and Finis R. Welch, "Closing the Gap: Forty Years of Economic Progress for Blacks" (Santa Monica, CA: The Rand Corporation, 1986).

17. Since the mid-1970s, the performance of the labor market has faltered badly. Average weekly earnings in constant dollars have fallen by about 14 percent from 1973 to 1985. Inflation and lagging productivity growth have accounted for much of this reduction, but the shift in the industry mix in the United States—away from manufacturing and toward the service sector—has also played a major role. From 1979 to 1985, the percentage of household heads who are expected to work, who hold jobs that pay less than is necessary to keep a family of four out of poverty has increased from about 20 percent to over 26 percent. (Sheldon Danziger and Peter Gottschalk, "Work, Poverty and the Working Poor," presented to the Employment and Housing Subcommittee of the House Committee on Government Operations, December 12, 1985.) A number of studies have documented an increase in the inequality of wages and earnings both in the economy as a whole, and, more importantly, within individual industries. As a result of these changes, some of the gains made by minorities in the 1960s and early 1970s have eroded. Several of these changes in labor market performance have been documented in *The Polarization of America: The Loss of Good Jobs, Falling Incomes and Rising Inequality* (Washington, DC: Industrial Union Department, AFL–CIO, 1986).

18. Smith and Welch, op. cit.

19. See Charles Brown, "Black-White Earnings Ratios Since the Civil Rights

Act of 1964: The Importance of Labor Market Dropouts," *Quarterly Journal of Economics* 99, no. 1 (February 1984): 31–44.

20. Earnings include wage, salary, and self-employment income. The data are for full-time, full-year workers. The ratios value earnings are in constant dollars. They are based on special tabulations by the author from the 1960 and 1980 Census of Population. After 1980, the data show an increase in the female-male ratio, but this is due more to erosion in male wages associated with the recession of the early 1980s than to increases in female wages. See Industrial Union Department (AFL–CIO), op. cit.

21. Income includes all reported census categories of income. The data are based on tabulations by the author from the 1960 and 1980 Census of Population. More recent data at this level of detail are unavailable.

22. Based on comparison of median weekly earnings of full-time and salary workers. Data are from the U.S. Bureau of Labor Statistics.

23. There is a vast literature on this topic. Good entry points are James D. Smith and Michael P. Ward, *Women's Wages and Work in the Twentieth Century* (Santa Monica, CA: The Rand Corporation, 1984); and Gary Becker, *A Treatise on the Family* (Cambridge, MA: Harvard University Press, 1981).

Chapter 3

1. Earnings include wage, salary, and self-employment income. The data are for full-time, full-year male workers. Youths are defined as workers eighteen to twenty-four years old; older workers as those forty-five to fifty-four years old. The ratios value earnings are in constant dollars. They are based on special tabulations by the author from the 1960 and 1980 Census of Population.

2. Data from James P. Smith and Finis R. Welch, "Closing the Gap: Forty Years of Economic Progress for Blacks" (Santa Monica, CA: The Rand Corporation, 1986), and from *Employment and Earnings* 34, no. 1 (January 1987).

3. An excellent review of the literature is: Charles L. Betsey, Robinson G. Hollister, Jr., and Mary R. Papageorgiou, eds., *Youth Employment and Training Programs: The YEPDA Years* (Washington, DC: National Research Council, National Academy Press, 1985). See also Richard Freeman and David Wise, *The Youth Labor Market Problem: Its Nature, Causes, and Consequences* (Chicago: University of Chicago Press, 1982); and Richard Freeman and Harry Holzer, eds., *The Black Youth Unemployment Crisis* (Chicago: University of Chicago Press, 1986).

4. The following are the best estimates available of the effect on the percentage of youth of various ages who are employed when the overall adult unemployment rate rises by one percent:

16–17 years	– 5 percent
18–19 years	– 2 percent
20–24 years	– 3 percent

Thus, every one-point increase in the adult unemployment rate—say, from 5 percent to 6 percent—reduces the percentage of sixteen- to seventeen-year-olds employed by 5 percent. Somewhat smaller, but still substantial, job losses are recorded for older youths. See Freeman and Wise, op. cit.

5. See Freeman and Wise, ibid.

6. Some researchers have found this reduction to have adversely affected employment opportunities of minority groups as much as the overcrowding effect associated with the baby boom. See Freeman and Wise, ibid., and Freeman and Holzer, op. cit.

7. Indeed, a paradox is that the recent drop in the real minimum wage caused by inflation might have hurt youth, both in terms of earnings and employment. The story runs as follows. First, because youth earnings are linked to the legislated minimum, their real earnings have dropped along with the set minimum. Second, as the wages available to youth drop, working appears less attractive to them compared to other uses of their time. Unemployment rates will rise as low-paying jobs are spurned, and some youth leave the labor force entirely. Evidence suggests that this has occurred to some degree, and must play a role in explaining why some youth have "dropped out" of the labor market, choosing instead crime and other "underground economy" activities.

8. This view is consistent with the writings of Professor William Julius Wilson, a sociologist at the University of Chicago, who speaks about the effects of the "catastrophic" increase of behavioral problems and cultural disintegration which has created a "ghetto underclass." This disintegration is associated with high rates of joblessness, teenage pregnancies, out-of-wedlock births, welfare dependency, female-headed families, and serious crime, one phenomenon building on and fostering the other. He quotes Kenneth B. Clark, the author of a 1965 study of the black ghetto: "The symptoms of lower-class society affect the dark ghettos of America—low aspirations, poor education, family instability, illegitimacy, unemployment, crime, drug addiction and alcoholism, frequent illness and early death." See William Julius Wilson, "The Urban Underclass in Advanced Industrial Society," in Paul Peterson, ed., *The New Urban Reality* (Washington, DC: The Brookings Institution, 1985); and Wilson, *The Truly Disadvantaged: The Inner City, the Underclass, and Public Policy* (Chicago: University of Chicago Press, 1987).

9. See Freeman and Wise, op. cit.

10. Irwin Garfinkel and Liz Uhr, "A New Approach to Child Support," *The Public Interest*, no. 75 (Spring 1984): 111–22.

11. Income includes all reported census categories of income. The data are based on tabulations by the author from the 1960 and 1980 Census of Population, plus 1980–1985 estimates of the change in the 1980 ratio based on tabulations from the 1986 Current Population Survey.

12. The 1967 data are from Sheldon Danziger and Peter Gottschalk, "How Have Families with Children Been Faring?" Institute for Research on Poverty Discussion Paper 801-86, University of Wisconsin–Madison, January 1986; the 1985 estimates are based on tabulations from the 1986 Current Population Survey.

13. Ibid.

14. Ibid.

15. U.S. Bureau of the Census, *Child Support and Alimony: 1985*, Series P-23, no. 152 (August 1987).

16. A somewhat more favorable picture of the effect of government policy on mother-only families would be revealed if changes in the value of in-kind benefits such as food stamps and Medicare were also accounted for. Although both have experienced some retrenchment since 1980, neither has experienced the budget cuts that have reduced cash transfers.

17. See Irwin Garfinkel and Sara McLanahan, *Single Mothers and Their Children: A New American Dilemma* (Washington, DC: Urban Institute Press, 1986) for a review and critique of the evidence on this issue. See also David Ellwood, *Poor Support: Poverty in the American Family* (New York: Basic Books, 1988.)

18. Charles Murray, *Losing Ground: American Social Policy, 1950–1980* (New York: Basic Books, 1984).

19. See Garfinkel and McLanahan, op. cit.

20. This appraisal parallels that in Garfinkel and McLanahan, ibid.

21. Samuel Preston, "Children and the Elderly: Divergent Paths for America's Dependents," *Demography* 21, no. 4 (November 1984): 435–57. A comprehensive discussion of the economic status of children and the nature of federal government support and assistance provided to them is: U.S. Congress, Congressional Budget Office, *Reducing Poverty Among Children* (Washington, DC: Congressional Budget Office, 1985). This report also discusses a large number of policy options for assisting children and their parents.

22. Gordon M. Fisher, "Developments in Money Income and Poverty in 1985 and Earlier Years," memorandum, U.S. Department of Health and Human Services, October 1986.

23. The 1967 data are from Sheldon Danziger and Peter Gottschalk, "How Have Families with Children Been Faring?," op. cit.; the 1985 estimates are based on tabulations from the 1986 Current Population Survey.

24. See, for example, Sheldon Danziger, Jacques van der Gaag, Eugene Smolensky, and Michael K. Taussig, "Implications of the Relative Economic Status of the Elderly for Transfer Policy," in Henry J. Aaron and Gary Burtless, eds., *Retirement and Economic Behavior* (Washington, DC: The Brookings Institution, 1984).

25. Joseph F. Quinn, "The Economic Status of the Elderly: Beware of the Mean," mimeo., Boston College, Chestnut Hill, MA, October 1983.

26. Karen Holden, Richard V. Burkhauser, and Daniel Myers, "Income Transitions at Older Stages of Life: The Dynamics of Poverty Among the Elderly," *The Gerontologist* 26, no. 3 (1986): 282–97. In 1978, the highest rates of poverty among the aged were for black females not living with their spouses (57 percent), black females who were divorced (52 percent), black females who were widows (47 percent), black women who were never married (35 percent), and black males not living with their spouses or never married (about 45 percent). See Jennifer Warlick, "Aged Women in Poverty: A Problem Without a Solu-

tion?," in William Brown and Laura Katz Olsen, eds., *Aging and Public Policy: The Politics of Growing Old in America* (Westport, CT: Greenwood Press, 1983).

27. Income includes all reported census categories of income. The data are based on tabulations by the author from the 1960 and 1980 Census of Population, plus 1980–1985 estimates of the change in the 1980 values based on tabulations from the 1980 and 1986 Current Population Survey.

28. This pattern of "left-behind" elderly persists even though the overall level of inequality among the aged population has fallen over the past two decades. In 1967, the Gini coefficient for the sixty-five-and-over population was .458; by 1983, it had fallen to .406. ("Changes in the Money Income of the Aged and Nonaged," Studies in Income Distribution, Social Security Administration, 1986.) It is the rapid rise in the well-being of most of the elderly in contrast to the persistent low income of these left-behind groups which causes this to be a problem of social concern. This is in spite of the coverage of most of the poor elderly by the Supplemental Security Income (SSI) program, a means-tested support program.

29. Indeed, the numbers shown in the table are themselves means. They conceal the fact that some of those in the last two rows fare far worse than even these averages reveal. Some of them have no Social Security coverage at all, or receive very low benefits if they are covered. There is a floor, however, as provided by the SSI program.

Chapter 4

1. This discussion draws from and was influenced by John Palmer and Stephanie Gould, "The Economic Consequences of an Aging Society," *Daedalus* 115, no. 1 (Winter 1986), pp. 295–323. For some of the population characteristics I will discuss, the year 1995 or 2000 is the latest for which population forecasts are available.

2. The following data on population are from the 1984 Annual Report of the Board of Trustees of the Federal Old-Age and Survivors Insurance and Disability Insurance Trust Funds; and U.S. Bureau of the Census, Current Population Reports, Series P-25, Nos. 98, 310, and 952. The projections are based on the mid-range series of Census and the Social Security actuaries.

3. Consider, for example, the population of men in the prime working years aged twenty-five to fifty-four. In 1984, there were 45 million of them; by 1995 their number is expected to grow to 55 million—an annual growth rate of close to 2 percent per year. The number of women in this age group will grow nearly as fast. While the entire population of people older than sixteen is projected to grow by about 10 percent from 1984 to 1995, the population of those aged twenty-five to fifty-four will grow by about 22 percent.

4. Data are from Howard N. Fullerton, Jr., "The 1995 Labor Force: BLS' Latest Projections," *Monthly Labor Review*, November 1985.

5. See Robert Haveman and Barbara Wolfe, "Pension Policy and Retirement Choices: Anticipating Future Changes," mimeo., University of Wisconsin–Mad-

ison, 1986; and William Butz, Kevin McCarthy, Peter A. Morrison, and Mary Varana, "Demographic Challenges in America's Future" (Santa Monica, CA; The Rand Corporation, 1982).

6. See, J.R. Norsworthy, M. Harper, and R. Kunze, "The Slowdown in Productivity Growth: Analysis of Some Contributing Factors," *Brookings Papers on Economic Activity* 2, 1979, pp. 387–421; Gregory Christainsen and Robert Haveman, "Public Regulations and the Slowdown in Productivity Growth," *American Economic Review* (May 1981), pp. 320–25; and U.S. Congressional Budget Office, *Environmental Regulation and Economic Efficiency,* March, 1985, Washington, DC.

7. The U.S. Department of Labor projects that the median age of the labor force will increase from thirty-five to thirty-eight over the 1984–1995 period. By 1995, 74 percent of the nation's work force will be in the highest productivity prime age categories, as opposed to 66 percent in 1984 (and only 61 percent in 1970). See Fullerton, op. cit.

8. This estimate, of course, presumes that no major depressions or international financial collapse occurs in the interim, and that capital and labor markets will adjust to accommodate the expected growth in these resources and allocate them efficiently over sectors of the economy. Indeed, it assumes that fiscal and monetary policy will be accommodating over this period, providing sufficient aggregate demand to absorb the growth in these available resources. See Palmer and Gould, op. cit.

9. Smeeding has estimated that over 60 percent of this not-rich/not-poor group of aged lives with two or more of these forms of economic insecurity; he calls them "tweeners." Timothy Smeeding, "Nonmoney Income and the Elderly: The Case of the 'Tweeners,'" Institute for Research on Poverty, University of Wisconsin–Madison, Discussion Paper 759–84, 1984.

10. See Haveman and Wolfe, op. cit.

11. In 1950, private pension plans covered only about 10 million, or about one-fourth of private sector wage and salary workers. By 1980, 35 million, or nearly 50 percent of private sector workers, were covered. About 70 percent of nonagricultural paid workers employed more than half-time over twenty-five years are now covered. This growth is reflected in a rapid increase in the number of people receiving private pension benefits from less than 0.5 million people in 1950 to more than 10 million beneficiaries in 1980. Total assets of the funds have also skyrocketed from $2 billion in 1940 to $1,000 billion in 1985. By 2000, assets are expected to hit $4 trillion. See Alicia H. Munnell, "ERISA: Is It Consistent with Other National Goals?" in *The Employee Retirement Income Security Act of 1974: The First Decade,* Special Committee on Aging, U.S. Senate, Washington, DC: Government Printing Office, 1984.

12. This assumes that private pensions will remain secure in future years, a proposition that some observers challenge. See *National Journal,* August 29, 1987, pp. 2138–44.

13. Over the past twenty years, the asset holdings of the elderly have increased more rapidly than those for other age groups, and the distribution of these holdings has become more unequal. See Robert Haveman, Barbara Wolfe, Ross Finnie, and Edward Wolff, "The Well-being of Children and Disparities

Among Them: Changes over Two Decades—1962–83," in John Palmer, Timothy Smeeding, and Barbara Torrey, eds., *The Vulnerables: America's Young and Old in the Industrial World* (Washington, DC: Urban Institute Press, 1988); and Edward Wolff and Marcia Marley, "Long-Term Trends in U.S. Wealth Inequality: Methodological Issues and Results," mimeo., New York University, 1987.

14. Recall from Chapter 3 that while nearly 16 percent of women over 60 were in poverty in 1980—a figure only slightly above the national poverty rate —about 30 percent of older women who live alone were poor. Black elderly individuals had a poverty rate of about 40 percent. See Karen Holden, "Living Arrangements, Income, and Poverty of Older Women in the U.S., 1950–80," Institute for Research on Poverty, University of Wisconsin–Madison, Discussion Paper 804-86, 1986; and Sheldon Danziger et al., "Implications of the Relative Economic Status of the Elderly for Transfer Policy," in Henry Aaron and Gary Burtless, eds., *Retirement and Economic Behavior* (Washington, DC: The Brookings Institution, 1984). These aged poor people are in this situation for two main reasons. First, over their working lives, they did not have jobs that provided them Social Security or private pension coverage, or they were married to people without such jobs or coverage. Second, the Social Security survivors benefits for which elderly widows are eligible tend to be very low.

15. Recent changes in requirements for joint and survivor pensions could provide some additional protection for these lowest-income elderly.

16. This forecast is consistent with the analysis in Richard Easterlin, *Birth and Fortune: The Impact of Numbers on Personal Welfare*, 2d ed. (Chicago: University of Chicago Press, 1987).

17. Data from Fullerton, op. cit.

18. Richard Freeman and David Wise, *The Youth Labor Market Problem: Its Nature, Causes, and Consequences* (Chicago: University of Chicago Press, 1982).

19. This bleak outlook for minority youths is anticipated by a recent government report on future labor force trends (see Fullerton, op. cit., p. 22):

[Although] there should be relatively less competition [among youths for jobs], a greater proportion of the youth population is projected to be minority. To the extent that minorities live where there are fewer jobs,...their chances of employment could be lower than one would expect, even if openings for youth exist elsewhere.

20. Data are from Irwin Garfinkel and Sara McLanahan, *Single Mothers and Their Children: America's New Dilemma* (Washington, DC: Urban Institute Press, 1986).

21. Senator Daniel P. Moynihan, "Children and Welfare Reform," *Journal of the Institute of Socio-Economic Studies* 6, no. 1 (spring 1981). See also Daniel P. Moynihan, *Family and Nation* (New York: Harcourt Brace Jovanovich, 1986).

22. About 60 percent of those who enter mother-only family status for the first time are in poverty during the first year of that status. See T. Knieser, M. McElroy, and S. Wilcox, "Family Structure, Race, and the Feminization of Poverty," Institute for Research on Poverty, University of Wisconsin–Madison, Discussion Paper 810–86, 1986. See also Lenore J. Weitzman, *The Divorce*

Revolution: The Unexpected Social and Economic Consequences for Women and Children in America (New York: Free Press, 1985).

23. Richard Easterlin, "The Impact of Demographic Factors on the Family Environment of Children, 1940–1985," in R. Nelson and F. Skidmore, eds., *American Families and the Economy* (Washington, DC: National Academy Press, 1983). See also R. Easterlin, op. cit.

24. See Knieser, McElroy, and Wilcox, op. cit.

Chapter 5

1. The discussion will focus on the federal government and its policies. State governments, cities, and counties also redistribute, as do private insurance and charitable organizations, but they and their effects are both smaller and far more inscrutable than those of the federal government. Instead of a single identifiable entity, there are literally thousands of state and local creatures. While they perform numerous and valuable functions, redistribution of income, wealth, and power is not generally regarded as one of their major purposes or activities. Moreover, what we know about these entities and their effects is far more limited than what is known about the federal government. Data on them are not collected in one central place, and it is difficult to comprehend and to characterize the actions and impacts of thousands of spending programs and taxing policies. In part because of this complexity, researchers have spent far less time exploring the effects of state and local policies relative to those of federal policy.

2. See Robert D. Plotnick and Felicity Skidmore, *Progress Against Poverty: A Review of the 1964–1974 Decade* (New York: Academic Press, 1975); Robert Haveman, ed., *A Decade of Federal Antipoverty Programs: Achievements, Failures, and Lessons* (New York: Academic Press, 1977); Daniel P. Moynihan, *Maximum Feasible Misunderstanding* (New York: Free Press, 1969); and Sheldon Danziger and Daniel Weinberg, eds., *Fighting Poverty: What Works and What Doesn't* (Cambridge, MA: Harvard University Press, 1986).

3. See John Palmer and Isabel Sawhill, eds., *The Reagan Experiment: An Examination of Economic and Social Policies under the Reagan Administration* (Washington, DC: Urban Institute Press, 1982); John Palmer and Isabel Sawhill, eds., *The Reagan Record: An Assessment of America's Changing Domestic Priorities* (Cambridge, MA: Ballinger Publishing, 1984).

4. See Lawrence Friedman, "The Social and Political Context of the War on Poverty: An Overview," in Robert Haveman, ed., *A Decade . . .*, op. cit.

5. Robert Lampman has emphasized this important function of the War on Poverty. See his "What Does It Do for the Poor? A New Test for National Policy," in Eli Ginzberg and Robert Solow, eds., *The Great Society* (New York: Basic Books, 1974).

6. If interest on the national debt is excluded from the calculation, this figure rises to nearly 60 percent.

7. Stated in terms of spending as a percentage of the nation's output or GNP, the story is similar, but not so dramatic. In the early 1950s, federal payments to

individuals stood at about 7–8 percent of GNP; by the 1980s this had grown to 13 percent.

8. The numbers in the table are not precise estimates, but are a synthesis of results drawn from a variety of studies; a good dose of judgment is built into them. See Sheldon Danziger, Robert Haveman, and Robert Plotnick, "Antipoverty Policy: Effects on the Poor and the Nonpoor," in Danziger and Weinberg, eds., *Fighting Poverty...*, op. cit.; Robert Plotnick and Timothy Smeeding, "Poverty and Income Transfers: Past Trends and Future Prospects," *Public Policy* 27 (1979): 255–72; and U.S. Bureau of the Census, *Alternative Methods for Valuing Selected In-Kind Transfer Benefits and Measuring Their Effects on Poverty,* Technical Paper 50, 1982.

9. The official U.S. poverty measure compares a family's actual money income with an officially designated cutoff level which is judged necessary to remove the family from poverty. If actual income is below the cutoff (which takes into account the size and composition of the family), the family is said to be poor. See Plotnick and Skidmore, op. cit., for a description and critique of this measure.

10. This estimate overstates the effect of transfers on poverty, as it does not take into account the reduced earnings of the recipients of transfers due to labor supply disincentives. Conversely, if in-kind benefits such as food stamps and Medicaid were included as benefits, the poverty-reducing impact of government would be larger.

11. This evaluation of the effect of government policy on equality has concentrated on the role of public expenditures, largely transfers, in reducing inequality. A wide variety of other government activities, often involving direct expenditures, has also contributed to closing gaps among groups. Basic educational opportunity grants, guaranteed student loans, compensatory education programs, affirmative action programs, and equal opportunity regulations are all designed to reduce gaps in a variety of dimensions among gender, racial, and income groups. There have been few if any studies of the effect of these programs on inequality of either results or opportunities. What does exist, however, is a plethora of studies that attempt to measure the effectiveness of these programs in closing racial and gender educational, housing, and employment gaps. See, for example, Orley Ashenfelter and James Heckman, "Measuring the Effect of an Anti-Discrimination Program," in Orley Ashenfelter and James Blum, eds., *Evaluating the Labor Market Effects of Social Programs* (Princeton, NJ: Industrial Relations Section, 1976); Glen Cain, "The Economic Analysis of Labor Market Discrimination: A Survey," in Orley Ashenfelter and Richard Layard, eds., *Handbook of Labor Economics* (Amsterdam: Elsevier Science Publishers, 1986); James Coleman et al., *Equality of Educational Opportunity* (Washington, DC: Government Printing Office, 1966); W. Lee Hansen and Robert Lampman, "Basic Opportunity Grants in Higher Education: Good Intentions and Mixed Results," in Robert Haveman and Julius Margolis, eds., *Public Expenditures and Policy Analysis,* 3d ed. (Boston: Houghton-Mifflin, 1983); Stephen Mullin and Anita Summers, "Is More Better? The Effectiveness of Spending on Compensatory Education," *Phi Delta Kappan* 64 (1983): 339–47; Harvey Averch et al., *How Effective Is Schooling? A Critical Review and Synthesis of Research Findings* (Santa Monica, CA: The Rand Corporation, 1972); and Robert Crain and Rita Mahard, "Desegregation and Black Achievement: A Review of the Research,"

Law and Contemporary Problems 42, no. 2 (1978). The findings of these studies are mixed, but generally support the view that the employment and the education gaps among relevant groups have been narrowed because of these efforts, but that the extent of the inequality reduction is not substantial. The measurement of these effects is notoriously difficult, and the translation of the findings into any precise statement of the impact of the efforts on either inequality of outcome or inequality of opportunity is impossible.

12. See Eugene Steuerle and Paul Wilson, "The Taxation of Poor and Lower Income Families," in Jack Meyer, ed., *Ladders Out of Poverty* (Washington, DC: American Horizons Foundation, 1986).

13. This description of the major federal taxes draws heavily from Joseph Pechman, *Who Paid the Taxes, 1966–85?* (Washington, DC: The Brookings Institution, 1985). The passage of the Tax Reform Act of 1986 has made these estimates somewhat obsolete. They are the most recent available, however, and the general patterns which are described here continue to hold.

14. Ibid. See also Edgar Browning, "Pechman's Tax Incidence Study: A Note on the Data," *American Economic Review* 76 (December 1986): 1214–18, and Pechman's reply in the same issue.

15. These distributional patterns of federal taxes are shown in Figure 5 for these two sets of assumptions. On the horizontal axis, people are lined up by their incomes, from lowest to highest. The average tax rate borne by each income level is shown on the vertical axis. Even with the least progressive assumptions, the income tax is generally progressive over the bulk of the income distribution.

16. Figure 6 shows this declining progressiveness for the most progressive of Pechman's assumptions; Figure 7 for the most regressive.

17. Again, the Tax Reform Act of 1986 will have changed some of the specifics, but few of the overall patterns described here. While the special tax breaks have been reduced and the tax brackets indexed, the post-reform income tax has about the same degree of progressivity as the pre-reform system. The reform benefited both low- and high-income groups.

18. This conclusion holds irrespective of whether one uses the most regressive or the most progressive of Pechman's assumptions.

19. Figure 8 is a helpful way of thinking about these questions. Panel (a) depicts the distribution of income from only market sources—wages and salaries, interest, dividends, rent. This distribution is a picture of how the market would allocate income if there were no government. It has the standard characteristics of an income distribution. There is a big hump toward the middle representing the large number of middle-class families. The right side trails off slowly, with people on the tail representing the very rich in society. In panel (b), the effect of the tax system on this distribution is shown as the dashed line, which results from subtracting the taxes paid by each family from their market income. The after-tax distribution has shifted to the left, and because the tax system takes more from the rich than from the poor, it is more pinched than the distribution of market incomes. The tax system is somewhat equalizing; it brings us somewhat together in income terms.

Figure 5
Income Levels and Total Taxes Paid, 1980

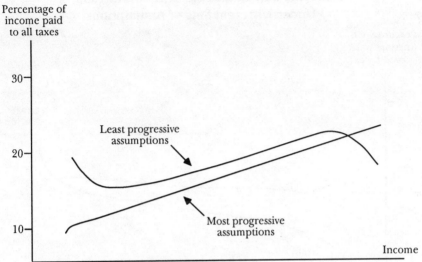

Percentage of
income paid
to all taxes

30–

20–

10–

Least progressive
assumptions

Most progressive
assumptions

Income

Source: Joseph Pechman, *Who Paid the Taxes, 1966–85?* (Washington, DC: The Brookings Institution, 1985).

Then, in panel (c), government benefits are added to the after-tax incomes of households. This yields the distribution of income after taxes and after government spending. Just as taxes tend to equalize, so do the benefits of government spending. The heavy dashed line, sometimes called "final income," is even more pinched than the after-tax line. By comparing the distribution of final income with the distribution of market income, the overall effect of the government on inequality can be seen. Because of government, there are more of us bunched up in the middle, fewer of us that are very rich or very poor. Government has moderated the extremes.

20. The following discussion draws heavily from Morgan Reynolds and Eugene Smolensky, *Public Expenditures, Taxes, and the Distribution of Income: The United States, 1950, 1961, 1970* (New York: Academic Press, 1977). See also Patricia Ruggles and Michael O'Higgins, "The Distribution of Public Expenditure Among Households in the United States," *Review of Income and Wealth,* series 27 (June 1981): 137–64. The diagram gives a picture of the general impact of the fisc over time, and not a precise representation of the numerical estimates.

21. The line shows the *average* effect of government on people with different incomes. Some families at any given income level will be above the line, while others will be below it.

Chapter 6

1. This way of thinking about the nation's income redistribution system has been emphasized by Robert Lampman, *Social Welfare Spending: Accounting for*

Figure 6
Income and Taxes Paid in 1966 and 1985,
Under Different Sets of Assumptions

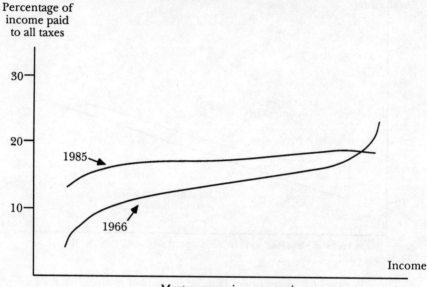

Most progressive assumptions

Figure 7

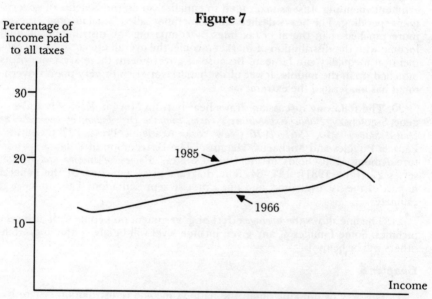

Least progressive assumptions

Source: Pechman, op. cit.

Figure 8
Government's Effect on Overall Income Distribution for Individuals

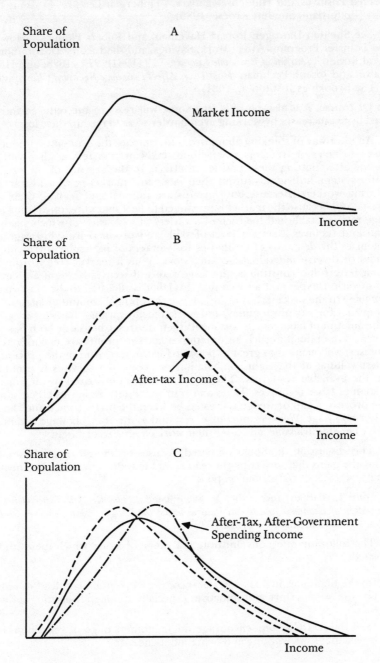

Changes from 1950 to 1978 (New York: Academic Press, 1984). See also Robert Haveman, "Does the Welfare State Increase Economic Welfare?: Reflections on Observed Positives and Hidden Negatives," Tinbergen Lecture, Erasmus University (Rotterdam: Stenfert Kroese, 1985).

2. See Sheldon Danziger, Robert Haveman, and Robert Plotnick, "How Income Transfer Programs Affect Work, Savings, and the Income Distribution: A Critical Review," *Journal of Economic Literature* 19 (1981): 975–1028; and Henry J. Aaron and Joseph Pechman, *How Taxes Affect Economic Behavior* (Washington, DC: The Brookings Institution, 1981).

3. Of course, it is also possible that some will react to the reduced income caused by tax increases by working even harder so as to recoup their loss.

4. Another way of thinking about this is to compare the economy without the increase in taxes or transfers—or without taxes or transfers at all—with the economy after putting these policies in effect. In the absence of the tax and transfer system, individuals supply their labor to a market in which businesses are hiring workers. Because both groups are rational and seeking their own interests, and because the market is presumed to be a smoothly functioning one, a wage rate is established for each of a variety of jobs, each of which yields an output and requires a certain level of skills and productivity. This wage rate harmonizes the demands of businesses for workers of particular sorts with the supplies of diverse individuals seeking work. With a market free to function without fetters and constraints, the wage rate will secure the right amount of labor of various types and see to it that this labor is allocated to the most appropriate jobs. In the process, businesses secure the optimal amount of labor of the right quality for any given outlay, and workers with various characteristics supply the amount of labor which best meets their desires. Choices by both business and labor are optimal in such an unfettered market: profits are maximized for businesses; well-being is as great as possible for workers. And in the process the greatest volume of the right combination of goods and services is produced given the available resources. The result can be summarized as an efficient allocation of labor resources. Taxes and transfers interfere in this efficient allocation process; a gap or wedge is created between the market wage and the net (or after-tax) wage. Workers, of course, respond to the after-tax wage and to the transfer benefits available, and alter their work choices accordingly.

5. This discussion, it should be noted, focuses on the efficiency losses, neglecting the gains that society might reap from the reduction in market inequality that is a result of redistribution policy.

6. John L. Palmer and Isabel V. Sawhill, eds., *The Reagan Experiment: An Examination of Economic and Social Policies under the Reagan Administration* (Washington, DC: Urban Institute Press, 1982).

7. The following questions illustrate the range of issues which these studies addressed:

- Do the high marginal tax rates of income and payroll taxes lead to reductions in work effort and initiative, especially for higher-earning individuals?

- Does the AFDC system encourage single mothers to go or remain on welfare rather than working and being independent?

- Does the Social Security system cause older workers to retire early or to decrease their work time in years before or after age sixty-five?
- Does the unemployment compensation system encourage workers to engage in activities which increase their probability of being laid-off, and once unemployed, does it discourage their job search efforts?
- Do disability transfers induce older workers to magnify their health problems in order to secure transfer benefits as opposed to working?

A sampling and critique of a number of these studies is found in Glen Cain and Harold Watts, eds., *Income Maintenance and Labor Supply: Econometric Studies* (New York: Academic Press, 1973); and Mark Killingsworth, *Labor Supply* (New York: Cambridge University Press, 1983).

8. Michael Boskin, "Social Security and Retirement Decisions," *Economic Inquiry* 15 (1977): 1–25. See also Michael Boskin and Michael Hurd, "The Effect of Social Security on Early Retirement," *Journal of Public Economics* 10, no. 3 (1978): 361–77.

9. Donald Parsons, "The Decline in Male Labor Force Participation," *Journal of Political Economy* 88 (1980): 117–34.

10. The labor force participation rate of men aged forty-five to sixty-two fell from 86 percent in 1950 to 71 percent in 1980.

11. Jerry A. Hausman, "Labor Supply," in Henry Aaron and Joseph Pechman, eds., *How Taxes Affect Economic Behavior* (Washington, DC: The Brookings Institution, 1981).

12. See, for example, Gary Burtless and Robert Moffitt, "The Effect of Social Security Benefits on the Labor Supply of the Aged," in Henry Aaron and Gary Burtless, eds., *Retirement and Economic Behavior* (Washington, DC: The Brookings Institution, 1984); Robert Haveman and Barbara Wolfe, "Disability Transfers and Early Retirement: A Causal Relationship?" *Journal of Public Economics* 24 (1984): 46–66; and Robert Triest, "The Effect of Income Taxation on Labor Supply," Ph.D. dissertation, University of Wisconsin, 1987.

13. See Danziger, Haveman, and Plotnick, op. cit. See also Henry Aaron, *Economic Effects of Social Security* (Washington, DC: The Brookings Institution, 1982).

14. See Robert Lampman, "Labor Supply and Social Welfare Benefits in the United States," Special Report no. 22, Institute for Research on Poverty, University of Wisconsin–Madison, 1978.

15. This conclusion is especially true if the system is a pay-as-you-go system, such as that of the United States. Such a system is financed by taxes raised concurrently with the benefits being paid; hence there is no reserve fund of contributions—themselves savings—to offset the reduction in private saving.

16. Martin Feldstein, "Social Security, Induced Retirement and Aggregate Capital Accumulation," *Journal of Political Economy* 84 (1974): 905–26.

17. Dean Leimer and Selig Lesnoy, "Social Security and Private Saving: New Time-Series Evidence," *Journal of Political Economy* 90 (1982): 606–29.

18. See Danziger, Haveman, and Plotnick, op. cit.

19. Michael Boskin, "Taxation, Saving, and the Rate of Interest," *Journal of Political Economy* 86 (1978): 533–44. See also Michael Boskin and Marc Robinson, "Social Security and Private Saving: Analytical Issues, Econometric Evidence, and Policy Implications," U.S. Congress, Joint Economic Committee, Special Study on Economic Change, Vol. 8, *Social Security and Pensions* (1980): 38–64.

20. See Ingemar Hansson, "An Evaluation of the Evidence on the Impact of Taxation on Capital Formation," in Hans Van der Kar and Barbara Wolfe, eds., *The Relevance of Public Finance* (Detroit, MI: Wayne State University Press, 1987).

21. See Edgar Feige, *The Unobserved Economy* (New York: Cambridge University Press, forthcoming). The Tax Reform Act of 1986, by broadening the tax base and lowering marginal tax rates, may retard this growth.

22. This case can be made slightly more complicated by assuming that the home redecorator is able to establish eligibility for public disability benefits. The disability program pays about one-half of her regular earnings, or $10,000, but imposes strict limits on the amount that she is allowed to work while receiving benefits. Now, engaging in unreported work really pays off. Say that the worker now settled for $14,000 per year, if she could be sure this would go unreported. Her take-home income would now rise to $24,000 ($14,000 in earnings plus $10,000 in benefits). Moreover, her customers could obtain her services for only $14,000 per year. The gain from "going underground" to both worker and customers becomes enormous; the loss to the government is even larger.

23. George Gilder, *Wealth and Poverty* (New York: Basic Books, 1981); and Charles Murray, *Losing Ground: American Social Policy, 1950–1980* (New York: Basic Books, 1984).

24. William Julius Wilson and Kathleen M. Neckerman, "Poverty and Family Structure: The Widening Gap between Evidence and Public Policy Issues," in Sheldon Danziger and Daniel Weinberg, eds., *Fighting Poverty: What Works and What Doesn't* (Cambridge, MA: Harvard University Press, 1986).

25. See Irwin Garfinkel and Sara McLanahan, *Single Mothers and Their Children: A New American Dilemma* (Washington, DC: Urban Institute Press, 1986), which provides a comprehensive review of the evidence on this issue.

26. Professors Richard and Peggy Musgrave have estimated the administrative cost of federal taxes to be about 50 cents for each $100 of revenue raised. See Richard Musgrave and Peggy Musgrave, *Public Finance in Theory and Practice*, 4th ed. (New York: McGraw-Hill, 1984). In addition to the costs borne by government, there is the expenditure of time and resources both to comply with the law and to take advantage of its many special provisions. Professors Slemrod and Sorum estimated that simple compliance with the income tax—record-keeping required to complete the tax form plus the completion and filing of the form—took an average of over twenty hours per return. They found that, in 1982, the time spent on compliance was about 2 billion hours, and the total cost of compliance was between $17 and $27 billion. See Joel Slemrod and Nikki Sorum, "The Compliance Cost of the U.S. Individual Income Tax System," *National Tax Journal* 37 (1984): 461–74.

27. These costs have been estimated at less than 2 percent of the benefits paid. See B. O. Schobel, "Administrative Expenses Under OASDI," *Social Security Bulletin* 44 (March 1981): 21–28.

28. Robert Lampman, *Social Welfare Spending*, op. cit., p. 111. To be precise, Lampman found the administrative and compliance costs of increasing the scale of the transfer system from its 1950 size to its 1980 size to be about 1 percent of GNP. In light of the results of Slemrod and Sorum, this figure seems low.

29. Indeed, in the early 1980s—before the 1986 reform—tax preferences in the federal income and corporation tax programs totaled about 90 percent of the revenue actually collected; stated alternatively, given the tax rate structure, nearly twice as much revenue would have been collected if these loopholes had not existed.
Professor Dan Usher of Queen's University in Canada has succinctly described the costs of tax avoidance as including: "The labor of hiding taxable objects from the tax collector, payments to lawyers and accountants for discovering profitable loopholes in the law, loss of income in switching from more taxed, more profitable endeavors to less taxed, less profitable endeavors, expenditure on litigation, and the risk of punishment from tax evasion" (quoted from "Tax Evasion and the Marginal Cost of Public Funds," D.P. 637, pp. 2–3, Queen's University, January 1986).

30. Lawrence Lindsey, "Estimating the Behavioral Response of Taxpayers to Changes in Tax Rates: 1982–1984, With Implications for the Revenue Maximizing Tax Rate," *Journal of Public Economics* 33 (1987): 173–206. From the large microeconomic tax models of the Treasury Department, Lindsey measured what total personal income tax revenues would be after the 1981 tax cut if individuals did *not* engage in less tax avoidance activities in response to the lower tax rates. He then compared these estimated revenues with the actual post-1981 revenues which presumably incorporated a smaller amount of tax avoidance activities. If tax avoidance efforts do respond to tax rates, the actual tax revenues would be greater than the estimated revenues.

31. Altering the composition and amount of work, investment portfolio decisions, interest expenses and deductions reflecting alternative ways of financing consumption and investment, charitable deductions, and business and entertainment expenses are all examples.

32. Lindsey also attempted to determine which tax avoidance behaviors were being decreased in response to the lower tax rates. There was, of course, a labor supply response—with lower tax rates, people would work more. Lindsey, however, found that most of the jump in revenue was due to higher income people rearranging their compensation packages—taking more in the form of wages and salaries and less in tax-avoiding forms such as business expenses (for example, personal auto use disguised as a business expense or business travel or entertainment). Another big jump was attributed to people reporting more business income; for example, more honest reporting, less hiding of income in shelters and other arrangements, and less engaging in unreported activities. Finally, Lindsey found that higher income people took and reported more capital gains income than they would have in the presence of higher rates, and this too is likely to represent a gain in efficiency in asset markets. The quantitative magnitude of his estimates remains a subject of some dispute, however.

33. Edward Denison, *Accounting for United States Economic Growth, 1929–1969* (Washington, DC: The Brookings Institution, 1974).

34. Robert Lampman, *Social Welfare Spending,* op. cit., pp. 94–96.

35. Robert Haveman and Barbara Wolfe, "Schooling and Economic Well-Being: The Role of Non-Market Effects," *Journal of Human Resources* 19 (1984): 377–408.

36. Moses Abramovitz, "Welfare Quandaries and Productivity Concerns," *American Economic Review* 71 (1981): 1–17.

37. See Robert Kirkpatrick, "The Income Elasticity of the Poverty Line," *Review of Economics and Statistics* 55 (1973): 327–32; Aldi Hagenaars, *The Perception of Poverty* (Amsterdam: North-Holland Publishing, 1985); and Lee Rainwater, *What Money Buys: Inequality and the Social Meaning of Income* (New York: Basic Books, 1974).

38. This abstract discussion clearly ignores numerous complications introduced by recognizing that the "income redistribution system" is not a single measure, but rather a complex series of cash and in-kind transfers, subsidies, and publicly provided merit goods, together with the taxes which finance them, each with its own positive and negative effects. The general point it reveals is, nevertheless, an important one.

39. These calculations of an economic sort, it should be emphasized, may fail to reflect longer-term changes in beliefs, tastes, or perceptions that may accompany the evolution of the redistribution system. These dynamic or evolutionary effects, emphasized by social psychologists, would influence assessment of both the losses and the gains attributed to redistribution. It is these longer-term or generational changes which lend credence to such assertions as: "Welfare programs breed weak people," or "reducing inequality fosters acceptance, understanding and solidarity." To the extent that such effects are not captured in the gain and loss categories identified above, our framework would be at a loss to deal with them.

40. Jerry Hausman, "Labor Supply," op. cit.

41. Edgar Browning and William Johnson, "The Tradeoff Between Equality and Efficiency," *Journal of Political Economy* 92 (1984): 175–203.

42. See Gary Burtless and Robert Haveman, "Taxes and Transfers: How Much Economic Loss," *Challenge* (March/April 1987): 45–51; and Charles Ballard, "The Marginal Efficiency Cost of Redistribution," *American Economic Review* (forthcoming).

43. This notion of a $100 net economic loss for each $100 delivered to the poor seems a realistic one for a marginal expansion of the existing income redistribution system. A similar number can be arrived at by a different path. A recent review of all of the existing studies of the labor supply and efficiency effects of the benefit side of the nation's redistributive system concluded that, on average, $25 of output was lost for each $100 of expenditures (see Danziger, Haveman, and Plotnick, op. cit.). This figure does not include the losses from raising $100 of taxes to finance the expenditures. Existing studies suggest that this average loss might also be about $25. The average dollar passing through

the redistributive system, then, would seem to generate a loss of about fifty cents. But this is for the average dollar in the system; the losses on both the tax and spending sides for a *marginal* dollar are likely to be substantially larger than these average values—perhaps double. See Edgar Browning, "On the Marginal Welfare Cost of Taxation," *American Economic Review* 77, no. 1 (March 1987): 11–24, and Charles Ballard, John Shoven, and John Whalley, "General Equilibrium Computations of the Marginal Welfare Costs of Taxes in the United States," *American Economic Review* 75, no. 1 (March 1985): 128–38. If this is so, expanding the existing redistributive system by $100 could well lead to an output loss of an equal amount.

44. William Baumol, *Superfairness* (Cambridge, MA: MIT Press, 1986).

Chapter 7

1. The earned income tax credit subsidizes, through a refundable tax credit, the earnings of family heads. The rate of subsidy is 14 percent of earned income up to an earnings level of $6,214 in 1988 (implying a total grant of $870). After earnings of $9,840, the subsidy is reduced at a rate of 10¢ for every dollar earned. After $18,540 of earnings, there is no subsidy received.

2. The most prominent proposals for reform of the transfer system are discussed in Michael Barth, John Palmer, and George Carcagno, *Toward an Effective Income Support System: Problems, Prospects, and Choices* (Madison, WI: Institute for Research on Poverty, 1973); Irene Lurie, ed., *Integrating Income Maintenance Programs: Problems and Solutions* (New York: Academic Press, 1975); Irwin Garfinkel, ed., *Income-Tested Transfer Programs: The Case for and Against* (New York: Academic Press, 1982); Theodore Marmor, ed., *Poverty Policy* (Chicago: Aldine-Atherton, 1971); and Robert Haveman, *Poverty Policy and Poverty Research: The War on Poverty and the Social Sciences* (Madison, WI: University of Wisconsin Press, 1987). See also Daniel Patrick Moynihan, *Family and Nation* (New York: Harcourt Brace Jovanovich, 1986).

3. The following illustration gives a picture of how such a plan might work, even though the actual numbers have no particular significance:

- A refundable tax credit set at one-half to two-thirds of the poverty line for each family unit would be introduced into the personal income tax law.
- The available credit would fall by forty cents for each $1 of other income, and this "reduction rate" (analogous to the marginal tax rate) would be integrated into the tax schedule.
- Marginal tax rates starting at 20 percent and increasing to 40 percent would apply to income above the level at which the credit reaches zero.
- Several existing public spending programs—including AFDC, food stamps, Supplemental Security Income, and public housing—would be scaled back or eliminated.

4. The first concrete discussion of such a "credit income tax" plan in the United States is that of Earl R. Rolph, "The Case for a Negative Income Tax Device," *Industrial Relations* 6 (1967): 155–65. (Lady Rhys-Williams had discussed this idea in England in 1943 and 1953.) A high guarantee and uninte-

grated form of this scheme was proposed by George McGovern as part of his 1971 campaign for the presidency. It has many of the characteristics of the negative income tax plan proposed by Milton Friedman, in his *Capitalism and Freedom* (Chicago: University of Chicago Press, 1962), and incorporated into President Nixon's Family Assistance Plan and President Carter's Program for Better Jobs and Income.

5. See Lawrence Thompson, "The Social Security Reform Debate," *Journal of Economic Literature* 21, no. 4 (December 1983); Henry Aaron and Gary Burtless, eds., *Retirement and Economic Behavior* (Washington, DC: The Brookings Institution, 1984); Gary Burtless, ed., *Work, Health, and Income Among the Elderly* (Washington, DC: The Brookings Institution, 1987); and Peter J. Ferrara, *Social Security: The Inherent Contradiction* (Washington, DC: Cato Institute, 1980).

6. The 1977 and 1983 Amendments to the Social Security program were among the most far-reaching. Whereas earlier amendments extended coverage and expanded benefits, the recent changes confronted the financing crisis of the system caused by the "demographic transition"— the baby boom followed by baby bust, plus increased longevity. Both long- and short-term projected system deficits were eliminated by increasing the payroll tax, delaying indexing, increasing the retirement age, and taxing the benefits of high income recipients.

7. This high benefits-contribution ratio for current retirees exists because of three principal factors. First, the program was developed during the working lives of new retirees; hence, they were not required to contribute via payroll taxes over their entire working career. Second, economic growth has generated an increasing flow of income for the economy, and part of this has been shared with retired workers in the form of increased benefit payments. Third, the age structure of the population—in particular, the baby boom after World War II—means there has been and continues to be a relatively high proportion of workers to retirees.

The converse of the fairly enviable situation of current retirees is that future retirees will likely not fare so well; indeed, even after the 1983 amendments, some of them might well not get back the amount they have paid in. This result is especially true in the years after 2000, and clearly depends on the changes in economic growth and the benefit and financing provisions of the system over that period. This relatively bleak scenario for future retirees is due to the same "demographics" mentioned above. As the large group of workers represented by the baby-boomers retires there will be a relatively small number of younger workers in the labor force providing for their support. Because of the 1983 amendments, future revenues will be raised through increased tax rates on the still-working and postponement of the normal age of retirement. A substantial trust fund—up to 30 percent of GNP—will be built up in the years after 2010. Nevertheless, if economic growth does not materialize, downward pressure on per capita retirement benefits could be substantial. Of course, strong economic growth would help future retirees as it has current ones, and could at least offset the effects of the shift in the age distribution. All in all, in spite of recent changes in the program, future retirees have good reason to be concerned over how well the current system will provide for them when they retire. See Timothy McBride, "Old-Age and Survivors Insurance in the Demographic Transition: An Evaluation of Partial Reserve Funding on the Long-Run Financing

Policy for Social Security," Ph.D. dissertation, Department of Economics, University of Wisconsin–Madison, 1987.

8. It has been estimated that 40 percent of the consumption spending of the elderly is supported by Social Security benefits.

9. Studies have indicated that about 75 percent of older couples have a consumption level in retirement that is *at least* as great as that experienced during their working years. Up to one-third will experience consumption during retirement that is 130 percent or more of that during their working years. This relative affluence of many elderly is attributable to the receipt of Social Security in addition to private pensions and annuities. See Laurence Kotlikoff, Aria Spivak, and Larry Summers, "The Adequacy of Savings," *American Economic Review* 72, no. 5 (December 1982): 1056–69.

10. This early retirement pattern reflects both an "income effect" (the higher lifetime income of the aged due to the system allows them to "purchase" more retirement) and a "substitution effect" (the high benefit reduction penalties) on those recipients who continue to work. Sheldon Danziger, Robert Haveman, and Robert Plotnick, "How Income Transfers Affect Work, Savings, and the Income Distribution: A Critical Review," *Journal of Economic Literature* 19, no. 3 (September 1981): 975–1028, have reviewed this evidence. See also Henry Aaron, *Economic Effects of Social Security* (Washington, DC: The Brookings Institution, 1982), and a number of the papers in Henry Aaron and Gary Burtless, eds., *Retirement and Economic Behavior* (Washington, DC: The Brookings Institution, 1984).

11. This argument is made cogently in Laurence Kotlikoff, "Justifying Public Provision of Social Security," *Journal of Policy Analysis and Management* 6, no. 4 (1987): 674–89.

12. An alternative approach that would achieve many of the same objectives is known as the "two-tiered" retirement benefit system. In it, the welfare component of the system—currently the Supplemental Security Income (SSI) program—would have a minimum benefit equal to the poverty line, with this payment reduced by, say, 50 cents for each dollar of unearned income. This income-conditioning of the SSI benefit would significantly expand the cost and the number of recipients of this bottom tier of the system. With such a program addressing redistributional objectives, the second tier would be a low replacement rate benefit program, with a proportional rate structure. Benefits in this upper tier would be closely related to wages, ensuring a similar rate of return on earnings across income groups. The overall system would remain progressive, especially if the upper tier retirement benefits were treated as taxable income. See Alicia Munnell, *The Future of Social Security* (Washington, DC: The Brookings Institution, 1977), pp. 40–44. If the universal demogrant proposed here were in place, a two-tiered arrangement could be attained by raising the income guarantee to the poverty line for those above retirement age, scaling back the Social Security retirement benefit to a proportional, but lower, replacement rate, and making this retirement benefit taxable.

13. By itself, this proposed change in the Social Security system has some characteristics of the proposals of Peter Ferrara. See Peter J. Ferrara, *Social Security: The Inherent Contradiction* (Washington, DC: Cato Institute, 1980); Peter

J. Ferrara, ed., *Social Security: Prospects for Real Reform* (Washington, DC: Cato Institute, 1985). While his proposals ultimately envision the scrapping of the Social Security retirement system, those presented here do not. Moreover, these proposals are part of a set of comprehensive changes designed to reduce inequality, promote independence, and increase economic efficiency.

14. Recent research has suggested that much of the rapid growth in individual retirement accounts in the decade before 1986 represented new private saving. See Steven Venti and David Wise, "Have IRAs Decreased U.S. Saving? Evidence from Consumer Expenditure Surveys," National Bureau of Economic Research, Working Paper 2217, 1987. Other analysts, however, have concluded that, to a large extent, these accounts simply substituted for other forms of private saving, leading to only a small increase in the total private saving rate.

15. Samuel Preston, "Children and the Elderly: Divergent Paths for America's Dependents," *Demography* 21, no. 4 (November 1984): 435–57.

16. A comprehensive and insightful discussion of this problem is Irwin Garfinkel and Sara McLanahan, *Single Mothers and Their Children: A New American Dilemma* (Washington, DC: Urban Institute Press, 1986). See also U.S. House of Representatives, Committee on Ways and Means, *Children in Poverty*, May 22, 1985.

17. About one-half of single mothers who would seem to be eligible for such support have been awarded none, and a minority of those who have an award are actually collecting the amount they are due. As a result, absent parents have, more often than not, been able to avoid financial responsibility for the children they brought into being but do not live with.

18. This system was first proposed by Professor Irwin Garfinkel of the University of Wisconsin-Madison. His proposals have been implemented on an experimental basis in several locations in Wisconsin and are reflected in national legislation proposed by Senator Moynihan and passed by the Congress in 1988. See Irwin Garfinkel and Liz Uhr, "A New Approach to Child Support," *The Public Interest* 75 (Spring 1984): 11–22.

19. Because some absent parents wish they were, in fact, present, the proposed child-support system implies adjustment of existing child custody arrangements to assure increased uniformity and equity.

20. This child-support arrangement has major advantages relative to recent "workfare" proposals, although it is not inconsistent with them. The latter generally entail an additional set of rules tacked onto AFDC, whereby single parents are *forced* to work to remain eligible for support. The child-support program takes the less harsh approach of offering incentives to encourage single parents to work. Forcing someone who has clear incentives *not* to work to do so requires a cumbersome, expensive, and punitive bureaucracy, and is ultimately not likely to be successful in making single parents independent of public support. Moreover, I would argue that the work which would be done as a result of inducements is more socially useful when access is gained to the general labor market rather than the restricted "make-work" activities associated with workfare programs. When combined with the proposed youth capital account and low-skill employment subsidy programs (discussed below), the child

support system would strongly encourage single parents to make the transition from welfare to the labor market and would provide both the incentives and support necessary for this shift.

21. See Eli Ginzberg, ed., *Employing the Unemployed* (New York: Basic Books, 1980).

22. This is because only the first $6,000 of annual earnings was eligible for subsidization. For example, an employer would receive a subsidy of $3,000 (.5 × $6,000) for a worker paid both $6,000 and $12,000 per year. While 50 percent of the wages of the first worker were subsidized, the subsidy was paid on only 25 percent of the wages of the higher-paid worker.

23. Robert Haveman and John Bishop, "Selective Employment Subsidies: Can Okun's Law Be Repealed?", *American Economic Review* 69 (May 1979): 124–30; and Jeffrey M. Perloff and Michael Wachter, "The New Jobs Tax Credit: An Evaluation of the 1977–78 Wage Subsidy Program," *American Economic Review* 69 (May 1979): 173–79.

24. Changes in other aspects of the 1977–1978 program are also desirable. The program should be modified so as to increase the hiring incentive by increasing the amount of the subsidy which is paid on the wage base. In addition, the cap on the subsidy available to any single firm should be removed so that the marginal employment decisions of large firms are subsidized to the same extent as small firms. Finally, the wage basis on which the subsidy is paid should be changed so as to increase the marginal incentive for hiring low-wage workers.

25. Plans with similar characteristics have been discussed in John Bishop, "Vouchers for Creating Jobs, Education, and Training: VOCJET, An Employment Oriented Strategy for Reducing Poverty," Institute for Research on Poverty Special Report 17, 1977. See also John Palmer, ed., *Creating Jobs: Public Employment Programs and Wage Subsidies* (Washington, DC: The Brookings Institution, 1978) and the papers by Robert Lerman and David Betson and John Bishop in Robert Haveman and John Palmer, eds., *Jobs for Disadvantaged Workers: The Economics of Employment Subsidies* (Washington, DC: The Brookings Institution, 1982).

26. At the same time, however, employers, knowing the rules of the program, have incentive to seek out disadvantaged, low-skill workers and to favor them in hiring decisions. The advantage of such an employee-based plan, then, stems from the increased incentives to both workers to search for jobs and employers to hire them.

Other advantages of the employee-based plan are that firms would not significantly alter their personnel practices; particular populations would be targeted for special help; there would be no inequities across firms with some qualifying and others not; there would be no firm "threshold" problems; and particular workers would gain security due to the market advantage afforded by their vouchers.

In assessing such an arrangement, however, a number of questions also arise: Would coworkers resent certified workers? Would target group members already employed qualify for the subsidy? If not, how could artificially induced job turnover be avoided? Given the benefits from a worker-based subsidy plan, the answers to these questions would have to be strongly negative to warrant dropping the idea.

27. A further important argument in favor of this demand-side strategy is that both of the proposed subsidies work largely by offsetting the distortions and demand-reducing effects caused by minimum wage legislation, labor union power and practices, and economic discrimination. Instead, this two-pronged plan effectively and efficiently counteracts these distortions. The subsidies offered slice through wedges and boost deficient sectoral demand in ways which would bring productive workers—ones who should be working—into gainful employment. And this is achieved by making employment of these workers more attractive through a simultaneous, policy-induced reduction of employer hiring costs and increase of worker remuneration.

28. The basic idea lying behind this proposal is not a new one. Indeed, in 1968, Professor James Tobin, a Nobel Prize winner, discussed the merits of such an approach, but in more general terms than the proposal I offer here. James Tobin, "Raising the Incomes of the Poor," in Kermit Gordon, ed., *Agenda for the Nation* (Washington, DC: The Brookings Institution, 1970). His idea ran as follows:

> [A] principal objective...must be to increase the society's investment in human capital and to make the distribution of human capital much less unequal. I will confine myself to one suggestion. After high school, every youth in the nation—whatever the economic means of his parents or his earlier education—should have the opportunity to develop his capacity to earn income and to contribute to the society. To this end the federal government could make available to every young man and woman, on graduation from high school and in any case at the age of 19, an "endowment" of, for example, $5,000 [in 1968 dollars]. He could draw on this "National Youth Endowment" for authorized purposes until his twenty-eighth birthday; the period of eligibility would be extended to allow for military service. Authorized purposes would include higher education, vocational training, apprenticeship, and other forms of on-the-job training. To be eligible, educational and training programs would have to be approved by the federal agency administering the endowment. The endowment would pay tuition and other fees to the educational institutions or employers operating the programs; the individual could also draw on the fund for subsistence while enrolled in an approved program.
>
> This proposal...has a number of important advantages. Individuals are assisted directly and equally, rather than indirectly and haphazardly, through government financing of particular programs. The advantages of background and talent that fit certain young people for university education are not compounded by financial favoritism. Within the broad limits of approved programs, individuals are free to choose how to use the money the government is willing to invest in their development. No individual misses out because there happens to be no training courses where he lives, or because his parents' income barely exceeds some permissible maximum.

29. Youths would be required to secure prior approval for withdrawals from the account to insure that the proposed expenditures met guidelines for acceptable education, training, and health care activities. Moreover, to ensure that provision to buy both education/training and medical care—but to protect wasteful overspending on either—subsequent spending limits could be established (such as a maximum of 75 percent of the account spent on either major category).

Notes

30. The concept of a capital account for youths and its design was discussed extensively in William Klein, "A Proposal for a Universal Personal Capital Account," Institute for Research on Poverty, University of Wisconsin–Madison, Discussion Paper 422–77, 1977. My proposal draws heavily on his discussion.

31. The programs would support guidance and counseling centers to assist youths in choosing the training, education, and health care activities that best meet their needs and interests.

32. David Betson, David Greenberg, and Richard Kasten, "A Simulation Analysis of the Economic Efficiency and Distributional Effects of Alternative Program Structures: The Negative Income Tax Versus the Credit Income Tax," in Irwin Garfinkel, ed., *Income Tested Transfer Programs: The Case for and Against* (New York: Academic Press, 1982).

33. This is consistent with a recent study which estimated the budgetary cost of a small refundable tax credit—$350 per person—accompanied by the elimination of the personal exemption in the current income tax. When the reductions in welfare payments in response to the credit was taken into account, the net federal cost was estimated to be essentially zero. See Robert Lerman, "Reducing Poverty Without Welfare: A Reorientation of Income Support for Nonelderly Families," mimeo., Heller Graduate School, Brandeis University, December 1987.

34. U.S. House of Representatives, Committee on Ways and Means, *Background Material and Data on Programs Within the Jurisdiction of the Committee on Ways and Means* (Washington, DC: GPO, March 1987).

35. Irwin Garfinkel and Sara McLanahan, *Single Mothers and Their Children: A New American Dilemma* (Washington, DC: Urban Institute Press, 1986). See also Irwin Garfinkel, "The Role of Child Support Insurance in Antipoverty Policy," *Annals,* American Academy of Political and Social Science, vol. 479 (May 1985), pp. 119–31.

36. It should be noted, however, that if the collections from absent parents are regarded as an additional source of tax revenue, then the increase in tax revenue would, by definition, be the increased collections. Because households are required to pay income tax on their total income in the proposed plan, the required net increase in expenditures would be less than this amount.

37. Robert Lerman, op. cit.

38. David Betson and John Bishop, "Wage Incentive and Distributional Effects," in Robert Haveman and John Palmer, eds., *Jobs for Disadvantaged Workers: The Economics of Employment Subsidies* (Washington, DC: The Brookings Institution, 1982).

39. Robert Lerman, op. cit.

Appendix

1. This view is restricted to two educational levels per race-gender group (high school completion and college degree) to simplify the figures. A view of all educational levels would be consistent with the patterns shown in these figures.

2. For example, in 1980, white women with college degrees aged forty-five to fifty-four earned less than every similarly aged white male educational group, and earned only 44 percent of similarly educated white men.

3. See, for example, James P. Smith and Finis R. Welch, "Closing the Gap: Forty Years of Economic Progress for Blacks" (Santa Monica, CA: The Rand Corporation, 1986), pp. 21–42. This study focuses on those factors which have worked to improve the lot of blacks; less emphasis is given to those left behind. It deals only with black men, but much of its discussion is applicable to black women as well.

4. The rewards to educational attainment and the amount of schooling obtained are also closely related: As the benefits to education rise for black men, the amount obtained should rise commensurately, other things being equal. This is a critical step in progress toward equalizing labor market opportunities and outcomes.

5. See, for example, Richard R. Freeman, "Black Progress After 1964: Who Has Gained and Why?" in S. Rosen, ed., *Studies in Labor Markets* (Chicago: University of Chicago Press, 1981), pp. 447–94.

6. Smith and Welch (op. cit., pp. 42–57, especially p. 56) show that until recently black weekly wages were approximately 30 percent lower in the South than the North. One-half to two-thirds of this gap has now been eliminated. Smith and Welch ascribe the narrowing of the South-North differential to the narrowing of skill differentials between the two regions and a decrease of discrimination in the South.

7. John D. Kasarada, "Contemporary U.S. Migration and Urban Demographic-Job Opportunity Mismatches," paper prepared for hearings held by the Joint Economic Committee, Subcommittee on Economic Resources, Competitiveness, and Security Economics, September 18, 1986. See also Glen G. Cain, "Comments on Murray's Analysis of the War on Poverty on the Labor Market Behavior of the Poor," Institute for Research on Poverty, University of Wisconsin–Madison, Special Report 38, August 1984.

8. Smith and Welch, op. cit., pp. 99–100. See also the proceedings of a conference on the labor market effects of antidiscrimination legislation which appeared in the *Industrial and Labor Relations Review* 29 (July 1976).

9. Another factor in the apparent rise in earnings as well as in unemployment concerns a statistical artifact. Those who have been joining the black unemployment ranks are also those who would tend to have lower earnings were they working. Rising unemployment rates would thus be expected statistically to generate higher average earnings for workers, even though no one is actually doing better and the newly unemployed are doing worse. While this form of "selection bias" surely exists in the numbers presented here, an attempt has been made to provide a variety of perspectives; other research also adjusts for such artifacts and reaches generally the same conclusions. The statistical problem must be kept in mind, but is unlikely to be the principal explanation for the results described here. See, for example, Richard Butler and James Heckman, "Government's Impact on the Labor Market Status of Black Americans: A Critical Review," in *Equal Rights and Industrial Relations*, University of Wisconsin-Madison, Industrial Relations Research Institute, 1977, pp. 235–81. Further

data based on *all* workers rather than only those who worked full-time, full-year also indicate a rising trend in the black-white earnings ratio. See also Glen G. Cain, "The Economic Analysis of Labor Market Discrimination: A Survey," in Orley Ashenfelter and Richard Layard, eds., *The Handbook of Labor Economics* (Amsterdam: Elsevier, 1986).

10. See Gary S. Becker, "Human Capital, Effort and the Sexual Division of Labor," *Journal of Labor Economics* 3, no. 1 (January 1985), supplement, pp. 533–58, which presents a neoclassical economic model where such specialization is natural, optimal, and chosen. Additional references can be found there.

11. The classic work on this is Alan Blinder's article, "Wage Discrimination: Reduced Form and Structural Variables," *Journal of Human Resources* 8, no. 4 (Fall 1973), pp. 436–55. See Cain, 1987, op. cit., for a discussion of this issue. See also the following for an example of the debates which range on the roles of "choice" versus "discrimination" in the determination of women's labor market earnings: Solomon Polachek, "Occupational Self-Selection: A Human Capital Approach to Sex Differences in Occupational Structure," *Review of Economics and Statistics* 63 (1981), pp. 60–69; Paula England, "The Failure of Human Capital Theory to Explain Occupational Sex Segregation," *Journal of Human Resources* 17 (1982), pp. 3–370; Polachek, "Occupational Segregation: A Defense of Human Capital Predictions," *Journal of Human Resources* 20 (1985), pp. 437–440; and England, "Occupational Segregation: A Rejoinder," *Journal of Human Resources* 20 (1985), pp. 441–43.

12. The relationship between family size and well-being is complicated. Are black two-parent families relatively "worse off" because their larger size drives down their per capita relative income more than that of whites? If family size is a matter of choice, the presence of more children suggests an increase in well-being. But if family size is not totally a choice variable, the meaning of the per capita numbers is more ambiguous.

13. Sheldon Danziger and Peter Gottschalk, "How Have Families with Children Been Faring?" Institute for Research on Poverty Discussion Paper 801–86, University of Wisconsin–Madison, 1986. The paper, based on Current Population Survey data, was originally prepared for the Joint Economic Committee of the Congress. I am grateful for data updates provided by George Slotsve.

14. We have seen that black women reduced their earnings gap relative to white women by three-quarters from 1960 to 1980. This would boost the income of two-parent black families relative to white ones even if labor force participation rates (of women) were equal across races. Since the black rate was considerably higher, these gains were magnified. On the other hand, the greater rise in labor force participation of white women works in the opposite direction. The net effect was that changes in earnings of wives significantly reduced the black-white two-parent family income gap in the 1967–1984 period. (See Danziger and Gottschalk, op. cit., p. 33, for data from which relevant calculations can be made.)

15. See Irwin Garfinkel and Sara McLanahan, *Single Mothers and Their Children: A New American Dilemma* (Washington, DC: The Urban Institute Press, 1986) for a full discussion of these issues.

16. There is also the issue of equity within the divorced family. Lenore Weitzman claims, in *The Divorce Revolution* (New York: Free Press, 1985), that absent fathers typically experience a rise in economic well-being at the time of the marriage's dissolution, while the mother and children experience a large drop in well-being. While others dispute these findings, it is agreed by most researchers that the well-being of the father at least rises relative to his former wife and children.

17. See, for example, the following: *Children in Poverty*, the Congressional Research Service and the Congressional Budget Office, prepared for the House Committee on Ways and Means, 1985; *1987 Budget Perspectives: Federal Spending for the Human Resource Programs*, Congressional Research Service, February 1986; *Smaller Slices of the Pie*, Center on Budget and Policy Priorities, November 1985; Sheldon Danziger and Peter Gottschalk, "How Have Families with Children Been Faring?" Institute for Research on Poverty Discussion Paper 801-86, Madison, Wisconsin, 1986; *Falling Behind: A Report on How Blacks Have Fared Under the Reagan Policies*, Center on Budget and Policy Priorities, October 1984; John L. Palmer and Isabel V. Sawhill, eds., *The Reagan Record: An Assessment of America's Changing Domestic Priorities* (Urban Institute Press, August 1984); Margaret C. Simms, *The Economic Well-Being of Minorities During the Reagan Years* (Urban Institute Press, October 1984); *Safety Net Programs: Are They Reaching Poor Children?*, Report for Select Committee on Children, Youth, and Families, U.S House of Representatives, 1988.

18. Noncash benefits should also be considered for a full appraisal of government support. Food stamps in particular are almost equivalent to cash, and adding them to cash payments would yield a better measure of government assistance. Table A. 26 shows all government expenditures on AFDC and AFDC plus food stamps. The drops in AFDC appear on the surface to be more than offset by increases in food stamps, but food stamp benefits go to *all* poor (not just families with children). In addition, the rising poverty rates over this period imply that the food stamp benefits had to be shared by a rising number of people. It turns out that in the median state, combined AFDC and food stamp support dropped from 85 percent of the poverty level in the early 1970s to only 65 percent in 1985 (note these are *maximum* benefits available for a family of four; actual benefits would generally be lower). And, illustratively, food stamps went to only 59 percent of all poor households with children in 1982. (See *Children in Poverty*, op. cit., pp. 203, 230.)

19. The book by Garfinkel and McLanahan (op. cit.) contains an excellent review of the data and analysis pertaining to the rising number of mother-only families. See also Mary Jo Bane, "Household Composition and Poverty," in Sheldon Danziger and Daniel Weinberg, eds., *Fighting Poverty: What Works and What Doesn't* (Cambridge, MA: Harvard University Press, 1986).

20. In economic terms, the relative cost of separation and divorce has fallen, as the woman's greater earning power makes her independence more viable. It follows that women in some sense improve their well-being by choosing this course of action. It also follows that the present concern for the low incomes of mother-only families should have been previously directed to the plight of women who remained in undesirable marriages because of the lack of resources to do otherwise, as women can now "improve" their position by leaving. Of

course, other things are also changing, such as fathers feeling less financially responsible than before, which complicates such inferences.

21. See, for example, William Julius Wilson and Kathryn M. Neckerman, "Poverty and Family Structure: The Widening Gap Between Evidence and Public Policy Issues," in Danziger and Weinberg, 1986, op. cit.

22. Note that the changed behavior of black women is clearly, in economic jargon, the result of "*reduced* opportunities": a decline in the probability of, or benefits of, marriage, due to a reduction in the "supply" of suitable marriage partners. This contrasts somewhat with the situation of whites discussed above, where behavior is viewed partially as the result of the "*increased* opportunities" opened by expanded labor force participation and earnings. This difference suggests that the increase in the number of mother-only families represents a reduction in well-being of black mother-only families relative to whites. To repeat, other factors are at play which could render such inferences incorrect.

23. Garfinkel and McLanahan, op. cit., p. 45.

24. Charles Murray, *Losing Ground: American Social Policy 1950–1980* (New York: Basic Books, 1984). For a critical view, see, for example, Special Report no. 38 of the Institute for Research on Poverty, 1985, or the exchange between Murray and Robert Greenstein in the March 25 and April 8 issues of *The New Republic*.

25. See, for example, Garfinkel and McLanahan, op. cit., p. 45; or Wilson and Neckerman, op. cit., both of which review the literature in this area.

26. Reviews of the literature on youth labor market performance include Albert Rees, "An Essay on Youth Joblessness," *Journal of Economic Literature* 24, no. 2 (June 1986), pp. 613–28; Charles L. Betsey, Robinson G. Hollister, Jr., and Mary R. Papageorgiou, eds., *Youth Employment and Training Programs: The YEPDA Years* (Washington, DC: National Research Council, National Academy Press, 1985); David T. Ellwood and David A. Wise, "Youth Employment in the Seventies: The Changing Circumstances of Young Adults," NBER Working Paper no. 1055, 1983; Richard B. Freeman and David A. Wise, *The Youth Labor Market Problem: Its Nature, Causes, and Consequences*, NBER Conference Report, University of Chicago Press, 1982; and Robert D. Mare and Christopher Winship, "Racial Socioeconomic Convergence and the Paradox of Black Youth Joblessness: Enrollment, Enlistment, and Employment, 1964–1981," NORC Discussion Paper, 1983.

27. Similar patterns exist for young women, but are not shown.

28. See Betsey et al., op. cit., p. 53, and Ellwood and Wise, 1983, op. cit., pp. 15–19. Lester Thurow, among others, has formalized this in a model of "job queues," whereby youth are generally lined up behind older workers in terms of who gets any jobs available. See Lester Thurow, *Poverty and Discrimination* (Washington, DC: The Brookings Institution, 1969).

29. See Jonathan S. Leonard, "The Interaction of Residential Segregation and Employment Discrimination," NBER Working Paper no. 1274, 1984, and John D. Kasarda, "Contemporary U.S. Migration and Urban Demographic-Job Opportunity Mismatches," mimeo., 1986.

30. See, for example, Barry Bluestone and Bennett Harrison, *The Deindustrialization of America* (New York: Basic Books, 1982).

31. See Ellwood and Wise, op. cit.

32. See Betsey et al., op. cit., p. 54, for a discussion of this issue, and numerous references.

33. See Michael Wachter and C. Kim, "Time Series Changes in Youth Joblessness," in Freeman and Wise, op. cit.; Ellwood and Wise, op. cit.; Wong W. Tan and Michael P. Ward, *Forecasting the Wages of Young Men: The Effects of Cohort Size* (Santa Monica, CA: Rand Corporation, May 1985); Louise B. Russell, *The Baby Boom Generation and the Economy* (Washington, DC: The Brookings Institution, 1982); Smith and Ward, op. cit.; and Betsey et al., pp. 59 and 67.

34. See Betsey, et al., p. 58.

35. See, for example, Ellwood and Wise, op. cit., and Meyer and Wise, op. cit. See also Elijah Anderson, "The Social Context of Youth Employment Programs," in Hollister et al., op. cit., pp. 348–66, for discussion of the problems for blacks specifically in this regard. Some suggest that the rise of the black middle class, while creating positive role models in the abstract (for example, on television and in other media), has not left inner-city youths with personal contact with such success stories; living examples of such success have moved to the suburbs.

36. See Sheldon Danziger, Jacques van der Gaag, Eugene Smolensky, and Michael Taussig, "Implications of the Relative Economic Status of the Elderly for Transfer Policy," in Henry Aaron and Gary Burtless, eds., *Retirement and Economic Behavior* (Washington, DC: The Brookings Institution, 1984), and Timothy Smeeding, "Full Income Estimates of the Relative Well-Being of the Elderly and the Nonelderly," Institute for Research on Poverty, University of Wisconsin–Madison, Discussion Paper 779–85, for recent sophisticated adjustments of this sort. Danziger et al. use 1973 data to adjust money income rates of 0.49 up to an actual relative well-being ratio of almost unity. Smeeding uses 1979, and adjusts from 0.518 to slightly greater than unity.

37. Another perspective on the effect of government spending is provided by Table A.19. Pretransfer-poor elderly families received well over twice as much government income support as pretransfer-poor families with children in 1985.

38. It should be noted that, as Table 1 shows, government assistance makes up about two-fifths or less of the money income of elderly households, although these statistics omit important categories of real income, such as health care, and food stamps.

39. While relative money income of families headed by persons sixty-five years of age or older has risen since the mid-1960s, the reverse was true for the period before the 1960s. See Table 2. That is, over the entire postwar period, the elderly have had money income growth about equal to nonelderly households.

40. Bruce Jacobs, in a paper presented to the Working Seminar on the Family and American Welfare Policy at the American Enterprise Institute, "The

Table 1
Percentage Composition of Total Income for Elderly-Headed (≥ 65) Family Units, 1967, 1983, and 1984

	1967	*1983*	*1984*
Earnings	43	20	16
Social Security*	28	38	38
Property	15	24	28
Public assistance	2	1	—
Other (including pensions)	11	16	3
Pensions	—	—	15

Note: *OASDI and Railroad Retirement benefits.

Sources: For 1984, "Developments in Aging: 1985, vol. 3, A Report of the Special Committee on Aging," U.S. Senate, February 28, 1985, p. 45; for 1967 and 1983, Daniel B. Radner, "Changes in the Money Income of the Aged and Nonaged, 1967–1983," Studies in Income Distribution, No. 14, U.S. Department of Health and Human Services, Social Security Administration, September 1986, p. 39. The figures in the two sources are not directly comparable.

Table 2
Growth of Income for Families (in percent)

	Heads < 65 Years	*Heads ≥ 65 Years*
1947–1967	68	26
1967–1983	12	40
1947–1983	89	76

Note: These numbers do not include income adjustments for family size and other relevant factors.

Source: Daniel B. Radner, "Changes in the Money Income of the Aged and Nonaged, 1967–1983," Studies in Income Distribution, No. 14, U.S. Department of Health and Human Services, Social Security Administration, September 1986.

Elderly: How Do They Fare?" (October 1986), documents the importance of the media's preoccupation with the portion of the elderly population which was indigent. Thus the "compassionate stereotype" emerged as the dominant image of the elderly in the 1960s, to which voters and lawmakers responded.

41. See Samuel Preston, "Children and the Elderly: Divergent Paths for America's Dependents," *Demography* 21, no. 4 (November 1984), pp. 435–57.

Index

About the Author

Robert Haveman is the John Bascom Professor of Economics at the University of Wisconsin–Madison, and Director of the La Follette Institute of Public Affairs. He has been the Director of the Institute for Research on Poverty, a Brookings Research Professor, and the Tinbergen Professor of Economics at Erasmus University, Rotterdam. He is the author of several books and articles on the economics of and public policy toward poverty, inequality, and disadvantaged workers. His most recent book is *Poverty Policy and Poverty Research* (University of Wisconsin Press, 1987).